ON GUARD
FOR STUDENTS

*A Thinker's Guide
to the Christian Faith*

WILLIAM LANE CRAIG

David C Cook
transforming lives together

ON GUARD FOR STUDENTS
Published by David C Cook
4050 Lee Vance View
Colorado Springs, CO 80918 U.S.A.

David C Cook Distribution Canada
55 Woodslee Avenue, Paris, Ontario, Canada N3L 3E5

David C Cook U.K., Kingsway Communications
Eastbourne, East Sussex BN23 6NT, England

The graphic circle C logo is a registered trademark of David C Cook.

The website addresses recommended throughout this book are offered as a
resource to you. These websites are not intended in any way to be or imply an
endorsement on the part of David C Cook, nor do we vouch for their content.

LCCN 2014959543
ISBN 978-0-7814-1299-5
eISBN 978-0-7814-1329-9

© 2015 William Lane Craig
Material adapted from On Guard, first edition, by William
Lane Craig © 2010, published by David C Cook.
The Team: Andrew Stoddard, Andrew Meisenheimer, Jack Campbell, Nick Lee, Karen Athen
Cover Design: Amy Konyndyk
Cover Photo: iStock
Interior Portraits: Dan Schultz
Interior Sketches: Luke Flowers

Printed in the United States of America
First Edition 2015

2 3 4 5 6 7 8 9 10

041415-CS

CONTENTS

FOREWORD

This book is intended to be a sort of trail guide for students seeking to explore the truth of Christianity. So it is a book to be *studied*, not just read. You'll find numerous arguments in support of various positions throughout the text. In discussing each argument, I'll present a reason (or several reasons) to think that each step in the argument is true. Then I'll discuss the strongest objections to each step before coming to a conclusion.

So, for example, suppose we have the following argument.

1. All men are mortal.
2. Socrates is a man.
3. Therefore, Socrates is mortal.

This is what we call a logically valid argument. That is to say, if steps 1 and 2 are true, then the conclusion 3 is also true.

There are only about nine basic rules of logic that govern such arguments. So long as you obey the rules of logic, they *guarantee* that if the steps are true, then the conclusion is true as well. We then say that the conclusion *follows logically* from steps 1 and 2.

So the question then becomes: Are steps 1 and 2 in the above argument *true?* In support of step 1, we might present scientific and medical evidence for the fact that all men are mortal. In support of step 2, we might turn to historical evidence to prove that Socrates was a man. Along the way, we'd want to consider any objections to 1 or 2 and seek to answer them. For example, someone might deny step 2 because he believes that Socrates is just a mythical figure and not a real man. We'd have to show why the evidence suggests that this belief is mistaken.

The steps in the argument are called *premises*. If you obey the rules of logic, the conclusion will follow necessarily from the premises.

Now a person can always avoid any argument's conclusion simply by denying one of the argument's premises. Someone can't be forced to accept the conclusion if he's willing to pay the price of rejecting one of the premises. But when there's good evidence for the truth of the premises, the price of rejecting one of them just to avoid the conclusion may become uncomfortably high.

For example, the person who denies premise 2 of the above argument is embracing a historical skepticism that the vast majority of professional historians would find quite unjustified. So he can reject premise 2 if he wants to, but he pays the price of making himself look like a kook. Such a person can hardly condemn as irrational someone who *does* accept the truth of premise 2.

Now whether the price of denying an argument's premises is too high will vary from person to person. It's up to you to assess the cogency of the arguments I present. I won't feel bad if you disagree with me on various points. I want you to think for yourself. At least you will see what it will cost intellectually to resist the conclusions. If you find that price too high, then you may come to accept the conclusions of the arguments.

In presenting the arguments and evidence in this book, I've tried to be *simple* without being *simplistic*.

PREMISE

The steps of an argument that lead to the conclusion are called the *premises* of the argument.

ON GUARD FOR STUDENTS

Sometimes the material may be new and difficult for you. I'd encourage you to consider it in small bites, which are easier to digest. You might find it helpful to be part of a small group in which you can discuss the arguments.

At the end of most chapters you'll find an argument map or outline of the case presented in that chapter. Let me explain how to use the argument map. The map has a "swim lane" format that exhibits my argument in the left-hand lane labeled "Pro." The right-hand lane labeled "Con" exhibits the objections that might be raised by those against the argument. The arrows moving back and forth across the lanes trace the various pro and con responses that might be given. These maps will help you to see the big picture.

Consider, for example, the argument map following this foreword: In the left-hand lane we see the first premise of the argument: "All men are mortal." Following the arrow, we find the evidence given in support of that premise. In this case no response to this premise is offered, and so the "Con" lane remains blank. Next in the "Pro" lane comes the second premise: "Socrates is a man." Here the skeptic does have a response, and so in the "Con" lane we see the objection that "Socrates was just a mythological figure." Following the arrow, we find the answer to this objection, which states succinctly the historical evidence for Socrates' being a real man. Notice that only a very terse summary is provided; reading the argument maps will be no substitute for studying the arguments themselves as they are presented in the text. The argument maps just help you to see the big picture.

I hope that this book will be a great help to you in finding out the truth about God and Christianity.

William Lane Craig

SAMPLE ARGUMENT MAP

CHAPTER 1

WHO CARES?

Out, out, brief candle! Life's but a walking shadow, a poor player who struts and frets his hour upon the stage and then is heard no more. It is a tale told by an idiot, full of sound and fury, signifying nothing.
William Shakespeare, *Macbeth*, act 5, scene 5

The late 1980s saw a fundamental shift in the world order with the collapse of the Soviet Union and the fall of the Iron Curtain. We were living in Brussels, Belgium, at the time. It was exciting to be working in Europe when such historic, world-changing events were happening before our eyes. On a trip to St. Petersburg (formerly Leningrad) shortly after the Change, I visited the famous Russian cosmologist Andrei Grib, who is a Russian Orthodox Christian. As we strolled through the Hermitage, viewing its splendid treasures from Russia's Czarist past, I asked Andrei about the massive turning to God in Russia that followed immediately upon the fall of Communism. "Well," he said to me in his thick Russian accent, "in mathematics we have something called 'proof by the opposite.' You can prove something to be true by showing its opposite is false. For seventy years we have tried Marxist atheism in this country, and it didn't work. So everybody figured the opposite must be true!"

Part of the challenge of getting people in the West to think about God is that we've become so used to God that we just take him for granted. We never think to ask what the implications would be if God did *not* exist. As a result people tend to think that God is irrelevant. It doesn't matter whether God exists or not.

It's intriguing, therefore, that many atheist thinkers themselves have testified that the question of God's existence is a much-bigger deal than merely deciding whether to add one more item to our inventory of things—rather it's an issue that lies at the very center of life's meaning. It therefore touches each of us at the core of his being.

Professor Grib's "proof by the opposite" is also known as *reductio ad absurdum* (reduction to absurdity). This label is especially appropriate when it comes to the question of God's existence. For many atheist philosophers, like the French existentialists Jean-Paul Sartre and Albert Camus, have argued that if God does not exist, then life is absurd. Now Sartre and Camus didn't take this to be a proof of the opposite, namely, that God does exist. Rather they reached the grim conclusion that life really *is* absurd. Their analysis of human existence suggests that the question of God's existence is much more important than the average person realizes.

ALBERT CAMUS (1913–1960)

French existentialist novelist. Since there is no God, Camus regarded life as absurd. Life is not merely meaningless but twisted and cruel. Suicide is the only serious philosophical question. Despite life's absurdity, Camus argued against suicide and for promoting human brotherhood.

The conclusion that, given atheism, life is absurd would not prove that God exists, but it would reveal that the question of God's existence is the most important question a person can ask. If these atheist thinkers are right, then no one who truly grasped the implications of atheism could say, "Whatever!" about whether there is a God.

Of course, this atheist conclusion depends upon what we mean by "God." The nonexistence of the finite, all-too-human gods and goddesses of ancient

Greece and Rome would not make much impact upon the meaning and significance of our lives and would in many ways actually make life a whole lot easier! But when atheist philosophers use the word "God" in this present context, they mean an all-powerful, perfectly good Creator of the world who offers us eternal life, the God of traditional monotheism. If such a God does not exist, it is claimed, then life is absurd. That is to say, life has no ultimate meaning, value, or purpose.

These three notions—meaning, value, and purpose—though closely related, are distinct. *Meaning* has to do with significance, why something matters. *Value* has to do with good and evil, right and wrong. *Purpose* has to do with a goal, a reason for something.

Many atheist thinkers claim that if there is no God, then meaning, value, and purpose are ultimately human illusions. They're just in our heads. If atheism is true, then, life is really, objectively meaningless, value-less, and purposeless, despite our subjective beliefs to the contrary.

This claim is worth underscoring, since it's so frequently misunderstood. The point is not that atheists experience life as dull and meaningless, that they have no personal values or lead immoral lives, that they have no goals or purpose for living. On the contrary, life would be unbearable and unlivable without such beliefs. Rather the claim is that on atheism these beliefs are all subjective illusions: the *appearance* of meaning, value, and purpose, even though, objectively speaking, there really isn't any. The claim is that if God does not exist, our lives are ultimately meaningless, valueless,

Reductio ad absurdum, or reduction to absurdity, is a form of argument that proves a statement by demonstrating that its opposite is absurd.

Meaning has to do with significance, why something matters. *Value* has to do with good and evil, right and wrong. *Purpose* has to do with a goal, a reason for something.

and purposeless despite how desperately we cling to the illusion to the contrary.

The Absurdity of Life without God

OBJECTIVE
VERSUS
SUBJECTIVE

Something is *objective* if it's real or true independent of anyone's opinion about it. "Water is H_2O" is an objective fact.

Something is *subjective* if it's just a matter of personal opinion. "Vanilla tastes better than chocolate" is subjective.

We can keep these terms straight by remembering that "objective" is like an *object* which is really there, while "subjective" is like a *subject* or a person on whose opinion something depends.

It seems clear that if God does not exist, then both man and the universe are inevitably destined to die. For on atheism it's plausible that there are no supernatural beings or forces that can override nature's laws. Man, like all biological organisms, must die. Man's life is but a spark in the infinite darkness of an expanding universe, a spark that appears, flickers, and dies forever.

Therefore, everyone must come face-to-face with what theologian Paul Tillich has called "the threat of non-being." Though I know that I now exist, that I am alive, I also know that someday I will no longer exist, that I will no longer be, that I will die. This thought is staggering and threatening: to think that the person I call "myself" will cease to exist, that I will be no more!

Some people have tried to diminish the significance of one's impending death by comparing it to the period of nonexistence before our birth. Why, they blithely ask, should we be any more disturbed by the impending period of nonexistence *after* our death than the period of nonexistence *before* our birth?

I find this cheery suggestion difficult to take seriously. There is clearly an asymmetry here that makes all the difference in the world. Having come to exist, we rationally do not want to lose that which we have. But we are not concerned that at one time we did not have it because we hadn't yet come to exist. We celebrate birthdays but grieve at funerals because in one case something has been gained whereas in the other something has been lost. Coming to be and ceasing to be are clearly not symmetrical.

I still remember vividly the first time my father told me that someday I would die. Somehow as a child the thought had just never occurred to me. When he told me, I was filled with fear and unbearable sadness. And though he tried repeatedly to reassure me that this was a long way off, that didn't seem to matter. Whether sooner or later, the undeniable fact was that *I was going to die and be no more*, and the thought overwhelmed me.

Eventually, like all of us, I grew to simply accept the fact. We all learn to live with the inevitable. But the child's insight, I think, remains true. As Sartre observed, *several hours or several years make no difference once you have lost eternity.*

And the universe, too, faces a death of its own. Scientists tell us that the universe is expanding, and the galaxies are growing farther and farther apart. As it does so, it grows colder and colder, as its energy is used up. Eventually all the stars will burn out, and all matter will collapse into dead stars and black holes. There will be no light; there will be no heat; there will be no life; only the corpses of dead stars and galaxies, ever expanding into the endless darkness and the cold recesses of space—a universe in ruins.

This is not science fiction: if atheism is true, this is *really going to happen.* So not only is the life of each individual person destined to destruction; the entire human race and the whole edifice and accomplishment

A MAN SAID TO THE UNIVERSE

STEPHEN CRANE

A man said to the universe:
"Sir, I exist!"
"However," replied the universe,
"The fact has not created in me
A sense of obligation."

of human civilization is doomed. Like prisoners on death row, we await our unavoidable execution. There is no escape. There is no hope.

These plain scientific facts seem nearly incontestable. The question then becomes, what is the consequence of this? Many atheist thinkers have argued that it means that human life itself becomes absurd. It means that the life that we do have is without ultimate significance, value, or purpose. Let's unfold what they claim about each of these.

No Ultimate Meaning

If each individual person passes out of existence when he dies, then what ultimate meaning can be given to his life? Does it really matter in the end whether he ever existed at all? Now obviously, his life may be important *relative* to certain other events, but what's the *ultimate* significance of any of those events? If everything is destined to destruction, then what does it matter that you influenced anything? Ultimately it makes no difference.

Mankind is thus no more significant in the grand scheme of things than a swarm of mosquitoes or a barnyard of pigs. For their end is all the same. The same blind cosmic process that coughed them up in the first place will eventually swallow them all again. The contributions of the scientist to the advance of human knowledge, the researches of the doctor to alleviate pain and suffering, the efforts of the diplomat to secure peace in the world, the sacrifices of good people everywhere to better the lot of the human race—all these come to nothing. This is the predicament of modern man: because he ends in nothing, he is nothing.

But it's important to see that it's not just immortality that is at issue. Mere duration of existence doesn't make that existence meaningful. If man and the universe could exist forever, but if there were no

TALK ABOUT IT

Have you ever felt the darkness of despair, that your life is meaningless? How did you cope?

God, their existence would still have no ultimate significance. We could still ask of life, "So what?" There is no wider framework within which man's life can be seen to be significant.

I once read a science-fiction story that seems to illustrate the point. An astronaut was marooned on a barren chunk of rock lost in outer space. He had with him two vials: one containing poison and the other a potion that would make him live forever. Realizing his predicament, he gulped down the poison. But then to his horror, he discovered that he had swallowed the wrong vial—he had drunk the potion for immortality! And that meant he was cursed to exist forever—a meaningless, unending life.

Now if God does not exist, our lives seem to be just like that. They could go on and on and still be utterly without meaning. So it's not just immortality man needs if life is to be ultimately significant; we need God and immortality. And if God does not exist, then we have neither.

Thus, if there is no God, it's difficult to deny the atheist's claim, unpleasant as it may be to contemplate. Life itself becomes meaningless. Man and the universe are without ultimate significance.

No Ultimate Value

What about moral value? If human life ends at the grave—as seems very plausible given atheism—then it makes no ultimate difference whether you live as a Stalin or as a Mother Teresa. Since your destiny is ultimately unrelated to your behavior, you may as well just live as you please. As the Russian writer Fyodor Dostoyevsky put it: "If there is no immortality, then all things are permitted."

The state torturers in Soviet prisons understood this all too well. Richard Wurmbrand, a pastor who was tortured for his faith, reports:

> The cruelty of atheism is hard to believe when man has no faith in the reward of good or the punishment of evil. There is no reason to be human. There is no restraint from the depths of evil which is in man. The Communist torturers often said, "There is no God, no hereafter, no punishment for evil. We can do what

"If there is no immortality, then all things are permitted." —Fyodor Dostoyevsky

ON GUARD FOR STUDENTS

we wish." I have heard one torturer even say, "I thank God, in whom I don't believe, that I have lived to this hour when I can express all the evil in my heart." He expressed it in unbelievable brutality and torture inflicted on prisoners.[1]

Given the finality of death, it really does not matter how you live. So what do you say to someone who concludes that we may as well just live as we please, out of pure self-interest?

We might say that it's in our best self-interest to adopt a moral lifestyle. You scratch my back, and I'll scratch yours! But clearly, that's not always true: we all know situations in which self-interest runs smack in the face of morality. Moreover, if you're sufficiently powerful, like a Ferdinand Marcos or a Kim Jung Il or even a Donald Trump, then you can pretty much ignore the dictates of conscience and safely live in self-indulgence.

Historian Stewart C. Easton sums it up well when he writes, "There is no objective reason why man should be moral, unless morality 'pays off' in his social life or makes him 'feel good.' There is no objective reason why man should do anything save for the pleasure it affords him."[2]

But the problem becomes even worse. For, regardless of immortality, if there is no God, it's difficult to see what objective standard of right and wrong would exist. Given atheism, all we're confronted with is, in Jean-Paul Sartre's words, the bare, valueless fact of existence. Moral values are either just expressions of personal taste or the by-products of biological evolution and social conditioning.

After all, on the atheistic view, what's so special about human beings? They're just accidental by-products of nature which have evolved relatively recently on an infinitesimal speck of dust called planet Earth, lost somewhere in a hostile and mindless universe, and which are doomed to perish individually and collectively in a relatively short time. Richard Dawkins' assessment of human worth may be depressing, but why, on atheism, is he mistaken when he says, "There is at bottom no design, no purpose, no evil, no good, nothing but pointless indifference.... We are machines for propagating DNA.... It is every living object's sole reason for being"?[3]

In a world without God, who's to say whose values are right and whose are wrong? There doesn't seem to be any transcendent standard of objective right and wrong, only our culturally and personally relative, subjective judgments. Think of what that means! It means it's impossible to condemn war, oppression, or crime as evil. Nor can you praise generosity, self-sacrifice, and love as good. To kill someone or to love someone is morally equivalent. For in a universe without God, good and evil do not exist—there is only the bare, valueless fact of existence, and there is no one to say you are right and I am wrong.

TALK ABOUT IT

How would you live if you believed that humans are simply machines for propagating their DNA?

No Ultimate Purpose

Finally, what becomes of purpose in life if the atheist is correct? If death stands with open arms at the end of life's trail, then what is the goal of life? Is it all for nothing? Is there no reason for life? And what of the universe? Is it utterly pointless? If its destiny is a cold grave in the recesses of outer space, as modern science predicts, then the answer must be, yes—it is pointless. There is no goal, no purpose for the universe. The litter of a dead universe will just go on expanding and expanding—forever.

And what of man? Is there no purpose at all for the human race? Or will it simply peter out someday, lost in the oblivion of an indifferent universe? The English writer H. G. Wells foresaw such a prospect. In his novel *The Time Machine*, Wells' time traveler journeys far into the future to discover the destiny of man. All he finds is a dead earth, except for a few lichens and moss, orbiting a gigantic red sun. The only sounds are the rush of the wind and the gentle ripple of the sea. "Beyond these lifeless sounds," writes Wells, "the world was silent. Silent? It would be hard to convey the stillness of it. All the sounds of man, the bleating of sheep, the cries of birds, the hum of insects, the stir that makes the background of our lives—all that was over."[4] And so Wells' time traveler returned.

But to what?—to merely an earlier point on the same purposeless rush toward oblivion. When as a teenager I first read Wells' book, I thought, "No, no! It can't end that way!" But if there is no God, it *will* end that way, like it or not. This is reality in a universe without God: there is no hope; there is no purpose.

What is true of mankind as a whole is true of each of us individually: we are here to no purpose. If there is no God, then your life has no more purpose than that of an animal. As the ancient writer of Ecclesiastes put it: "The fate of the sons of men and the fate of beasts is the same. As one dies so dies the other; indeed, they all have the same breath and there is no advantage for man over beast, for all is vanity. All go to the same place. All came from the dust and all return to the dust" (Ecclesiastes 3:19–20 NASB). In this work the author shows the futility of pleasure, wealth, education, political fame, and honor in a life doomed to end in death. His verdict? "Vanity of vanities! All is vanity" (1:2b). If life ends at the grave, then we have no ultimate purpose for living.

But more than that: even if life did not end in death, without God life would still be without purpose. For man and the universe would then be simply accidents

OZYMANDIAS

Percy Bysshe Shelley

I met a traveller from an
antique land
Who said: Two vast and
trunkless legs of stone
Stand in the desert. Near
them on the sand
Half sunk, a shatter'd visage
lies, whose frown
And wrinkled lip and sneer of
cold command
Tell that its sculptor well
those passions read
Which yet survive, stamp'd
on these lifeless things,
The hand that mock'd them
and the heart that fed.
And on the pedestal these
words appear:
"My name is Ozymandias,
king of kings:
Look on my works, ye
Mighty, and despair!"
Nothing beside remains.
Round the decay
Of that colossal wreck,
boundless and bare,
The lone and level sands
stretch far away.

of chance, thrust into existence for no reason. Without God the universe is the result of a cosmic accident, a chance explosion. There is no reason for which it exists. As for man, he's a freak of nature—a blind product of matter plus time plus chance. If God does not exist, then you are just a miscarriage of nature, thrust into a purposeless universe to live a purposeless life.

Of course, you can always make up some purpose for your life. But that's not really the reason for which you exist. It's purely subjective.

So if atheism is right, man and the universe exist to no purpose—since the end of everything is death—and they came to be for no purpose, since they are only blind products of chance. In short, life is ultimately without reason.

I hope you begin to appreciate the gravity of the alternatives before us. For if God exists, then there is hope for man. But if God does not exist, then all we are left with is despair. As one writer has aptly put it, "If God is dead, then man is dead, too."

Living in Denial

But most people don't realize this fact. They continue on as though nothing has changed. I'm reminded of the story told by the nineteenth-century atheist philosopher Friedrich Nietzsche of a madman, who in the early morning hours burst into the marketplace, lantern in hand, crying, "I seek God! I seek God!" Since many of those standing about did not believe in God, he provoked much laughter. "Did God get lost?"

❧ ON GUARD FOR STUDENTS

they taunted him. "Or is he hiding? Or maybe he has gone on a voyage or emigrated!" Thus they yelled and laughed. Then, writes Nietzsche, the madman turned in their midst and pierced them with his eyes.

> "Whither is God?" he cried. "I shall tell you. We have killed him—you and I. All of us are his murderers. But how have we done this? How were we able to drink up the sea? Who gave us the sponge to wipe away the entire horizon? What did we do when we unchained this earth from its sun? Whither is it moving now? Away from all suns? Are we not plunging continually? Backward, sideward, forward, in all directions? Is there any up or down left? Are we not straying as through an infinite nothing? Do we not feel the breath of empty space? Has it not become colder? Is not night and more night coming on all the while? Must not lanterns be lit in the morning? Do we not hear anything yet of the noise of the gravediggers who are burying God? … God is dead.… And we have killed him. How shall we, the murderers of all murderers, comfort ourselves?"[5]

The crowd stared at the madman in silence and astonishment. At last he dashed his lantern to the ground. "I have come too early," he said. "This tremendous event is still on its way—it has not yet reached the ears of man."

People did not yet comprehend the consequences of the death of God; but Nietzsche predicted that someday modern man would realize the implications of atheism, and this realization would usher in an age of nihilism—the destruction of all meaning and value in life.

TALK ABOUT IT

Are the people you know willing to face up to the consequences of atheism? Why are they or aren't they?

Most people still do not reflect on the consequences of atheism and so, like the crowd in the marketplace, go unknowingly on their way. But when we realize, as did Nietzsche, what atheism implies, then his question presses hard upon us: How shall we, the murderers of all murderers, comfort ourselves?

The Practical Impossibility of Atheism

About the only solution the atheist can offer is that we face the absurdity of life and live bravely. The British philosopher Bertrand Russell, for example, believed that we have no choice but to build our lives upon "the firm foundation of unyielding despair." Only by recognizing that the world really is a terrible place can we successfully come to terms with life. Camus said that we should honestly recognize life's absurdity and then live in love for one another.

The fundamental problem with this solution, however, is that it's impossible to live consistently and happily within the framework of such a worldview. If you live consistently, you will not be happy; if you live happily, it is only because you are not consistent.

Francis Schaeffer has explained this point well. Modern man, says Schaeffer, resides in a two-story universe. In the lower story is the finite world without God; here life is absurd, as we have seen. In the upper story are meaning, value, and purpose. Now modern man lives in the lower story because he believes there is no God. But he cannot live happily in such an absurd world; therefore, he continually makes leaps of faith into the upper story to affirm meaning, value, and purpose, even though he has no right to, since he does not believe in God.

Let's look again, then, at each of the three areas in which we explored the absurdity of life without God, to see how difficult it is to live consistently and happily with an atheistic worldview.

Meaning of Life

First, the area of meaning. We saw that without God, life has no ultimate meaning. Yet atheist philosophers continue to live as though life does have meaning. For example, Sartre argued that one may create meaning for his life by freely choosing to follow a certain course of action. Sartre himself chose Marxism.

JEAN-PAUL SARTRE (1905–1980)

French existentialist philosopher. Taking Nietzsche's proclamation of God's death as given, Sartre denied that there are any objective values or meaning to life to be discovered. Rather each person is free to invent for himself whatever values and purposes he chooses. Sartre struggled to reconcile this apparent libertinism with his opposition to Nazi anti-Semitism.

Unfortunately, this is totally inconsistent. It is inconsistent to say life is objectively absurd and then to say you may create meaning for your life. If life really is absurd, then you're trapped in the lower story. To try to create meaning in life represents a leap to the upper story. But Sartre has no basis for this leap. Sartre's program is actually an exercise in self-delusion. For the universe doesn't really acquire meaning just because *I* happen to give it one. This is easy to see: for suppose I give the universe one meaning, and you give it another. Who's right? The answer, of course, is neither one. For the universe without God remains objectively meaningless, no matter how *we* happen to regard it. Sartre is really saying, "Let's *pretend* the universe has meaning." And this is just fooling yourself.

The point is this: if God does not exist, then life is objectively meaningless; but man cannot live consistently and happily knowing that life is meaningless; so in order to be happy he pretends life has meaning. But this is, of course, entirely inconsistent—for without God, man and the universe are without any real significance.

TALK ABOUT IT

Do you know anyone who thinks he can create his own meaning for his life? If so, how could you talk to him about whether this belief makes sense?

Value of Life

Turn now to the problem of value. Here is where the most blatant inconsistencies occur. First of all, atheistic humanists are totally inconsistent in affirming the traditional values of love and brotherhood. Camus has been rightly criticized for inconsistently holding to *both* the absurdity of life *and* the ethics of human love and brotherhood. The view that there are no values is logically incompatible with affirming the values of love and brotherhood. Bertrand Russell, too, was inconsistent. For although he was an atheist, he was an outspoken social critic, denouncing war and restrictions on sexual freedom. Russell admitted that he could not live as though ethical values were simply a matter of personal taste, and that he therefore found his own views "incredible." "I do not know the solution," he confessed.[6]

The point is that if there is no God, then objective right and wrong do not exist. As Dostoyevsky said, "All things are permitted." But people cannot live this way. So they make a leap of faith and affirm values anyway. And when they do so, they reveal the inadequacy of a world without God.

The horror of a world devoid of value was brought home to me with new intensity several years ago as I watched a BBC television documentary called *The Gathering*. It concerned the reunion of survivors of the Holocaust in Jerusalem, where they rediscovered lost friendships and shared their experiences. One former prisoner, a nurse, told of how she was made the gynecologist at Auschwitz. She observed that pregnant women were grouped together by the soldiers under the direction of Dr. Mengele and housed in the same barracks. Some time passed, and she noted that she no longer saw any of these women. She made inquiries. "Where are the pregnant women who were housed in that barracks?" "Haven't you heard?" came the reply. "Dr. Mengele used them for *vivisection*."

Another woman told of how Dr. Mengele had bound up her breasts so that she could not suckle her baby. The doctor wanted to learn how long an infant could survive without nourishment. Desperately this poor woman tried to keep her baby alive by giving it pieces of bread soaked in coffee, but to no avail. Each day the baby lost weight, a fact which was eagerly monitored by Dr. Mengele. A nurse then came secretly to this woman and told her, "I have arranged a way for you to get out of here, but you cannot take your baby with you. I have brought a morphine injection that you can give to your child to end its life." When the woman protested, the nurse was insistent: "Look, your baby is going to die anyway. At least save yourself." And so this mother felt compelled *to take the life of her own baby*. Dr. Mengele was furious when he learned of it because he had lost his experimental specimen, and he searched among the dead to find the baby's discarded corpse so that he could have one last weighing.

My heart was torn by these stories. One rabbi who survived the camp summed it up well when he said that at Auschwitz it was as though there existed a world in which all the Ten Commandments were reversed. Mankind had never seen such a hell.

And yet, if God does not exist, then in a sense, our world *is* Auschwitz: there is no right and wrong; *all things* are permitted.

But no atheist, no agnostic, can live consistently with such a view. Nietzsche himself, who proclaimed the necessity of living beyond good and evil, broke with his mentor Richard Wagner precisely over the issue of the composer's anti-Semitism and strident German nationalism. Similarly Sartre, writing in the aftermath of the Second World War, condemned anti-Semitism, declaring that a doctrine that leads to mass extermination is not merely an opinion or matter of personal taste, of equal value with its opposite. In his important essay "Existentialism Is a Humanism," Sartre struggles vainly to elude the contradiction between his denial of divinely pre-established values and his urgent desire to affirm the value of human persons. Like Russell, he could not live with the implications of his own denial of ethical absolutes.

Neither can the so-called "new atheists" like Richard Dawkins. For although he says that there is no evil, no good, nothing but pointless indifference, he is an unabashed moralist. He vigorously condemns such actions as the harassment and abuse of homosexuals, religious indoctrination of children, the Incan practice of human sacrifice, and prizing cultural diversity over the interests of Amish children. He even goes so far as to offer his own amended Ten Commandments for guiding moral behavior, all the while marvelously oblivious to the contradiction with his ethical subjectivism.[7]

> ### TALK ABOUT IT
> Why do you suppose that even smart atheists often don't care that their ideas about right and wrong are inconsistent?

Indeed, one will probably never find an atheist who lives consistently within his system. For a universe without moral accountability and devoid of value is unimaginably terrible.

Purpose of Life

Finally, let's look at the problem of purpose in life. The only way most people who deny purpose in life live happily is either by making up some purpose—which amounts to self-delusion, as we saw with Sartre—or by not carrying their view to its logical conclusions. The temptation to invest one's own petty plans and projects with objective significance and thereby to find some purpose to one's life is almost irresistible.

For example, the outspoken atheist and Nobel Prize–winning physicist Steven Weinberg, at the close of his much-acclaimed book *The First Three Minutes*, writes:

> It is almost irresistible for humans to believe that we have some special relation to the universe, that human life is not just a more-or-less farcical outcome of a chain of accidents reaching back to the first three minutes, but that somehow we were built in from the beginning.... It is very hard to realize that this is all just a tiny part of an overwhelmingly hostile universe. It is even harder to realize that this present universe has evolved from an unspeakably unfamiliar early condition, and faces a future extinction of endless cold or intolerable heat. The more the universe seems comprehensible, the more it also seems pointless.
>
> But if there is no solace in the fruits of our research, there is at least some consolation in the research itself. Men and women are not content to comfort themselves with tales of gods and giants, or to confine their thoughts to the daily affairs of life; they also build telescopes and satellites and accelerators and sit at their desks for endless hours working out the meaning of the data they gather. The effort to understand the universe is one of the very few things that lifts human life a little above the level of farce, and gives it some of the grace of tragedy.[8]

There's something strange about Weinberg's moving description of the human predicament: *tragedy* is an evaluative term. Weinberg sees the pursuit of scientific research as raising human life above the level of farce to the level of tragedy. But on atheism, what is the basis for such an evaluative differentiation? Weinberg evidently sees a life devoted to scientific pursuits as truly meaningful, and therefore it's too bad that such a noble pursuit should be extinguished. But why on atheism should the pursuit of science be any different from slouching about doing nothing? Since there is no objective purpose to human life, none of our pursuits has any objective significance, however important and dear they may seem to us subjectively. They're no more significant than shuffling deck chairs on the *Titanic*.

The Human Predicament

The dilemma of modern man is thus truly terrible. Man cannot live consistently and happily as though life were ultimately without meaning, value, or purpose. If we try to live consistently within the atheistic worldview, we shall find ourselves profoundly unhappy. If instead we manage to live happily, it is only by giving the lie to our worldview.

TALK ABOUT IT

Think of a movie you've seen recently. If you asked the main character, "Why does your life matter?" what do you think he or she would say?

Confronted with this dilemma, modern man flounders pathetically for some means of escape. In a remarkable address to the American Academy for the Advancement of Science in 1991, Dr. L. D. Rue, confronted with the predicament of modern man, boldly advocated that we deceive ourselves by means of some "Noble Lie" into thinking that we and the universe still have value.

According to Rue, "The lesson of the past two centuries is that intellectual and moral relativism is profoundly the case." He says that the consequence of this realization is that the quest for self-fulfillment and the quest for social coherence fall apart. This is because on the view of relativism the search for self-fulfillment becomes radically privatized: each person chooses his *own* set of values and meaning.

So what are we to do? Rue says there is on the one hand "the madhouse option," where self-fulfillment is pursued regardless of social coherence. On the other hand, there is "the totalitarian option," where social coherence is imposed at the expense of personal fulfillment. If we're to avoid these two options, he says, then we have no choice but to embrace some Noble Lie that will inspire us to live beyond selfish interests and so voluntarily achieve social coherence. A Noble Lie "is one that deceives us, tricks us, compels us beyond self-interest, beyond ego, beyond family, nation, [and] race." It is a lie, because it tells us that the universe is infused with value (which is a great fiction), because it makes a claim to universal truth (when there is none), and because it tells me not to live for self-interest (which is evidently false). "But without such lies, we cannot live."

This is the dreadful verdict pronounced over modern man. In order to survive, he must live in self-deception.

Back to Square One

So what do we do now? It seems to me that in light of the consequences of how we answer the question of God's existence, it is imperative that we go back to square one and ask what reasons there are for believing in God's existence or not. For maybe the atheist is wrong. Maybe God exists after all. I know, I know: none of what we've said gives us grounds for thinking that God does exist. Indeed, the atheist might say that theism is itself a Noble Lie by which we deceive ourselves. But apart from examining the arguments for and against God, how can the atheist justifiably make

NOBLE LIE

A Noble Lie "is one that deceives us, tricks us, compels us beyond self-interest, beyond ego, beyond family, nation, [and] race."
—Dr. L. D. Rue

such an accusation? How does he know that God does not exist? Shouldn't we at least look at the evidence?

That is surely correct. Some philosophers have even argued that if the evidence for these two options were absolutely equal, a rational person ought to choose to believe in God. That is, if the evidence is equal, it seems positively irrational to prefer death, futility, and destruction to life, meaningfulness, and happiness. As Pascal said, we have nothing to lose and infinity to gain.

But my aim in this chapter is more modest than that. I only hope to have gotten you *to think* about these issues, to realize that the question of God's existence has profound consequences for our lives and that therefore we cannot afford to be indifferent about it. What I've at least done is to clearly spell out the alternatives. If God does not exist, then life is futile. If God does exist, then life is meaningful. Only the second of these two alternatives enables us to live happily and consistently. Therefore, it makes a huge *difference* whether God exists, a difference we should care about.

Who cares? You should.

1. Richard Wurmbrand, *Tortured for Christ* (London: Hodder & Stoughton, 1967), 34.
2. Stewart C. Easton, *The Western Heritage*, 2nd ed. (New York: Holt, Rinehart, & Winston, 1966), 878.
3. Cited in Lewis Wolpert, *Six Impossible Things before Breakfast*, 215. Unfortunately, Wolpert's reference is mistaken. The quotation seems to be a pastiche from Richard Dawkins, *River Out of Eden: A Darwinian View of Life* (New York: Basic Books, 1996), 133; and Richard Dawkins, "The Ultraviolet Garden," Lecture 4 of 7 Royal Institution Christmas Lectures (1992), http://physicshead.blogspot.com/2007/01/richard-dawkins-lecture-4-ultraviolet.html. Thanks to my assistant Joe Gorra for tracking down this reference!
4. H. G. Wells, *The Time Machine* (New York: Berkeley, 1957), chap. 11.
5. Friedrich Nietzsche, "The Gay Science," in *The Portable Nietzsche*, ed. and trans. W. Kaufmann (New York: Viking, 1954), 95.
6. Bertrand Russell, letter to the *Observer*, October 6, 1957.
7. Richard Dawkins, *The God Delusion* (New York: Houghton-Mifflin, 2006), 23, 264, 313–17, 326, 328, 330.
8. Steven Weinberg, *The First Three Minutes* (London: Andre Deutsch, 1977), 154–55.

I. If God does not exist, then all human life as well as every individual life will eventually be destroyed.

II. If there is no God and no life beyond the grave, then life itself has no objective meaning, value, or purpose.

  A. Meaning

    1. Without immortality your life has no ultimate significance and makes no difference to the world's outcome.

    2. Without God there is no broader framework within which man's life can be seen to matter.

  B. Value

    1. Without immortality there is no moral accountability, and your moral choices become inconsequential.

    2. Without God moral values are just delusions ingrained into us by evolution and social conditioning.

  C. Purpose

    1. Without immortality your only destination is extinction in death.

    2. Without God there is no purpose for which you came into this world.

III. It is impossible to live consistently and happily with an atheistic worldview.

  A. If we live happily as atheists, it is only by inconsistently affirming meaning, value, and purpose for our lives, despite the lack of foundation for them.

  B. If we live consistently as atheists, we shall be profoundly unhappy and even in despair because we know our lives are really meaningless, worthless, and purposeless.

IV. Biblical Christianity challenges the worldview of modern man.

A. According to biblical Christianity God exists and life does not end at the grave.

B. Biblical Christianity thereby affirms the two conditions sufficient for a meaningful, valuable, and purposeful life: God and immortality.

C. Biblical Christianity therefore supplies a framework within which one can live consistently and happily.

D. So why not look into the truth of biblical Christianity?

CHAPTER 2

WHY DOES ANYTHING AT ALL EXIST?

Why are there beings rather than nothing? That is the question. Clearly it is no ordinary question. "Why are there beings, why is there anything at all, rather than nothing?"—obviously this is the first of all questions.

Martin Heidegger, *Introduction to Metaphysics*

Keokuk, Iowa, was a great place to grow up as a boy. On the banks of the mighty Mississippi River, in the southeastern toe of Iowa that hangs down over Missouri, Keokuk is in Mark Twain territory. As kids, we had every kind of pet we could catch: frogs, toads, snakes, salamanders, rabbits, birds, stray dogs and cats that wandered by our house, even a bat and a possum. You could see the stars clearly at night in Keokuk, too. I remember as a boy looking up at the stars, innumerable in the black night, and thinking, "Where did all of this come from?" It seemed to me instinctively that there had to be an explanation for why all this exists.

Only years later did I realize that my boyhood question, as well as its answer, had occupied the minds of the greatest philosophers for centuries. For example, G. W. Leibniz, co-discoverer of the calculus and a towering intellect of eighteenth-century Europe, wrote: "The first question which should rightly be asked is: *Why is there something rather than nothing?*" In other words, why does anything at all exist? This, for Leibniz, is the most basic question that anyone can ask.

So we shall begin our inquiry where Leibniz said we should begin, despite the difficulty of the question. Bear with me and it will all be worth it. Why does anything at all exist? Leibniz came to the conclusion that the answer is to be found, not in the universe of created things, but in God. God exists necessarily and is the explanation for why anything else exists.

Leibniz's Argument

We can put Leibniz's thinking into the form of a simple argument. This has the advantage of making his logic very clear and focusing our attention on the crucial steps of his reasoning. (You'll find an argument map at the end of this chapter.)

GOTTFRIED WILHELM LEIBNIZ

Gottfried Wilhelm Leibniz (1646–1716) was a German philosopher, mathematician, and logician. He invented differential and integral calculus at about the same time Sir Isaac Newton did. In fact, he spent the last five years of his life defending himself against the accusation that he had stolen Newton's ideas and published them. Today most historians agree that Leibniz did invent calculus independently.

Here are the premises of Leibniz's argument:

1. Everything that exists has an explanation of its existence.
2. If the universe has an explanation of its existence, that explanation is God.
3. The universe exists.

That's it! Now what follows logically from these three premises?

Well, look at premises 1 and 3. If *everything that exists has an explanation of its existence* and *the universe exists*, then it logically follows that:

TALK ABOUT IT

Which of the three premises have you heard atheists challenge? On what basis did they do so?

4. The universe has an explanation of its existence.

Now notice that premise 2 says that *if the universe has an explanation of its existence, that explanation is God.* And 4 says *the universe does have an explanation of its existence.* So from 2 and 4 the conclusion logically follows:

5. Therefore, the explanation of the universe's existence is God.

Is this a good argument? Well, that all depends on what you mean by a good argument. You can always deny the conclusion of any argument simply by denying one of the premises. But if we follow the evidence where it leads, we shall accept the premises if they are, in light of the evidence, more plausible than their negations. The premises of a good argument, then, don't need to be certain, but just more plausibly true than false.

To be a good argument, then, an argument must meet three conditions: (1) its conclusion follows from its premises by the rules of logic; (2) its premises are true; and (3) in light of the evidence its premises are more plausible than not.

Now Leibniz's argument is a logically airtight argument. That is to say, if the three premises are true, then the conclusion follows logically. It doesn't matter if we don't like the conclusion. It doesn't matter if we have other objections to God's existence. So long as we agree with the three premises, we have to accept the conclusion.

So are the premises more plausibly true than false? Premise 3 is, I think, undeniable for any sincere seeker after truth. Obviously the universe exists! So the whole question comes down to this: Are premises 1 and 2 more plausibly true or false? Well, let's look at them.

PREMISE 1

Everything that exists has an explanation of its existence.

An Objection to Premise 1

At first blush premise 1 might seem vulnerable in an obvious way. If everything that exists has an explanation of its existence and God exists, then God must have an explanation of his existence! But that seems absurd, for then the explanation of God's existence would have to be some other being greater than God. But that's impossible, since God is supposed to be the greatest being conceivable, certainly greater than anything else that exists! So premise 1 must be false. *Some* things must be able to exist without any explanation. The theist will say that God exists inexplicably. The atheist will say, "Why not stop with the universe? The universe just exists inexplicably." So we seem to reach a stalemate.

Not so fast! This obvious objection to premise 1 is based, I think, on a misunderstanding of what Leibniz meant by an "explanation." In Leibniz's view there are two kinds of things: (a) things which exist necessarily and (b) things which are produced by some external cause. Let me explain.

NECESSARY OR CONTINGENT

Things that *exist necessarily* exist by a necessity of their own nature. It belongs to their very nature to exist. Things that *exist contingently* can fail to exist and so need an external cause to explain why they do in fact exist.

(a) Things which exist necessarily exist by a necessity of their own nature. It's impossible for them not to exist. Philosophers call such things metaphysically necessary beings. Examples? Many mathematicians think that numbers, sets, and other mathematical entities exist in this way. It's hotly debated whether such mathematical entities really do exist. But virtually everyone agrees that if there really are such things as numbers, sets, and so on, they don't just happen to exist. No matter how the physical universe might have been, there would still be numbers. So they exist either necessarily or not at all.

(b) By contrast, things that are caused to exist by something else don't exist necessarily. They exist because something else has produced them. If their causes were removed, then they would not exist. Examples? Familiar physical objects like people, planets, and galaxies belong in this category. Unlike mathematical entities like numbers, these things would not still exist, no matter how the universe were changed.

So when Leibniz says that everything that exists has an explanation of its existence, the explanation may be found *either* in the necessity of a thing's nature or else in some external cause. So premise 1 could be more fully stated in the following way:

> 1. Everything that exists has an explanation of its existence, either in the necessity of its own nature or in an external cause.

But now the objection falls to the ground. The explanation of God's existence, if he exists, lies in the necessity of his own nature. As even the atheist recognizes, it's impossible for God to have a cause. So Leibniz's argument is really an argument for God as a metaphysically necessary, uncaused being.

Far from undermining Leibniz's argument, the atheist's objection to premise 1 actually helps to clarify and magnify the concept of God. For if God exists, he is a necessarily existing, uncaused being.

TALK ABOUT IT

If he exists at all, why is it impossible for God to have a cause?

Grounds for Premise 1

So what grounds might be offered for thinking that premise 1 is true? Well, when you reflect on it, premise 1 has a sort of self-evidence about it. Imagine that you're hiking through the woods and you come across a ball lying on the forest floor. You would naturally wonder how it came to be there. If one of your hiking partners said to you, "It just exists inexplicably! Forget about it!" you'd either think that he was nuts or figure that he just wanted you to keep moving. No one would take seriously the suggestion that the ball existed there with literally no explanation.

Now suppose you increase the size of the ball in this story so that it's the size of a car. That wouldn't do anything to satisfy or remove the demand for an explanation. Suppose it were the size of a house. Same problem. Suppose it were the size of a continent or a planet. Same problem. Suppose it were the size of the entire universe. Same problem. Merely increasing the size of the ball does nothing to affect the need of an explanation.

The Taxicab Fallacy

So how do atheists usually reply to Leibniz's argument? The typical atheist response to Leibniz's argument is to deny that premise 1 applies to the universe. Sometimes atheists will say that premise 1 is true of everything *in* the universe but is not true *of* the universe itself. Everything in the universe has an explanation, but the universe itself has no explanation.

But this response commits what has been aptly called "the taxicab fallacy." For as the nineteenth-century atheist philosopher Arthur Schopenhauer quipped, premise 1 can't be dismissed like a hack once you've arrived at your desired destination! You can't say everything has an explanation of its existence and then suddenly exempt the universe.

It would be arbitrary for the atheist to claim that the universe is the exception to the rule. (Recall that Leibniz does *not* make God an exception to premise 1.) The illustration of the ball in the woods showed that merely increasing the size of the object to be explained, even until it becomes the universe itself, does nothing to remove the need for some explanation of its existence.

Notice, too, how unscientific this atheist response is. For modern cosmology (the study of the universe) is devoted to the search for an explanation of the universe's existence. The atheist attitude, if adopted, would cripple science.

So some atheists have tried to *justify* making the universe an exception to premise 1. This is a more reasonable approach, since it seeks to give a reason for making the universe an exception to the rule. So what justification have atheists given for exempting the universe from premise 1? They say that it's *impossible* for the universe to have an explanation of its existence. For the explanation of the universe would have to be some prior state of affairs in which the universe did not yet exist. But that would be nothingness, and nothingness cannot be the explanation of anything. So the universe must just exist inexplicably.

The problem is that this line of attack is obviously fallacious. For it just assumes that the universe is all there is, so that if there were no universe there would be nothing. In other words, the objection assumes that atheism is true! The atheist is thus begging the question, arguing in a circle.

FALLACY

A *fallacy* is an error in reasoning. Fallacies can be either formal or informal. A formal fallacy involves breaking the rules of logic. An informal fallacy involves an argumentative tactic that is illicit, such as reasoning in a circle. The "taxicab fallacy" would be an informal fallacy.

COSMOLOGY

Cosmology is the study of the large-scale structure and development of the universe. The Greek word *kosmos* means "orderly arrangement" or "world." Pythagoras may have been the first person to use this word to refer to the universe.

TALK ABOUT IT

It's hard to imagine nothing. We can imagine empty space, but empty space is something, not nothing. Try to imagine that only God exists. Not the universe, not empty space, not even time. What goes on in your head when you try to conceive of this? Now suppose that not even God exists.

Leibniz would agree that the explanation of the universe must be a prior state of affairs in which the universe did not exist. But that state of affairs, he would say, is God and his will, not nothingness.

So it seems to me that premise 1 is more plausibly true than false.

PREMISE 2

If the universe has an explanation of its existence, that explanation is God.

Atheists Agree with Premise 2

What, then, about premise 2, that *if the universe has an explanation of its existence, that explanation is God*? When I first encountered the present formulation of Leibniz's argument, this seemed to me the obviously weak premise. Like the *Deus ex machina* in ancient Greek plays, God suddenly appears out of nowhere in this premise. Why should we think premise 2 more plausibly true than false?

What I failed at first to realize is that premise 2 is, in fact, logically equivalent to the typical *atheist* response to Leibniz's argument. Two statements are logically equivalent if it is impossible for one to be true and the other one to be false. They stand or fall together. So what do atheists almost always say in response to Leibniz's argument? As we have just seen, the atheist typically asserts the following:

> A. If atheism is true, the universe has
> no explanation of its existence.

LOGICAL EQUIVALENCE

Two statements are logically equivalent if it is impossible for one to be true and the other false. They are either both true or both false.
One of the most important logical equivalences is called *contraposition*. It tells us that any statement of the form "If P, then Q" is logically equivalent to "If not-Q, then not-P." The example in the text of statements A and B is an example of contraposition.

❧ ON GUARD FOR STUDENTS

This is precisely what the atheist says in response to premise 1. The universe is the exception to the rule. The universe just exists inexplicably. But this is logically equivalent to saying:

> B. If the universe has an explanation of its existence, then atheism is not true.

So you can't affirm (A) and deny (B).

But (B) is virtually synonymous with premise 2! (Just compare them.) So by saying in response to premise 1 that, given atheism, the universe has no explanation, the atheist is implicitly admitting premise 2, that if the universe does have an explanation, then God exists.

Besides that, premise 2 is very plausible in its own right. For think of what the universe is: *all* of space-time reality, including *all* matter and energy. Leibniz is using the word "universe" as an all-inclusive term for space-time reality, regardless of whether our observable universe is part of a larger multiverse. It follows that if the all-inclusive universe has an explanation of its existence, there must be a nonphysical, immaterial being beyond space and time.

Now there are only two candidates that could possibly fit that description: either an abstract object like a number or else an unembodied mind or consciousness. But abstract objects can't cause anything. That's part of what it means to be abstract. The number 7, for example, can't cause any effects. So it follows logically

ABSTRACT VERSUS CONCRETE OBJECTS

Philosophers distinguish objects as being either abstract or concrete. The defining difference between them is that abstract objects are causally effete, or impotent, whereas concrete objects can cause effects in the world. Various objects have been identified by different philosophers as abstract, principally mathematical entities like numbers, sets, and functions, but also propositions, properties, fictional characters, and even musical and literary works.

that the cause of the existence of the universe must be a transcendent Mind, which is what believers understand God to be.

I hope you begin to grasp the power of Leibniz's argument. If successful, it proves the existence of a metaphysically necessary, uncaused, timeless, spaceless, immaterial, Personal Creator of the universe. This is truly mind-blowing!

Atheist Alternative

The atheist has one alternative open to him at this point. He can retrace his steps, withdraw his objection to premise 1, and say instead that, yes, the universe *does* have an explanation of its existence. But that explanation is: the universe exists by a necessity of its own nature. The universe could serve as a sort of God-substitute which exists necessarily.

Now this would be a very radical step to take, and I can't think of any contemporary atheist who has in fact adopted this line. A few years ago at a Philosophy of Time conference at City College in Santa Barbara, I thought that Professor Adolf Grünbaum, a vociferous atheistic philosopher of science from the University of Pittsburgh, was flirting with this idea. But when I raised the question from the floor whether he thought the universe existed necessarily, he was quite indignant at the suggestion. "Of course not!" he snapped and went on to give the typical atheist response that the universe just exists without any explanation.

The reason atheists are not eager to embrace this alternative is clear. As we look about the universe, none of the things that make it up, whether stars, planets, galaxies, dust, radiation, or what have you, seems to exist necessarily. They could all fail to exist; indeed, at some point in the past, when the universe was very dense, none of them did exist.

TALK ABOUT IT

Do you know anyone who believes that the universe or the world is a God-substitute (like Gaia or the Force from *Star Wars*)? What leads them to believe that?

But, the atheist might insist, what about the matter out of which these things are made? Maybe the matter exists necessarily, and all these things are just different configurations of matter. The problem with this suggestion is that, according to the standard model of subatomic physics, matter itself is composed of fundamental particles such as quarks. The universe is just the collection of all these particles arranged in different ways. But then a new question arises: Couldn't a different collection of fundamental particles have existed instead of this one? Does each and every one of these particles exist necessarily?

	I	II	III	
Quarks	U up	C charm	t top	γ photon
	d down	s strange	b bottom	g gluon
Leptons	νe electron neutrino	νμ muon neutrino	ντ tau neutrino	Z^0 weak force
	e electron	μ muon	τ tau	$W^{\pm}$ weak force
				Bosons

Notice what the atheist cannot say at this point. He cannot say that the fundamental particles are just configurations of matter which could have been different, even though the matter of which the particles are composed exists necessarily. He can't say this because particles aren't composed of anything! They just *are* the basic units of matter. So if a fundamental particle doesn't exist, the matter doesn't exist.

Now it seems obvious that a different collection of particles could have existed instead of the collection that does exist. But if that were the case, then a different universe would have existed.

To see the point, think about your desk. Could your desk have been made of ice? Notice that I'm not asking if you could have had an ice desk in the place of your wooden desk that had the same size and shape. Rather I'm asking if your very desk, the one made of wood, if *that* desk could have been made of ice. The answer seems obviously, no. The ice desk would be a different desk, not the same desk.

Similarly, a universe made up of different particles, even if identically arranged as in this universe, would be a different universe. It follows, then, that the universe does not exist by a necessity of its own nature.

So atheists have not been so bold as to deny premise 2 and say that the universe exists necessarily. Premise 2 also seems to be plausibly true.

TALK ABOUT IT

Ask a physics teacher: Why do elementary particles exist? Is it impossible for them not to exist? (Be prepared for the possibility that your physics teacher doesn't want to have this conversation.)

Conclusion

But given the truth of the three premises, the conclusion is logically inescapable: *God is the explanation of the existence of the universe.* This is no ill-defined flying spaghetti monster. The argument implies that God is an uncaused, unembodied Mind who transcends the physical universe and even space and time themselves and who exists necessarily. This conclusion is staggering. Leibniz has expanded our minds far beyond the mundane affairs of daily life. In the next chapter our minds will be stretched further still, as we try to grasp the infinite and discover the beginning of the universe.

TALK ABOUT IT

How has this chapter shown that God:
Is unembodied Mind?
Transcends the universe?
Created the universe?

LEIBNIZ'S COSMOLOGICAL ARGUMENT

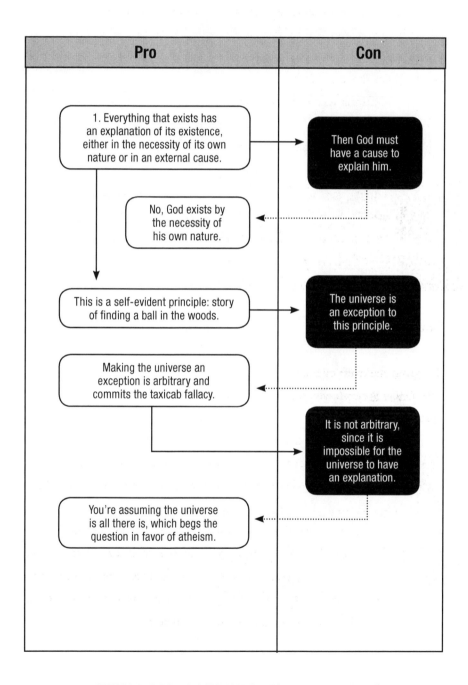

Pro	Con
1. Everything that exists has an explanation of its existence, either in the necessity of its own nature or in an external cause.	Then God must have a cause to explain him.
No, God exists by the necessity of his own nature.	
This is a self-evident principle: story of finding a ball in the woods.	The universe is an exception to this principle.
Making the universe an exception is arbitrary and commits the taxicab fallacy.	
	It is not arbitrary, since it is impossible for the universe to have an explanation.
You're assuming the universe is all there is, which begs the question in favor of atheism.	

LEIBNIZ'S COSMOLOGICAL ARGUMENT (cont.)

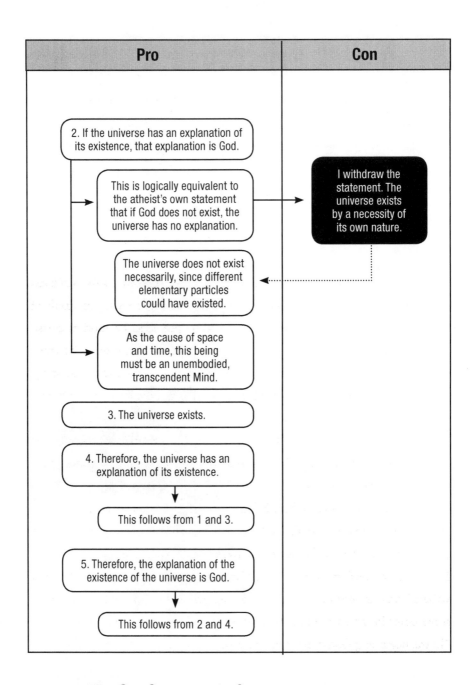

Pro	Con
2. If the universe has an explanation of its existence, that explanation is God.	
This is logically equivalent to the atheist's own statement that if God does not exist, the universe has no explanation.	I withdraw the statement. The universe exists by a necessity of its own nature.
The universe does not exist necessarily, since different elementary particles could have existed.	
As the cause of space and time, this being must be an unembodied, transcendent Mind.	
3. The universe exists.	
4. Therefore, the universe has an explanation of its existence.	
This follows from 1 and 3.	
5. Therefore, the explanation of the existence of the universe is God.	
This follows from 2 and 4.	

CHAPTER 3

WHY DID THE UNIVERSE BEGIN?

An infinite number of real parts of time, passing in succession, and exhausted one after another, appears so evident a contradiction, that no man, one should think, whose judgement is not corrupted, instead of being improved, by the sciences, would ever be able to admit of it.

David Hume, *An Enquiry concerning Human Understanding*

As a boy I not only wondered at the existence of the cosmos. I also wondered about how it began. I remember lying in bed at night trying to think of a beginningless universe. Every event would be preceded by another event, back and back into the past, with no stopping point—or, more accurately, no starting point! An infinite past with no beginning. My mind reeled at the prospect. It just seemed inconceivable to me. There must have been a beginning at some point, I thought, in order for everything to get started.

Again, little did I suspect that for centuries—millennia, really—men had grappled with the idea of an infinite past and the question of whether there was an absolute beginning.

Ancient Greek philosophers believed that matter was necessary and uncreated and therefore eternal. God may be responsible for introducing order into the cosmos, but he did not create the universe itself. This Greek view was in contrast to even more ancient Jewish thought about the subject. Hebrew writers held that the universe had not always existed but was created by God at some point in the past. As the first verse of the Hebrew holy scriptures states: "In the beginning God created the heavens and the earth" (Genesis 1:1).

Eventually these two competing traditions began to interact. There arose within Western philosophy an ongoing debate that lasted for well over a thousand years about whether or not the universe had a beginning. This debate played itself out among Jews and Muslims as well as Christians, both Catholic and Protestant. It finally sputtered to something of an inconclusive end in the thought of the great eighteenth-century German philosopher Immanuel Kant. He held, ironically, that there are rationally compelling arguments for *both* sides, thereby exposing the bankruptcy of reason itself!

Al-Ghazali's Argument

What is the argument that provoked such debate? Let's allow one of its greatest medieval champions to speak for himself. Al-Ghazali was a twelfth-century Muslim theologian from Persia, or modern-day Iran. He was concerned that Muslim philosophers of his day were being influenced by ancient Greek philosophy to deny God's creation of the universe. They held that the universe flows necessarily out of God and therefore is beginningless.

After thoroughly studying the teachings of these philosophers, Ghazali wrote a withering critique of their views entitled *The Incoherence of the Philosophers*. In this fascinating book, he argues that the idea of a beginningless

ABÛ HÂMID MUHAMMAD IBN MUHAMMAD AL-GHAZÂLÎ

Al-Ghazali was born sometime between AD 1055 and 1058 in Persia. By his midthirties his learnedness had come to the attention of the grand vizier of the Seljuks, who appointed him to teach at a prestigious madrassa in Baghdad. He became influential at court and a confidant of the sultan. But his study of Sufi literature led him to conclude that it was impossible to live by the high ethics of his religion while enjoying the riches of powerful men, because he was supporting their corrupt rule. So in 1095 he left Baghdad to lead a simpler life. He taught in minor schools until 1106, when he returned to a prominent madrassa to, he said, correct theological confusion among the public. He died in his hometown in 1111.

universe is absurd. The universe must have had a beginning, and, since nothing begins to exist without a cause, there must be a transcendent Creator of the universe.

Ghazali frames his argument simply: "Every being which begins has a cause for its beginning; now the world is a being which begins; therefore, it possesses a cause for its beginning."[1]

Once again, we can summarize Ghazali's reasoning in three simple steps:

1. Whatever begins to exist has a cause of its beginning.
2. The universe began to exist.
3. Therefore, the universe has a cause of its beginning.

This argument is logically airtight. If the two premises are true, then the conclusion necessarily follows. So anybody who wants to deny the conclusion has to regard either premise 1 or premise 2 as false. So the whole question is: Are these two premises more plausibly true or false? Let's examine each premise in turn.

PREMISE 1

Whatever begins to exist has a cause.

It seems to me that the first premise, that *whatever begins to exist has a cause of its beginning*, is almost undeniable for any sincere seeker after truth. For something to come into being *without any cause whatsoever* would be to come into being from nothing. That is surely impossible. Here are three reasons in support of this premise:

1. *Something cannot come from nothing.* To claim that something can come into being from nothing is worse than magic. When a magician pulls a rabbit out of a hat, at least you've got the magician, not to mention the hat! But if you deny premise 1, you've got to think that the whole universe just appeared at some point in the past for no reason whatsoever. But nobody

sincerely believes that things, say, a horse or an Eskimo village, can just pop into being without a cause.

Sometimes skeptics will respond to this point by saying that in physics subatomic particles (so-called "virtual particles") come into being from nothing. Or certain theories of the origin of the universe are sometimes described in popular magazines as getting something from nothing, so that the universe is the exception to the proverb "There ain't no free lunch."

This skeptical response represents a deliberate abuse of science. The theories in question have to do with particles' (or the universe's) originating as a fluctuation of a physical system, such as the subatomic vacuum. The vacuum in modern physics is not what the layman understands by "vacuum," namely, nothing. Rather in physics the vacuum is a sea of fluctuating energy governed by physical laws and having a physical structure. To tell laymen that on such theories something comes from nothing is a misrepresentation of those theories.

Properly speaking, the word "nothing" is a term of universal negation. It means "not anything." So, for example, if I say, "I had nothing for lunch today," I mean, "I didn't have anything for lunch today." If you read an account of World War II in which it says that "nothing stopped the German advance from sweeping across Belgium," it means that the German advance was not stopped by anything. If a theologian tells you that "God created the universe out of nothing," he means that God's creation of the universe was not out of anything. The word "nothing," to repeat, is simply a term of universal negation, meaning "not anything."

POP SCIENCE

You have to be very, very leery of popular articles and television shows on scientific theories. In order to communicate these highly technical theories to laymen, writers inevitably have to resort to metaphors and word pictures that can be grossly misleading and inaccurate. The claim that physics shows that something can come from "nothing" is a case in point.

ON GUARD FOR STUDENTS

There's a whole series of similar words of universal negation in English: "Nobody" means not anybody. "None" means not one. "Nowhere" means not anywhere. "No place" means not in any place.

Now because the word "nothing" is grammatically a pronoun, we can use it as the subject or direct object of a sentence. By misusing these words, not as terms of universal negation, but as words referring to something, you can generate all sorts of funny situations. If you say, "I saw nobody in the hall," the wiseacre replies, "Yeah, he's been hanging around there a lot lately!" If you say, "I had nothing for lunch today," he says, "Really? How did it taste?"

These sorts of puns are as old as literature itself. In Homer's *Odyssey*, Odysseus introduces himself to the Cyclops as "No man" or "Nobody." One night Odysseus puts out the Cyclops' eye. His fellow Cyclopses hear him screaming and yell to him, "What's the matter with you, making so much noise that we can't sleep?" The Cyclops answers, "Nobody is killing me! Nobody is killing me!" They reply, "If nobody is attacking you, then you must be sick, and there's nothing we can do about it!"

In Euripides' version of the story, he composes a sort of Abbott and Costello "Who's on first?" routine:

> "Why are you crying out, Cyclops?"
> "Nobody has undone me!"
> "Then there is no one hurting you after all."
> "Nobody is blinding me!"
> "Then you're not blind."
> "As blind as you!"
> "How could nobody have made you blind?"
> "You're mocking me! But where is this Nobody?"
> "Nowhere, Cyclops!"

The use of these words of negation like "nothing," "nobody," and "no one" as substantive words referring to something *is a joke*.

How astonishing, then, to find that some contemporary popularizers of science, whose mother tongue is English, have used these terms precisely as substantive terms of reference. They've told us with a straight face, for example, that:

> "There are a variety of forms of nothing, [and] they all have physical definitions."
> "The laws of quantum mechanics tell us that nothing is unstable."
> "Seventy percent of the dominant stuff in the universe is nothing."
> "There's nothing there, but it has energy."
> "Nothing weighs something."
> "Nothing is almost everything."[2]

All of these claims take the word "nothing" to be a substantive term referring to something, for example, the quantum vacuum or quantum fields. These are physical realities and therefore clearly something. To call these realities nothing is at best misleading, guaranteed to confuse laypeople, and at worst a deliberate misrepresentation of science. Such statements do not even begin to address, much less answer, Leibniz's question as to why there is something rather than nothing.

2. *If something can come into being from nothing, then it becomes inexplicable why just anything or everything doesn't come into being from nothing.* Think about it: Why don't bicycles and Beethoven and root beer just pop into being from nothing? Why is it only universes that can come into being from nothing? What makes nothingness so discriminatory? There can't be anything about nothingness that favors universes, for nothingness doesn't have any properties. Nor can anything constrain nothingness, for there isn't anything to be constrained! Remember: "nothing" means not anything.

I've heard atheists respond to this argument by saying that premise 1 is true of everything *in* the universe but not *of* the universe. But this is just the old taxicab fallacy that we encountered in chapter 2. You can't dismiss the causal principle as you would a cab once you get to the universe. Premise 1 is not merely a physical law of nature, like the law of gravity, which only applies in the universe. Rather it's a metaphysical principle that governs all being, all reality.

At this point the atheist is likely to retort, "All right, if everything has a cause, what is God's cause?" I'm always amazed at the self-congratulatory attitude with which students pose this question. They imagine that they've said something important or profound, when all they've done is misunderstand the premise. Premise 1 does not say that everything has a cause. Rather it says that everything *that begins to exist* has a cause. Something that is eternal wouldn't need a cause, since it never came into being.

Ghazali would therefore respond to the question by saying that God is eternal and uncaused. This is not special pleading for God, since this is exactly what the atheist has traditionally said about the universe: it is eternal and uncaused. The problem is that if we now have good evidence that the universe is not eternal but had a beginning, then the atheist is backed into the corner of saying the universe sprang into being without a cause, which is absurd.

> *Metaphysics* is the branch of philosophy devoted to exploring questions about the nature of ultimate reality. Prominent issues in metaphysics include the nature of existence, the nature of time and space, the relation of mind and body, the reality of abstract objects, and the existence of God.

> ### TALK ABOUT IT
> Why do you suppose so many smart people think it makes sense that the universe may have popped into being from nothing, without a cause?

TALK ABOUT IT

What would you say to someone who says that nothing ever begins to exist, since everything is made of prior material constituents?

3. Common experience and scientific evidence confirm the truth of premise 1. Premise 1 is constantly verified and never falsified. It's hard to understand how any atheist committed to modern science could deny that premise 1 is more plausibly true than false in light of the evidence.

I've heard some skeptics respond to this third point by charging that it commits the fallacy of composition. Reasoning by composition involves inferring that because every *part* of a thing has a certain property, therefore the *whole* thing has that property. For example, someone might wrongly infer that because every part of an elephant is light in weight, the entire elephant is light in weight.

This third point, by contrast, does not infer that because every part of the universe has a cause, therefore the whole universe has a cause. In fact, it doesn't even refer to the universe, much less its parts!

Rather this third point is classic inductive reasoning, which underlies all of science. One infers from a random sample of items some property shared by every item of that sort. The sort in question is *things that begin to exist.* They always have causes. So the generalization that *whatever begins to exist has a cause of its beginning* is powerfully supported by the inductive evidence. The objection is based on a confusion between inductive reasoning (which is sound reasoning) and reasoning by composition (which is fallacious reasoning).

So I think that the first premise of the argument is clearly true. If the price of denying the argument's conclusion is denying premise 1, then atheism is philosophically bankrupt.

PREMISE 2

The universe began to exist.

The more controversial premise in the argument is premise 2, that *the universe began to exist.* This is by no means obvious. So let's look at two philosophical arguments and two scientific arguments which have been offered in defense of this premise.

First Philosophical Argument

Ghazali argued that if the universe never began to exist, then there has been an infinite number of past events prior to today. But, he argued, an infinite number of things cannot exist. Ghazali recognized that a *potentially* infinite number of things could exist, but he denied that an *actually* infinite number of things could exist. Let me explain the difference.

Potential versus Actual Infinity

When we say that something is *potentially* infinite, infinity serves merely as an ideal limit which is never reached. For example, you could divide any finite distance in half, and then into fourths, and then into eighths, and then into sixteenths, and so on to infinity. The number of divisions is potentially infinite, in the sense that you could go on dividing endlessly. But you would never arrive at an "infinitieth" division. You would never have an actually infinite number of parts or divisions.

Now Ghazali has no problem with the existence of merely potential infinites, for these are just ideal limits. But he argued that if an actually infinite number of things could exist, then various absurdities would result. If we're to avoid these absurdities, then we must deny that an actually infinite number of things exist. That implies that the number of past events cannot be actually infinite. Therefore, the universe cannot be beginningless; rather the universe began to exist.

An Objection from Modern Math

It's very frequently alleged that this kind of argument has been invalidated by developments in modern mathematics. In modern set theory the use of actually infinite sets is commonplace. For example, the set of the natural numbers {0, 1, 2, …} has an actually infinite number of members in it. The number of members in this set is not merely potentially infinite, according to modern set theory; rather the number of members is actually infinite. Many people have inferred that these developments undermine Ghazali's argument.

But is that really the case? Modern set theory shows that if you adopt certain axioms and rules, then you can *talk* about actually infinite collections in a consistent way, without contradicting yourself. All this accomplishes is showing how to set up a certain *universe of discourse* for talking consistently about actual infinites. But it does absolutely nothing to show that such mathematical entities really exist or that an actually infinite number of things can really exist. If Ghazali is right, then this universe of discourse may be regarded as just a fictional realm, like the world of Sherlock Holmes, or something that exists only in your mind.

Moreover, Ghazali's claim is not that the existence of an actually infinite number of things involves a *logical* contradiction but that it is *really* impossible. To give an analogy, the claim that *something came into existence from nothing* is not strictly logically contradictory, but nonetheless it is really impossible. These modern mathematical developments, far from undermining Ghazali's argument, can actually strengthen it by providing us insight into the strange nature of the actual infinite.

Hilbert's Hotel

The way in which Ghazali brings out the real impossibility of an actually infinite number of things is by imagining what it would be like if such a collection could exist and then drawing out the absurd consequences. Let me share one of my favorite illustrations called "Hilbert's Hotel," the brainchild of the great German mathematician David Hilbert.

Hilbert first invites us to imagine an ordinary hotel with a finite number of rooms. Suppose, furthermore, that all the rooms are full. If a new guest shows up at the desk asking for a room, the manager says, "Sorry, all the rooms are full," and that's the end of the story.

But now, says Hilbert, let's imagine a hotel with an infinite number of rooms, and let's suppose once again that *all the rooms are full.* This fact must be clearly appreci-

ated. There is not a single vacancy throughout the entire infinite hotel; every room already has somebody in it. Now suppose a new guest shows up at the front desk, asking for a room. "No problem," says the manager. He moves the person who was staying in room #1 into room #2, the person who was staying in room #2 into room #3, the person who was staying in room #3 into room #4, and so on to infinity. As a result of these room changes, room #1 now becomes vacant, and the new guest gratefully checks in. But before he arrived, all the rooms were already full!

It gets worse! Let's now suppose, Hilbert says, that an *infinity* of new guests shows up at the front desk, asking for rooms. "No problem, no problem!" says the manager. He moves the person who was staying in room #1 into room #2, the person who was staying in room #2 into room #4, the person who was staying in room #3 into room #6, each time moving the person into the room number twice his own. Since any number multiplied by two is an even number, all the guests wind up in even-numbered rooms. As a result, all the odd-numbered rooms become vacant, and the infinity of new guests is easily accommodated. In fact, the manager could do this *an infinite number of times* and always accommodate infinitely more guests. And yet, before they arrived, all the rooms were already full!

As a student once remarked to me, Hilbert's Hotel, if it could exist, would have to have a sign posted outside: "No Vacancy (Guests Welcome)."

But Hilbert's Hotel is even stranger than the great German mathematician made it out to be. For just ask yourself the question: What would happen if some of the guests start to *check out*? Suppose all the guests in the odd-numbered rooms check out. In this case an infinite number of people has left the hotel; indeed, as many left as remained behind. And yet, there are no fewer people in the hotel. The number is just infinite! Now suppose the manager doesn't like having a half-empty hotel (it looks bad for business). No matter! By moving the guests as before, only this time in reverse order, he converts his half-empty hotel into one that is bursting at the seams!

Now you might think that by these maneuvers the manager could always keep his strange hotel fully occupied. But you'd be wrong. For suppose the guests in rooms #4, 5, 6 … check out. At a single stroke the hotel would be virtually emptied, the guest register reduced to just three names, and the infinite converted to finitude. And yet it would be true that the *same number* of guests checked out this time as when all the guests in the odd-numbered rooms checked out! Can such a hotel exist in reality?

Hilbert's Hotel is absurd. Since nothing hangs on the illustration's involving a hotel, the argument can be generalized to show that the existence of an actually infinite number of things is absurd.

Responses to Hilbert's Hotel

Sometimes students react to Hilbert's Hotel by saying that these absurdities result because the concept of infinity is beyond us and we can't understand it. But this reaction is mistaken and naïve. As I said, infinite set theory is a highly developed and well-understood branch of modern mathematics. The absurdities result because we *do* understand the nature of the actual infinite. Hilbert was a smart guy, and he knew well how to illustrate the bizarre consequences of the existence of an actually infinite number of things.

Really, the only thing the critic can do at this point is to just bite the bullet and say that a Hilbert's Hotel is not absurd. Sometimes critics will try to justify this move by saying that if an actual infinite could exist, then such situations are exactly what we should expect. But this justification is inadequate, I think. Hilbert would, of course, agree that *if* an actual infinite could exist, the situation with his imaginary hotel is what we would expect. Otherwise, it wouldn't be a good illustration! But the question is whether such a hotel is really possible.

Moreover, the critics can't just bite the bullet when it comes to situations like the guests' checking out of the hotel. For here we have a logical contradiction: we subtract *identical quantities* from *identical quantities* and come up with *non-identical results*. That's why subtraction of infinity from infinity is

TALK ABOUT IT

Ghazali shows that an infinite number of past events is impossible. What about the future? Is it actually or merely potentially infinite? How is eternity different from an infinite number of moments in time?

prohibited in transfinite arithmetic. But while we may slap the hand of the mathematician who tries to break the rules, we can't stop real people from checking out of a real hotel!

So I think Ghazali's first argument is a good one. It shows that the number of past events must be finite. Therefore, the universe must have had a beginning.

We can summarize Ghazali's argument as follows:

1. An actual infinite cannot exist.
2. An infinite temporal regress of events is an actual infinite.
3. Therefore an infinite temporal regress of events cannot exist.

Second Philosophical Argument

Ghazali has a second, independent argument for the beginning of the universe. So those who deny that the universe began to exist have to refute not only his first argument, but his second one as well, since it is independent of the first one.

Counting to (or from) Infinity

The series of past events, Ghazali observes, has been formed by adding one event after another. The series of past events is like a sequence of dominoes falling one after another until the last domino, today, is reached. But, he argues, no series which is formed by adding one member after another can be actually infinite. For you cannot pass through an infinite number of elements one at a time.

This is easy to see in the case of trying to count to infinity. No matter how high you count, there is always an infinity of numbers left to count.

But if you can't count *to* infinity, how could you count down *from* infinity? This would be like someone's claiming to have counted down all the negative numbers, ending at zero: …, -3, -2, -1, 0. This seems crazy. For before he could count 0, he would have to count -1, and before he could count -1, he would have to count -2, and so on, back to infinity. Before any number could be counted, an infinity of numbers will have to have been counted first. You just get driven back and back into the past, so that no number could ever be counted.

But then the final domino could never fall if an infinite number of dominoes had to fall first. So today could never be reached. But obviously here we are! This shows that the series of past events must be finite and have a beginning.

An Objection

Some critics have responded to this argument by pointing out that even in a beginningless past, every event in the past is only a finite distance from the present. Compare the series of negative numbers: …, -3, -2, -1, 0. It's beginningless; nevertheless, any number you pick, say, -11 or -1,000,000 or whatever, is only finitely distant from zero. But the finite distance from any past event to the present is easily crossed, just as you can count down to zero from any negative number you pick. Therefore, there's no problem in the lapsing of an infinite past.

THE FALLACY OF
COMPOSITION

Each *part* of an elephant
may not be heavy, but that
doesn't mean the *whole*
elephant isn't heavy!

This objection commits the logical fallacy called "the fallacy of composition." As explained above, this is the fallacy of confusing a property of *a part* with a property of *the whole*. Recall our illustration: every part of an elephant may be light in weight, but that doesn't mean the whole elephant is light in weight!

In the case at hand, just because every finite *part* of a series can be crossed or counted down doesn't mean the *whole* infinite series can be crossed or counted. The critics have committed an elementary logical fallacy. The question is not how any finite part of the past can be formed by adding one event after another, but how the whole, beginningless past could be completed by adding one event after another.

Two More Absurdities

Ghazali sought to heighten the impossibility of forming an infinite past by giving illustrations of the absurdities that would result if it could be done. For example, suppose that for every one orbit that Saturn completes around the sun Jupiter completes two. The longer they orbit, the further Saturn falls behind. If they continue to orbit forever, they will approach a limit at which Saturn is infinitely far behind Jupiter. Of course, they will never actually arrive at this limit.

But now turn the story around: suppose Jupiter and Saturn have been orbiting the sun from eternity past. Which will have completed the most orbits? The answer is that the number of their orbits is exactly the same: infinity! (We can't slip out of this argument by saying that infinity is not a number. In modern mathematics it *is* a number, the number of elements in the set {0, 1, 2, 3, …}.) But that seems absurd, for the longer they orbit, the greater the disparity grows. So how does the number of orbits magically become equal by making them orbit from eternity past?

Another illustration: suppose we meet someone who claims to have been counting down from eternity past and is now finishing: …, -3, -2, -1, 0! Whew! Why, we may ask, is he just finishing his countdown today? Why didn't he finish yesterday or the day before? After all, by then an infinite amount of time had already elapsed. So if the man were counting at a rate of one number per second, he's already had an infinite number of seconds to finish his countdown. He should already be done! In fact, at *any* point in the past, he has already had infinite time and so should already have finished. But then at no point in the past can we find the man finishing his countdown, which contradicts the hypothesis that he has been counting from eternity.

Philosophers Alexander Pruss and Robert Koons have defended an engaging contemporary version of Ghazali's argument called the Grim Reaper Paradox. Imagine that there are infinitely many Grim Reapers. You are alive at midnight. Grim Reaper 1 will strike you dead at 1:00 a.m. if you are still alive at that time. Grim Reaper 2 will strike you dead at 12:30 a.m. if you are still alive then. Grim Reaper 3 will strike you dead at 12:15 a.m., and so on. Such a situation seems clearly conceivable—given the possibility of an actually infinite number of things—but leads to an impossibility: you cannot survive past midnight, and yet you cannot be killed by any Grim Reaper at any time. Pruss and Koons show how to reformulate the paradox so that the Grim Reapers are spread out over infinite time rather than over a single hour, for example, by having each Grim Reaper swing his scythe on January 1 of each past year if you have managed to live that long.

These illustrations only strengthen Ghazali's claim that no series which is formed by adding one member after another can be actually infinite. Since the series of past events has been formed by adding one event after another, it can't be actually infinite. It must have had a beginning. So we have a second good argument for premise 2, that *the universe began to exist.* We can summarize this argument as follows:

> 1. A collection formed by successive addition cannot be an actual infinite.
> 2. The temporal series of events is a collection formed by successive addition.
> 3. Therefore, the temporal series of events cannot be an actual infinite.

First Scientific Argument

One of the most astonishing developments of modern astronomy, which Ghazali could never have anticipated, is that we now have strong scientific evidence for the beginning of the universe. Yes, science provides some of the most dramatic evidence for the second premise of the argument. The first scientific confirmation of the universe's beginning comes from the expansion of the universe.

The "Big Bang"

All throughout history men have assumed that the universe as a whole was unchanging. Of course, things *in* the universe were moving about and changing, but the universe itself was just there, so to speak. This was also Albert Einstein's assumption when he first began to apply his new theory of gravity, called the General Theory of Relativity, to the universe in 1917.

But Einstein found there was something terribly amiss. His equations described a universe which was either blowing up like a balloon or else collapsing in upon itself. Perplexed, Einstein "solved" the problem by fudging his equations, adding a new term to enable the universe to walk the tightrope between exploding and imploding.

During the 1920s the Russian mathematician Alexander Friedman and the Belgian astronomer Georges LeMaître decided to take Einstein's equations at face value, and as a result they came up independently with models of an expanding universe. In 1929 the American astronomer Edwin Hubble, through tireless observations at Mt. Wilson Observatory, made a startling discovery which verified Friedman and LeMaître's theory. He found that the light from distant galaxies appeared to be redder than expected. This "redshift" in the light was most plausibly due to the stretching of the light waves as the galaxies are moving away from us. Wherever Hubble trained his telescope in the night sky, he observed this same redshift in the light from the galaxies. It appeared that we are at the center of a cosmic explosion, and all of the other galaxies are flying away from us at fantastic speeds!

Now according to the Friedman-LeMaître model, we are not *really* at the center of the universe. Rather an observer in *any* galaxy will

TALK ABOUT IT

Why do you suppose Einstein might have been uncomfortable with the idea that the universe wasn't permanent and unchanging?

look out and see the other galaxies moving away from him. There is no center to the universe. This is because, according to the theory, it is really space itself which is expanding. The galaxies are actually at rest in space, but they recede from one another as space itself expands. To get a picture of this difficult idea, imagine a balloon with buttons glued to its surface (Fig. 1).

Fig. 1. Illustration of an expanding universe. The buttons are glued to the surface of the balloon, so they're stuck in place. They don't move across its surface. Nevertheless, as the balloon inflates, the buttons grow farther and farther apart. The *surface* of the balloon has no center. An observer on any button will see the other buttons receding from him and so feel as if he were at the center of the expansion.

The buttons are stuck to the surface of the balloon and so don't move across the surface. But as you blow up the balloon, the buttons will grow farther and farther and farther apart because the balloon gets bigger and bigger. Notice that there's no center of the balloon's surface. (There is a center point inside the balloon, but we're focusing just on the *surface* of the balloon.) But an observer on any button will feel as if he were at the center of the expansion because he'll look out and see the other buttons all moving away from him.

Now the two-dimensional surface of the balloon is an illustration of our three-dimensional space, and the buttons represent the galaxies in space. The galaxies are actually at rest in space, but they recede from one another as space itself expands. Just as there is no center of the balloon's surface, so there is no center of the universe.

The Friedman-LeMaître model eventually came to be known as the Big Bang theory. But that name can be misleading. Thinking of the expansion of the universe as a sort of explosion could mislead us into thinking that the galaxies are moving out into a pre-existing, empty space from a central point. That would be

TALK ABOUT IT

Given that the name "Big Bang" is misleading, why do you suppose it has caught on? What might be a better name for the theory?

a complete misunderstanding of the model. The Big Bang did not occur at some point in a pre-existing empty space.

(You might say, "But what about the central point in the interior of the balloon?" Ah, you're forgetting that it's the *surface* of the balloon which is the analogy to space! The balloon's two-dimensional surface happens to exist in a three-dimensional world, into which it is expanding. But in the Friedman-LeMaître model, there is no higher, four-dimensional world into which our three-dimensional space is expanding. So there's just nothing corresponding to the space outside or inside the balloon.)

So we mustn't be misled into thinking of the Big Bang as the explosion of a super-dense pellet of matter into empty space. The theory is much more radical than that.

The Beginning of Time

As you trace the expansion of the universe back in time, everything gets closer and closer together. If our balloon had no minimum size but could just keep shrinking and shrinking, eventually the distance between any two points on the balloon's surface would shrink to zero. According to the Friedman-LeMaître model, that's what happens to space as you go back in time. Eventually the distance between any two points in space becomes zero. You can't get any closer than that! So at that point you've reached the boundary of space and time. Space and time cannot be extended any further back than that. It is literally the beginning of space and time.

Try to get your mind around the idea that empty space itself is expanding right now, while you're reading this book.

To get a picture of this we can portray our three-dimensional space as a two-dimensional surface which shrinks as you go back in time (Fig. 2).

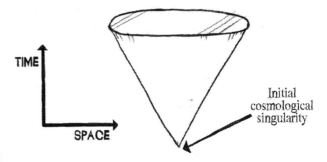

Fig. 2. Geometrical representation of space-time. The two-dimensional disc represents our three-dimensional space. The vertical dimension represents time. As one goes back in time, space shrinks until the distance between any two points is zero. Space-time thus has the geometry of a cone. The point of the cone is the boundary of space and time.

ST. AUGUSTINE

Why didn't God make the world sooner? In the early fifth century AD, Augustine of Hippo answered that God did not make the universe at a point in time, but "simultaneously with time." That is, he believed God had created space and time together. Modern cosmologists have come to agree that he was right about space and time, and therefore it is meaningless to ask why the Big Bang didn't happen earlier than it did.

Eventually, the distance between any two points in space becomes zero. So space-time can be represented geometrically as a cone. What's significant about this is that while a cone can be extended indefinitely in one direction, it has a boundary point in the other direction. Because this direction represents time and the boundary point lies in the past, the model implies that past time is finite and had a beginning.

Because space-time is the arena in which all matter and energy exist, the beginning of space-time is also the beginning of all matter and energy. It's the beginning of the universe.

Notice that there's simply nothing prior to the initial boundary of space-time. Let's not be misled

ON GUARD FOR STUDENTS

by words. When cosmologists say, "There is nothing prior to the initial boundary," they do *not* mean that there is some state of affairs prior to it, and that is a state of nothingness. That would be to treat nothing as though it were something! Rather they mean that at the boundary point, it is false that "There is something prior to this point."

The standard Big Bang model thus predicts an absolute beginning of the universe. If this model is correct, then we have amazing scientific confirmation of the second premise of Ghazali's *kalam* cosmological argument.

Is the Standard Model Correct?

So is the model correct, or, more importantly, is it correct in predicting a beginning of the universe? We've already seen that the redshift in the light from distant galaxies provides powerful evidence for the Big Bang. In addition, the best explanation for the abundance of certain light elements like helium in the universe is that they were formed in the hot, dense Big Bang. Finally, the discovery in 1965 of a cosmic background of microwave radiation is best explained as a vestige of the Big Bang.

Nevertheless, the standard Big Bang model will need to be modified in various ways. The model is based, as we've seen, on Einstein's General Theory of Relativity. But Einstein's theory breaks down when space is shrunk down to subatomic proportions. We'll need to introduce subatomic physics at that point to formulate

A CHRISTIAN-JEWISH-MUSLIM ARGUMENT

The *kalam* cosmological argument originated in the efforts of ancient Christian philosophers like John Philoponus of Alexandria to refute Aristotle's doctrine of the eternity of the universe. When Islam swept over Egypt, it absorbed this tradition and developed sophisticated versions of the argument. Jews lived alongside Muslims in medieval Spain and eventually mediated this tradition back to the Christian West, where it was championed by St. Bonaventura. Since Christians, Jews, and Muslims share a common belief in creation, the *kalam* cosmological argument has enjoyed great intersectarian appeal and helps to build bridges for sharing one's faith with Jews and especially Muslims.

a quantum theory of gravity, and no one is sure how this is to be done. Moreover, the expansion of the universe is probably not constant, as in the standard model. It's probably accelerating and may have had a brief moment of super-rapid expansion in the past.

But none of these adjustments need affect the fundamental prediction of the absolute beginning of the universe. Indeed, physicists have proposed scores of alternative models over the decades since Friedman and LeMaître's work, and those that do not have an absolute beginning have been repeatedly shown to be unworkable. Put more positively, the only viable non-standard models are those that involve an absolute beginning to the universe. That beginning may or may not involve a beginning *point*. But on theories (such as Stephen Hawking's "no boundary" proposal) that do not have a point-like beginning, the past is still finite, not infinite. The universe has not existed forever according to such theories but came into existence, even if it didn't do so at a sharply defined point.

In a sense, the history of twentieth-century cosmology can be seen as a series of one failed attempt after another to avoid the absolute beginning predicted by the standard Big Bang model. Unfortunately, the impression arises in the minds of laymen that the field of cosmology is in constant turnover, with no lasting results. What the layman doesn't understand is that this parade of failed theories only serves to *confirm* the prediction of the standard model that the universe began to exist. That prediction has now stood for nearly one hundred years, during a period of enormous advances

"At first the scientific community was very reluctant to accept the idea of a birth of the universe."

"Not only did the Big Bang model seem to give in to the Judeo-Christian idea of a beginning of the world, but it also seemed to have to call for an act of supernatural creation...."

"It took time, observational evidence, and careful verification of predictions made by the Big Bang model to convince the scientific community to accept the idea of a cosmic genesis."

"... [T]he Big Bang is a very successful model ... that imposed itself on a reluctant scientific community."[3]
—J. M. Wersinger, Assoc. Prof. of Physics, Auburn University

in observational astronomy and creative theoretical work in astrophysics.

Meanwhile, a series of remarkable singularity theorems has increasingly tightened the loop around empirically tenable models by showing that under more and more generalized conditions, a beginning is inevitable. In 2003 Arvind Borde, Alan Guth, and Alexander Vilenkin were able to show that any universe which is, on average, in a state of cosmic expansion throughout each history cannot be infinite in the past but must have a beginning. That goes for multiverse scenarios, too. In 2012 Vilenkin showed that models which do not meet this one condition still fail for other reasons to avert the beginning of the universe. Vilenkin concluded, "None of these scenarios can actually be past eternal."[4] "All the evidence we have says that the universe had a beginning."[5]

The Borde-Guth-Vilenkin theorem proves that classical space-time, under a single, very general condition, cannot be extended to past infinity but must reach a boundary at some time in the finite past. Now either there was something on the other side of that boundary or not. If not, then that boundary just is the beginning of the universe. If there was something on the other side, then it will be a region described by the yet-to-be-discovered theory of quantum gravity. In that case, Vilenkin says, *it* will be the beginning of the universe. Either way, the universe began to exist.

We can fully expect that new theories will be proposed, attempting to avoid the universe's beginning. Such proposals are to be welcomed and tested.

MULTIVERSE

Some cosmologists speculate that our observable universe is just an expanding bubble in a much-wider sea of energy, which is also expanding. Since this wider universe contains many other bubbles in addition to ours, it is often called a multiverse. The Borde-Guth-Vilenkin theorem also applies to the multiverse as a whole, not just to the individual bubbles within it. Thus, even if there is a multiverse, it cannot be eternal in the past but must have had a beginning. We'll return to the question of whether there is a multiverse in the next chapter.

Of course, scientific results are always provisional. Nevertheless, it's pretty clear which way the evidence points. Today the proponent of Ghazali's cosmological argument stands comfortably within the scientific mainstream in holding that the universe began to exist.

Second Scientific Argument

As if this weren't enough, there is actually a second scientific confirmation of the beginning of the universe, this one from the second law of thermodynamics. According to the second law, unless energy is being fed into a system, that system will become increasingly disorderly. For example, if you had a bottle that was a closed vacuum inside and you injected into it some molecules of gas, the gas would spread itself evenly throughout the bottle. The chances that the molecules would all huddle together in one corner of the bottle are practically nil. This is because there are many more ways in which the molecules could exist in a disorderly state than in an orderly state.

Now already in the nineteenth-century, scientists realized that the second law implied a grim prediction for the future of the universe. Given enough time, all the energy in the universe will spread itself out evenly throughout the universe, just as the gas spreads itself out evenly throughout the bottle. The universe will become a featureless soup in which no life is possible. Once the universe reaches such a state, no significant further change is possible. It is a state of *equilibrium*. Scientists called this the "heat death" of the universe.

THE LAWS OF
THERMODYNAMICS

The science of thermodynamics is rooted in the work of the German physicist Rudolf Clausius (1822–1888), who is credited with formulating the second law. There are three fundamental laws of thermodynamics: The first law states that the energy in a physical system can be neither created nor destroyed. This is known as the conservation of energy. The second law states that a closed system will tend toward increasing disorder, or entropy, until it reaches equilibrium. The third law states that as a system approaches the temperature of absolute zero, its entropy approaches a certain minimum value.

But this unwelcome prediction raised a further puzzle: if, given enough time, the universe *will* inevitably stagnate in a state of heat death, then why, if it has existed forever, is it not *now* in a state of heat death? If in a finite amount of time, the universe *will* reach equilibrium, then, given infinite past time, it should by now *already be* in a state of equilibrium. But it's not. We're in a state of *dis*equilibrium, where energy is still available to be used and the universe has an orderly structure.

Boltzmann's Many Worlds Hypothesis

The nineteenth-century Austrian physicist Ludwig Boltzmann proposed a daring solution to this problem. Boltzmann suggested that perhaps the universe *is*, in fact, in a state of overall equilibrium. Nevertheless, by chance alone, there will arise more-orderly pockets of disequilibrium here and there. Boltzmann refers to these isolated regions of disequilibrium as "worlds." Our universe just happens to be one of these worlds. Eventually, in accordance with the second law, it will revert to the overall state of equilibrium.

Contemporary physicists have universally rejected Boltzmann's daring Many Worlds Hypothesis as an explanation of the observed disequilibrium of the universe. Its fatal flaw is that if our world is just a chance fluctuation from a state of overall equilibrium, then we ought to be observing a much-smaller universe. Why? Because a small fluctuation from equilibrium is vastly more probable than the huge, sustained fluctuation necessary to create the universe we see, and yet a small

EQUILIBRIUM

Equilibrium is a state in which all forces are in balance and there is therefore no change. In the case of the universe, equilibrium would be the point at which the temperature and pressure are the same everywhere in the universe. No galaxies. No stars. No planets.

fluctuation would be sufficient for our existence. For example, a fluctuation that formed a world no bigger than our solar system would be enough for us to be alive and would be incomprehensibly more likely to occur than a fluctuation that formed the whole universe we see!

In fact, Boltzmann's hypothesis, if consistently carried out, would lead to a strange sort of illusionism: in all probability we really *do* inhabit a smaller world, and the stars and the planets we observe are just illusions, mere images on the heavens. For that sort of world is much more probable than a universe which has, in defiance of the second law of thermodynamics, moved away from equilibrium for billions of years to form the universe we observe.

Contemporary End of the World Scenarios

The discovery of the expansion of the universe in the 1920s modified the sort of heat death predicted on the basis of the second law, but it didn't alter the fundamental question.

If the universe will expand forever, then it will never actually arrive at equilibrium. Because the volume of space is constantly growing, the matter and energy always have more room to spread out. Nevertheless, as the universe expands, its available energy is used up and it becomes increasingly cold, dark, dilute, and dead. It will eventually become a thin gas of subatomic particles endlessly expanding in absolute darkness.

By contrast, if the universe is not expanding fast enough, the expansion will slow down, come to a halt, and then gravity will begin to pull everything together again in a catastrophic Big Crunch. Eventually everything in the universe will coalesce into a gigantic black hole, from which the universe will never rebound.

Whether its end will be in fire or ice, the fundamental question remains the same: If, given sufficient time, the universe will reach such a state, why is it not now in such a condition, if it has existed forever?

Recent discoveries indicate that the cosmic expansion is actually speeding up. Because the volume of space is increasing so rapidly, the universe actually becomes farther and farther from an equilibrium state in which matter and energy are evenly distributed. But the acceleration of the universe's expansion only hastens its demise. For now the different regions of the universe become increasingly isolated from one another in space, and each marooned region becomes dark, cold, dilute, and dead. So again, why isn't our region in such a state if the universe has already existed for infinite time?

The Beginning of the Universe and Attempts to Avoid It

The obvious implication of all this is that the question is based on a false assumption, namely, that the universe has existed for infinite time. Today most physicists would say that the matter and energy were simply put into the universe as an initial condition, and the universe has been following the path plotted by the second law ever since its beginning a finite time ago.

Of course, attempts have been made to avoid the beginning of the universe predicted on the basis of the second law of thermodynamics. But none of them has been successful. Skeptics might hold out hope that quantum gravity will serve to avert the implications of the second law of thermodynamics. But in 2013, the cosmologist Aron Wall of the University of California was able to formulate a new singularity theorem which seems to close the door on that possibility. Wall shows that, given the validity of the generalized second law of thermodynamics in quantum gravity, the universe must have begun to exist, unless one postulates *a reversal of the arrow of time* (time runs backward!) at some point in the past, which, he rightly observes, involves a thermodynamic beginning in time which "would seem to raise the same sorts of philosophical questions that any other sort of beginning in time would."[6] Wall reports that his results require the validity of only certain basic concepts, so that "it is reasonable to believe that the results will hold in a complete theory of quantum gravity."[7]

So once again the scientific evidence confirms the truth of the second premise of Ghazali's cosmological argument. This evidence is especially impressive because thermodynamics is so well understood by physicists that it is practically a completed field of science. This makes it highly unlikely that these findings will be reversed.

Conclusion

On the basis, therefore, of both philosophical and scientific evidence, we have good grounds for believing that the universe began to exist. Since whatever begins to exist has a cause of its beginning, it follows that the universe has a cause of its beginning.

Is the Universe Self-Caused?

The prominent atheist philosopher Daniel Dennett actually agrees that the universe has a cause of its beginning. But he thinks that the cause of the universe's beginning to exist is: itself! Yes, he's serious. In what he calls "the ultimate boot-strapping trick," he claims that the universe created itself.

Dennett's view is nonsense. Notice that he's not saying that the universe just came into being from nothing. No, he's saying that the universe brought itself into being. But this is impossible, for in order to create itself, the universe would have to already exist. It would have to exist before it existed. Dennett's view is logically incoherent.

The Personal Creator of the Universe

The cause of the universe must therefore be a transcendent cause beyond the universe. What can we

EASTERN THINKING

Some people dismiss this kind of logical argument as an example of Western thinking. In the East, they say, people pursuing enlightenment can see beyond the confinements of logic. Note, though, that Ghazali was from Persia (modern Iran), and that India today is producing vast numbers of scientists and engineers who use exactly the rules of logic and the evidence of science that we have been using. Why do you suppose so many Westerners are drawn to the nonlogic of belief systems like Zen Buddhism?

know about the nature of this cause? First, this cause must be itself uncaused because, as we've seen, an infinite series of causes is impossible. It is therefore the Uncaused First Cause. It must transcend space and time, since it created space and time. Therefore, it must be immaterial and nonphysical. It must be unimaginably powerful, since it created all matter and energy.

Finally, this Uncaused First Cause must also arguably be a personal being. We've already seen one reason for this conclusion in the previous chapter. Only a Mind could fit the description just given.

But let me also share a reason given by Ghazali for why the First Cause must be personal: it's the only way to explain how a timeless cause can produce a temporal effect with a beginning like the universe.

Here's the problem: if a cause is sufficient to produce its effect, then if the cause is there, the effect must be there, too. For example, the cause of water's freezing is the temperature's being below 0 degrees Celsius. If the temperature has always been below 0 degrees, then any water around would be frozen from eternity. It would be impossible for the water to *begin* to freeze just a finite time ago. Now the cause of the universe is permanently there, since it is timeless. So why isn't the universe permanently there as well? Why did the universe come into being only 14 billion years ago? Why isn't it as permanent as its cause?

Ghazali maintained that the answer to this problem is that the First Cause must be a personal being with freedom of the will. His creating the universe is a free act which is independent of any prior determining conditions. So his act of creating can be something spontaneous and new. Freedom of the will enables one to get an effect with a beginning from a permanent, timeless cause. Thus, we are brought not merely to a transcendent cause of the universe but to its Personal Creator.

This is admittedly hard for us to imagine. But one way to think about it is to envision God existing alone without the universe as changeless and timeless. His free act of creation is a temporal event simultaneous with the universe's coming into being. Therefore, God enters into time when he creates the universe. God is thus timeless without the universe and in time with the universe.

Ghazali's cosmological argument thus gives us powerful grounds for believing in the existence of a beginningless, uncaused, timeless, spaceless, changeless, immaterial, enormously powerful Personal Creator of the universe. It complements and reinforces Leibniz's version of the cosmological argument.

1. Al-Ghazali, *Kitab al-Iqtisad fi'l-I'tiqad*, cited in S. de Beaurecueil, "Gazzali et S. Thomas d'Aquin: Essai sur la preuve de l'existence de Dieu proposée dans l'Iqtisad et sa comparaison avec les 'voies' Thomiste," *Bulletin de l'Institut Francais d'Archaeologie Orientale* 46 (1947): 203.
2. All of these statements belong to atheist physicist Lawrence Krauss. For references, see the video of our dialogue "Why Is There Something rather than Nothing?" at www.youtube.com/watch?v=V82uGzgoajI (accessed March 9, 2015).
3. J. M. Wersinger, "Genesis: The Origin of the Universe," *National Forum* (Winter 1996), 11, 9, 12.
4. Audrey Mithani and Alexander Vilenkin, "Did the Universe Have a Beginning?," arXiv:1204.4658v1 [hep-th] April 20, 2012, Cornell University, http://arxiv.org/pdf/1204.4658.pdf, 5. For an accessible video, see www.youtube.com/watch?v=NXCQelhKJ7A (accessed March 9, 2015), where Vilenkin concluded, "There are no models at this time that provide a satisfactory model for a universe without a beginning."
5. Alexander Vilenkin, cited in Lisa Grossman, "Why Physicists Can't Avoid a Creation Event," *New Scientist*, January 11, 2012.
6. Aron C. Wall, "The Generalized Second Law Implies a Quantum Singularity Theorem," arXiv:1010.5513v3 [gr-qc] 24 (January 2013): 38.
7. Wall, "Generalized Second Law," 4.

THE *KALAM* COSMOLOGICAL ARGUMENT

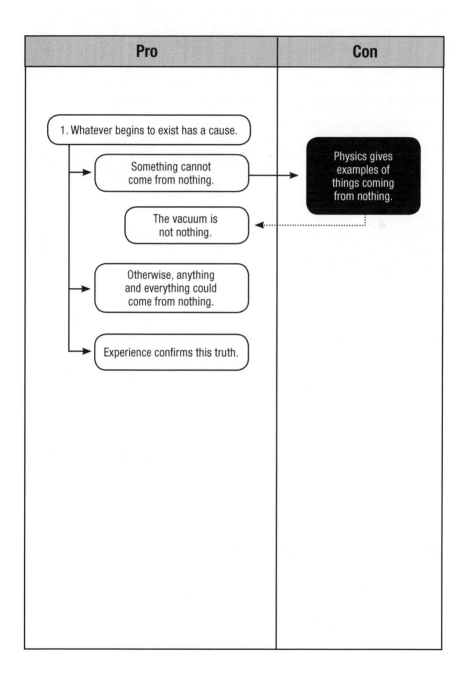

Pro	Con

1. Whatever begins to exist has a cause.

Something cannot come from nothing.

The vacuum is not nothing.

Otherwise, anything and everything could come from nothing.

Experience confirms this truth.

Physics gives examples of things coming from nothing.

THE *KALAM* COSMOLOGICAL ARGUMENT (cont.)

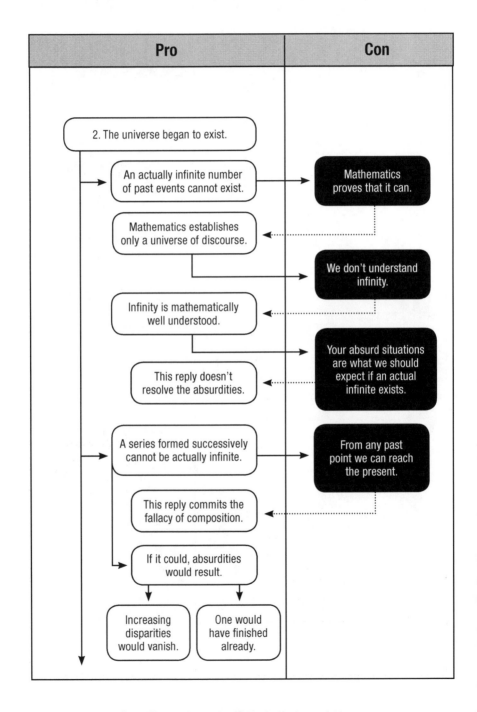

Pro	Con

2. The universe began to exist.

An actually infinite number of past events cannot exist.

Mathematics proves that it can.

Mathematics establishes only a universe of discourse.

We don't understand infinity.

Infinity is mathematically well understood.

Your absurd situations are what we should expect if an actual infinite exists.

This reply doesn't resolve the absurdities.

A series formed successively cannot be actually infinite.

From any past point we can reach the present.

This reply commits the fallacy of composition.

If it could, absurdities would result.

Increasing disparities would vanish.

One would have finished already.

THE *KALAM* COSMOLOGICAL ARGUMENT (cont.)

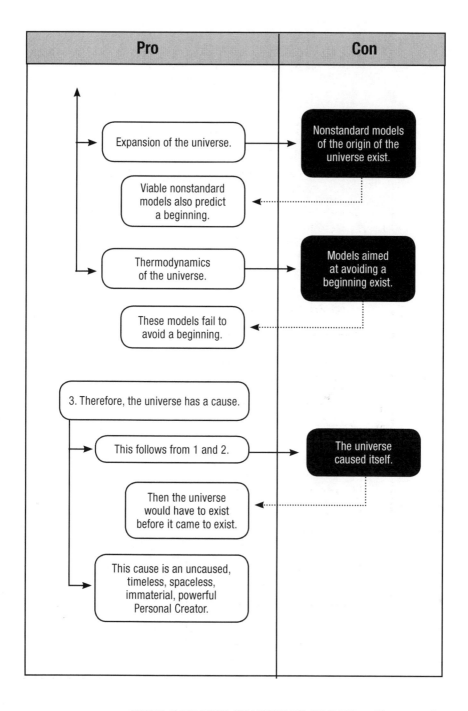

Pro	Con
Expansion of the universe.	Nonstandard models of the origin of the universe exist.
Viable nonstandard models also predict a beginning.	
Thermodynamics of the universe.	Models aimed at avoiding a beginning exist.
These models fail to avoid a beginning.	
3. Therefore, the universe has a cause.	
This follows from 1 and 2.	The universe caused itself.
Then the universe would have to exist before it came to exist.	
This cause is an uncaused, timeless, spaceless, immaterial, powerful Personal Creator.	

CHAPTER 4

WHY IS THE UNIVERSE FINE-TUNED FOR LIFE?

There is for me powerful evidence that there is something going on behind it all ... it seems as though somebody has fine-tuned nature's numbers to make the universe. The impression of design is overwhelming.

Paul Davies, *Cosmic Blueprint*

Ancient Greek philosophers were struck with the order that pervades the cosmos. The stars and the planets in their constant revolution across the night sky were especially awesome to the ancients. Anyone who has personally studied the heavens must lend a sympathetic ear to these men of antiquity, who gazed up into the night sky, as yet undimmed by pollution and the glare of city lights, and watched the slow but irresistible turn of the cosmos, replete with its planets, stars, and familiar constellations, across their view and wondered, *What is the cause of all this?*

Plato's Academy lavished extensive time and thought on the study of astronomy because, Plato believed, it was the science that would awaken man to his divine destiny. According to Plato, there are two things that lead men to believe in God: the argument from the existence of the soul, and the argument "from the order of the motion of the stars, and of all things under the dominion of the Mind which ordered the universe."[1] Plato employed these arguments to refute atheism and concluded that there must be a "best soul" who is the "Maker and Father of all," the "King," who ordered the primordial chaos into the rational cosmos that we observe today.[2]

An even more magnificent statement of divine design is to be found in a fragment from a lost work of Aristotle entitled *On Philosophy*. Aristotle, too, was filled with wonder at the majestic sweep of the glittering host across the night sky of ancient Greece. He concluded that the cause of this cosmic order was divine intelligence. He imagined the impact that the sight of the world would have upon a race of men who had lived underground and never beheld the sky. He believed that they would "most certainly … have judged both that there exist gods and that all these marvelous works are the handiwork of the gods."

Aristotle

"When thus they would suddenly gain sight of the earth, seas, and the sky; when they should come to know the grandeur of the clouds and the might of the winds; when they should behold the sun and should learn its grandeur and beauty as well as its power to cause the day by shedding light over the sky; and again, when the night had darkened the lands and they should behold the whole of the sky spangled and adorned with stars; and when they should see the changing lights of the moon as it waxes and wanes, and the risings and settings of all these celestial bodies, their courses fixed and changeless through-out all eternity—when they should behold all these things, most certainly they would have judged both that there exist gods and that all these marvelous works are the handiwork of the gods" (*On Philosophy*).

In his *Metaphysics* Aristotle proceeded to argue that there must be a First Uncaused Cause which is God—a living, intel-ligent, immaterial, eternal, and most good being who is the source of order in the cosmos.

TALK ABOUT IT

Go outside at night and look up at the sky. How is what you see different from what Aristotle might have seen? How do you think this difference affects the way people today think and feel about the stars and planets?

Reading the works of these ancient philosophers, one cannot help but think of the apostle Paul's words in his letter to the church in Rome: "Ever since the creation of the world his invisible nature, namely, his eternal power and deity, has been clearly perceived in the things that have been made" (Romans 1:20). From earliest times men wholly ignorant of the Bible have concluded on the basis of the design in the universe that God must exist.

The Rebirth of Design

Today many astronomers, as a result of recent discoveries, are coming to a similar conclusion.

Scientists used to think that whatever the very early universe might have been like, given sufficient time and some luck, intelligent life forms like our-selves would eventually evolve somewhere. As a result of discoveries over the last half century, we now know that that assumption was wrong. In fact, quite the opposite is true.

Astronomers have been stunned by the discovery of how complex and delicate a balance of initial conditions must be present in the Big Bang itself if the universe is to permit the evolution and existence of intelligent life anywhere at all in the cosmos. This delicate balance of initial conditions has come to be known as the "fine-tuning" of the universe for life. We've come to discover that the universe is fine-tuned for the existence of intelligent, interactive life with a complexity and delicacy that literally defy human comprehension.

Two Kinds of Fine-Tuning

There are two kinds of fine-tuning. The first involves the constants of nature and the second involves certain arbitrary physical quantities.

Nature's Constants

First, the constants of nature. What is a constant? When the laws of nature are expressed as mathematical equations, you find appearing in them certain symbols which stand for unchanging quantities, like the force of gravity, the electromagnetic force, and the subatomic "weak" force. These unchanging quantities are called constants. The value of these constants is not determined by the laws of nature. There could be universes governed by the same laws of nature even

CONSTANTS OF NATURE

When the laws of nature are expressed as mathematical equations, certain constants feature prominently in them. Consider, for example, Newton's famous law of gravity. It states: $F = Gm_1m_2/r^2$. According to this equation the force of gravity symbolized by F is equal to the value of the gravitational constant G multiplied by the masses of the two bodies that are being attracted to each other divided by the distance between them squared. The masses and the distance may vary depending on what objects you're talking about, but the value of G is constant.

though these constants had very different values. So the actual values of the various constants are not determined by nature's laws. Depending on the values of those constants, universes governed by the same laws of nature will look very different.

Arbitrary Quantities

In addition to the constants, there are certain arbitrary quantities which are just put in as initial conditions on which the laws of nature operate. Because these quantities are arbitrary, they're also not determined by the laws of nature. An example would be the amount of thermodynamic disorder (or entropy) in the early universe. It's just given in the Big Bang as an initial condition, and the laws of nature then take over and determine how the universe will develop from there. If the initial quantities had been different, then the laws would predict that a quite different universe would evolve.

Definition of "Fine-Tuning"

Now what scientists have been surprised to discover is that these constants and quantities must fall into an extraordinarily narrow range of values if the universe is to permit the existence of intelligent, interactive forms of life. This is what is meant by the fine-tuning of the universe.

The term "fine-tuned" thus does *not* mean "designed"—much less "designed for man"! The expression is a neutral term which doesn't say anything about what the purpose of the universe is or how the fine-tuning is best explained. "Fine-tuning" just means that the range of life-permitting values for these constants and quantities is extremely narrow. If the value of even one of these

> ### TALK ABOUT IT
> Imagine a universe in which the gravitational constant, G, was considerably stronger than in our universe. Do you think there could be galaxies in that universe? Why?

The term *fine-tuned* does
not mean "designed." The
expression is a neutral term
that doesn't say anything
about how the fine-tuning is
best explained. *Fine-tuning*
just means that the range
of life-permitting values for
the constants and quantities
is extremely narrow. If the
value of even one of these
constants or quantities were
to be altered by a hair's
breadth, the delicate balance
required for the existence
of life would be upset and
the universe would be life-
prohibiting instead.

constants or quantities were to be altered by less than a hair's breadth, the delicate balance required for the existence of life would be upset and the universe would be life-prohibiting instead.

Examples of Fine-Tuning

So fine-tuning in this neutral sense is uncontroversial and well-established. Physics abounds with examples of fine-tuning. Before I share a few, let me give you some numbers to give you a feel for the delicacy of the fine-tuning. The number of seconds in the entire history of the universe is around 10^{17} (that's 1 followed by seventeen zeroes: 100,000,000,000,000,000). The number of subatomic particles in the entire known universe is said to be around 10^{80} (1 followed by eighty zeroes). These are simply incomprehensible numbers.

Now with those numbers in mind, consider the following. The atomic weak force is so finely tuned that an alteration in its value by even one part out of 10^{100} would have prevented a life-permitting universe! Similarly, a change in the value of the so-called cosmological constant, which drives the acceleration of the universe's expansion, by as little as one part in 10^{120} would have rendered the universe life-prohibiting. Here's a corker: Roger Penrose of Oxford University has calculated that the odds of the universe's initial low entropy condition's existing by chance is on the order of one chance out of $10^{10(123)}$, a number which is so inconceivable that to call it astronomical would be a wild understatement.

The fine-tuning here is beyond comprehension. Having an accuracy of even one part out of 10^{60} is like firing a bullet toward the other side of the observable universe, twenty billion light-years away, and nailing a one-inch bull's-eye!

TALK ABOUT IT

How does it affect you to know that the universe is so precisely fine-tuned?

The examples of fine-tuning are so many and so various that they aren't likely to disappear with the advance of science. Like it or not, fine-tuning is just a fact of life which is scientifically well-established.

A Possible Objection

Now you might be thinking, *But if the constants and quantities had had different values, then maybe different forms of life might have evolved.* But that underestimates the truly disastrous consequences of a change in the values of these constants and quantities.

When scientists talk about a universe's being life-permitting, they're not talking about just present forms of life. By "life" scientists just mean the property of organisms to take in food, extract energy from it, grow, adapt to their environment, and reproduce. Anything that can fulfill those functions counts as life. And the point is, in order for life so-defined to exist, whatever form it might take, the constants and quantities of the universe have to be unbelievably fine-tuned. Otherwise disaster results. In the absence of fine-tuning not even matter, not even chemistry, would exist, much less planets where life might evolve.

A FLY ON THE WALL

The philosopher John Leslie gives the following illustration to show why we needn't be concerned with universes governed by different laws of nature. Imagine a solitary fly, resting on a large, blank area of the wall. A single shot is fired, and the bullet strikes the fly. Now even if the rest of the wall outside the blank area is covered with flies, so that a randomly fired bullet would probably hit one, nevertheless it remains highly improbable that a single, randomly fired bullet would strike the solitary fly within the large, blank area. A life-permitting universe is like that solitary fly on the wall. When we consider universes governed by our laws of nature, almost all of them are life-prohibiting. So the odds that a universe selected randomly out of this lot would be life-permitting are practically nil.

Another Objection

Sometimes people will object, "But maybe in a universe governed by *different* laws of nature, such disastrous consequences might not result." But this objection betrays a misunderstanding of the argument.

We're not concerned with universes governed by *different* laws of nature. We have no idea what such universes might be like! Rather we're concerned solely with universes governed by the *same* laws of nature but with *different* values of the constants and arbitrary quantities.

The philosopher John Leslie gives the following illustration: imagine a solitary fly, resting on a large, blank area of the wall. A single shot is fired, and the bullet strikes the fly. Now even if the rest of the wall outside the blank area is covered with flies, so that a randomly fired bullet would probably hit one, nevertheless it remains highly improbable that a single, randomly fired bullet would strike the solitary fly within the large, blank area.

In the same way, we need only concern ourselves with universes governed by the same laws of nature in order to determine how likely it is that one of them should be life-permitting. Because the laws are the same, we can determine what would happen if the constants and quantities were to be altered. And the results turn out to be disastrous. A life-permitting universe is like that solitary fly on the wall.

An Argument for Design

The question we face, then, is this: What is the best explanation of the cosmic fine-tuning? Many people think that the reason the universe is finely tuned for life is because it was intended to be life-permitting by an intelligent Designer.

But design is not the only explanatory option. There are also physical necessity and chance. These are the three live options in the contemporary literature on fine-tuning. The key to inferring to design as the best explanation will be eliminating the other two alternatives.

Accordingly, we can formulate a very simple three-step argument:

> 1. The fine-tuning of the universe is due to either physical necessity, chance, or design.
> 2. It is not due to physical necessity or chance.
> 3. Therefore, it is due to design.

This is a logically valid argument, whose conclusion follows necessarily from the two premises. So the only question is whether those premises are more plausibly true than false. So let's look at them.

PREMISE 1

The fine-tuning of the universe is due to either physical necessity, chance, or design.

The first premise, that *the fine-tuning of the universe is due to either physical necessity, chance, or design,* is unobjectionable because it just lists the three alternatives available for explaining the fine-tuning. If someone has a fourth alternative, he's welcome to add it to the list, and then we'll consider it when we come to premise 2. But there doesn't seem to be another alternative to the three listed here.

Notice that by focusing on cosmic fine-tuning this argument avoids the whole emotionally charged issue of biological evolution. The argument from fine-tuning, if successful, will show that the evolution of intelligent

TALK ABOUT IT

In popular culture, where do you see chance promoted as an explanation for our world? What about necessity? What about design? Which of these ideas do you think gets the most airtime at the popular level?

AN END RUN AROUND EVOLUTION

Notice that by focusing on cosmic fine-tuning this argument does an end run around the whole emotionally charged issue of biological evolution. The argument from fine-tuning, if successful, will show that the evolution of intelligent life anywhere in the cosmos depends upon the design of the initial cosmic conditions. Any design arguments based on the origin of life, the origin of biological complexity, the origin of consciousness, and so on, will simply layer on more improbability, making it all the more unlikely that all this can be explained apart from a Designer.

life *anywhere* in the cosmos depends upon the design of the initial cosmic conditions. Any design arguments based on the origin of life, the origin of biological complexity, the origin of consciousness, and so on, will simply layer on more improbability, making it all the more unlikely that all this can be explained apart from a Designer.

PREMISE 2

The fine-tuning is not due to physical necessity or chance.

So the crucial premise is the second premise, that *the fine-tuning is not due to physical necessity or chance.* Let's examine each of these alternatives in turn.

Physical Necessity?

According to the first alternative, physical necessity, the universe *has* to be life-permitting. The constants and quantities must have the values they do, so that a life-prohibiting universe is physically impossible.

Implausibility of This Alternative

Now on the face of it, this alternative seems fantastically implausible. It would require us to say that a life-prohibiting universe is a physical impossibility. But why take such a radical view? The constants, we've seen, are not determined by the laws of nature. So why couldn't they be different? Moreover, the arbitrary quantities are just boundary conditions on which the laws of nature operate. Nothing seems to make them necessary. So the opponent of design is taking a radical line that requires some proof. But there is none. The alternative is put forward as a bare possibility.

Theories of Everything

Sometimes scientists do talk of a yet-to-be-discovered "theory of everything" (TOE). But like so many of the colorful names given to scientific theories, this label is very misleading. A successful TOE would enable us to unify the four basic forces of nature (gravity, the weak force, the strong force, and electromagnetism) into a single force carried by a single kind of particle. But it wouldn't even attempt to explain literally everything. For example, the most promising candidate for a TOE to date, so-called M-theory or superstring theory, only works if there are eleven dimensions. But the theory itself cannot explain why just that particular number of dimensions should exist.

Moreover, M-theory doesn't predict uniquely a life-permitting universe. It permits a vast range of around 10^{500} different possible universes, all consistent with the same laws but varying in the values of the constants of nature. Almost all of these possible universes are life-prohibiting.

This so-called "cosmic landscape" of worlds permitted by M-theory has become something of a phenom lately. It's important to understand that the landscape is just a range of possibilities. Some people have misinterpreted it to mean that all these different universes actually exist. Some have thought it undermines the argument for design because the landscape must include life-permitting worlds like ours. But the cosmic landscape is not real; it's just a list of possibilities. It describes the range of universes which are consistent with M-theory.

That range is so huge (10^{500} different possibilities) that some explanation is needed why a life-permitting universe exists, since life-permitting universes are a practically infinitesimal part of the landscape. So you can't say that life-permitting universes are physically necessary because on M-theory, at least, that's clearly false.

So there is no evidence that a life-permitting universe is physically necessary. Quite the contrary, all the evidence indicates that life-prohibiting universes are not only possible but far, far more likely than any life-permitting universe.

Chance?

That leads to the second alternative: Could the fine-tuning be due simply to chance? According to this alternative, it's just an accident that all the constants and quantities fell into the life-permitting range. We basically just lucked out!

The fundamental problem here is that the chances of a life-permitting universe's existing are so remote that this alternative becomes unreasonable.

Improbability of a Life-Permitting Universe

Sometimes people object that it's meaningless to speak of the probability of a fine-tuned universe's existing because there is, after all, only one universe. So you can't say that 1 out of every 10 universes, for example, is life-permitting.

But the following illustration from the physicist John Barrow clarifies the sense in which a life-permitting

The so-called "cosmic landscape" of worlds permitted by M-theory has become something of a phenom lately. It's important to understand that the landscape is just a range of possibilities. Some people have misinterpreted it to mean that all these different universes actually exist. Some have thought it undermines the argument for design because the landscape must include life-permitting worlds like ours. But the cosmic landscape is not real; it's just a list of possibilities. It describes the range of universes that are consistent with M-theory.

ON GUARD FOR STUDENTS

universe is improbable. Take a sheet of paper and put a red dot on it. That dot represents our universe.

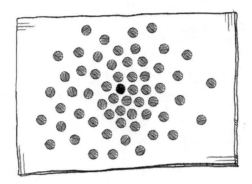

Now alter slightly one or more of the finely tuned constants and physical quantities which we've been discussing. As a result we have a description of another universe, which we can represent as a new dot in the neighborhood of the first. If that new set of constants and quantities describes a life-permitting universe, make it a red dot; if it describes a universe which is life-prohibiting, make it a blue dot. Now repeat the procedure over and over again until the sheet is filled with dots. What you wind up with is a sea of blue with only a few pin-points of red. That's the sense in which it is overwhelmingly improbable that the universe should be life-permitting. There are simply vastly more life-prohibiting universes in our local area of possible universes than there are life-permitting universes.

Lottery Illustrations

Sometimes people will appeal to the example of a lottery in order to justify the chance alternative. In a lottery where all the tickets are sold, it's fantastically improbable that any one person should win, yet *somebody* has to win! It would be unjustified for the winner, whoever he may be, to say, "The odds against my winning were twenty million to one. And yet I won! The lottery must have been rigged!"

In the same way, they say, *some* universe out of the range of possible universes has to exist. The winner of the universe lottery would also be unjustified to think that because his universe exists, this must have been the result of design, not chance. *All* the universes are equally improbable, but one of them, by chance, has to win.

This analogy is actually very helpful because it enables us to see clearly where the advocate of chance has misunderstood the argument for design and to offer a better, more accurate analogy in its place. Contrary to popular impression, the argument for design is not trying to explain why *this* particular universe exists. Rather it's trying to explain why a life-permitting universe exists. The lottery analogy was misconceived because it focused on why a particular person won.

The correct analogy would be a lottery in which billions and billions and billions of white ping-pong balls were mixed together with just one or two red ping-pong balls, and you were told that one ball will be randomly selected out of the horde. If it's red, you'll be allowed to live; if it's white, you'll be shot.

Now notice that any particular ball which is randomly selected is equally improbable: no matter which ball rolls down the chute, the odds against that particular ball are fantastically improbable. But some ball must roll down the chute. This is the point illustrated by the first lottery analogy. That point, however, is irrelevant because we're not trying to explain why *this particular* ball was picked.

The relevant point is that whichever ball rolls down the chute, it is overwhelmingly more probable that *it will be white rather than red*. Getting a *particular* red ball is no more improbable than getting any *particular* white ball. But it is incomprehensibly more probable that you will get a white ball instead of a red one. So if a red ball rolls down the chute, you certainly should suspect that the lottery was rigged to let you live.

If you still don't see the point of this analogy, then imagine that in order to be allowed to live, a red ball had to be randomly picked five times in a row. (If the odds against getting a red ball even once are great enough, happening five times rather than once won't really affect the probabilities significantly.) If such a thing actually happened, everyone would recognize that it did not happen by chance.

So in the correct analogy, we're not interested in why you got the particular ball you did. Rather we're puzzled by why, against overwhelming odds, you got a life-permitting ball rather than a life-prohibiting ball. That question is just not addressed by saying, "Well, some ball had to be picked!"

In the same way, some universe has to exist, but whichever universe exists, it is incomprehensibly more probable that it will be life-prohibiting rather than life-permitting. So we still need some explanation why a life-permitting universe exists.

REINFORCING THE LOTTERY STORY

If you're having difficulty seeing the point of the lottery analogy in the text, then imagine that in order for you to live, the red ball had to be randomly picked five times in a row. If the odds against getting the red ball even once are great enough, then getting it five times rather than once won't affect the probabilities significantly. But if you got the red ball five times in a row, everyone would recognize that it didn't happen by chance!

Is an Explanation Needed?

THE ANTHROPIC PRINCIPLE

We can observe only those values of the fundamental constants and quantities that are compatible with our existence.

Some people have argued that no explanation is needed for why we observe a life-permitting universe because that's the only kind of universe we *can* observe! If the universe were not life-permitting, then we wouldn't be here to ask about it. (This is the so-called Anthropic Principle, which says that we can observe only properties of the universe which are compatible with our existence.)

This reasoning is fallacious. The fact that we can observe only life-permitting universes does nothing to eliminate the need of an explanation for why a life-permitting universe exists.

Again, an illustration can help. Imagine you're traveling abroad and arrested for hacking into a foreign country's national security system. You're dragged in front of a firing squad of one hundred trained marksmen standing at point-blank range. You hear the command given, "Ready! Aim! Fire!" and you hear the deafening sound of the guns. And then you observe that you're still alive! That all of the one hundred marksmen missed! Now what would you conclude?

"Well, I guess I shouldn't be surprised that they all missed! After all, if they hadn't all missed, I wouldn't be here to be surprised about it! Nothing more to be explained here!"

Of course not! It's true that you shouldn't be surprised that you don't observe that you're dead, since if you were dead, you wouldn't be able to observe it. But you should still be surprised that you do observe that you are alive, in light of the enormous improbability that all the marksmen would miss. Indeed, you'd probably conclude that they all missed *on purpose*, that the whole thing was a setup, engineered for some purpose by someone.

The Many Worlds Hypothesis

Theorists have therefore come to recognize that the Anthropic Principle cannot eliminate the need of an explanation of the fine-tuning *unless* it's conjoined with a Many Worlds Hypothesis. According to that hypothesis, our universe is but one member of a World Ensemble or "multiverse" of randomly ordered universes, preferably infinite in number. If all of these other universes really exist, then by chance alone life-permitting worlds will appear somewhere in the World Ensemble. Since only finely tuned universes have observers in them, any observers existing in the World Ensemble will naturally observe their worlds to be finely tuned. So no appeal to design is necessary to explain fine-tuning. It's pure chance.

It's worth pausing for a moment to reflect on what is happening here. The current debate over fine-tuning has now become a debate over the Many Worlds Hypothesis. This hypothesis is at the heart of the discussion today. In order to explain fine-tuning we are being asked to believe not merely that there are other unobservable universes, but that there is an infinite number of such worlds and, moreover, that they randomly vary in their fundamental constants and quantities. All this is needed to guarantee that a life-permitting universe like ours will appear by chance in the ensemble.

University of Cape Town astrophysicist George Ellis (whom one cosmologist described to me as the person who knows more about cosmology than any other man alive) has indicted the Many Worlds Hypothesis as "unproveable," as involving "much too much untestable speculation about the existence of infinities of entities," and as based upon "ill-defined and untestable probability measures."[3] Ellis adds, "Nothing is wrong with scientifically based philosophical speculation, which is what multiverse proposals are. But we should name it for what it is."[4]

This is really quite extraordinary. It's a sort of backhanded compliment to the design hypothesis. For otherwise sober scientists would not be flocking to adopt so speculative and extravagant a view as the Many Worlds Hypothesis unless they felt absolutely compelled to. The fact that many theorists are turning to the Many Worlds Hypothesis to rescue the alternative of chance is perhaps the best evidence that the appeal to chance is in trouble. The odds against the existence of a life-permitting universe are just too great to be faced unless you embrace the metaphysical hypothesis of a World Ensemble.

So the next time someone says of the fine-tuning, "It could have happened by chance!" or "The improbable happens!" or "It was just dumb luck!" ask him, "Then why do the proponents of chance feel compelled to embrace an extravagance like the Many Worlds Hypothesis in order to defend the alternative of chance?"

First Response to the Many Worlds Hypothesis

So how does the Many Worlds Hypothesis fare as an explanation of the observed fine-tuning? One problem with the Many Worlds Hypothesis is that it just kicks the can down the road. For now we must ask whether the multiverse itself also involves fine-tuning. In order to be scientifically credible, the Many Worlds Hypothesis must offer some plausible mechanism for generating the many worlds. But if the Many Worlds Hypothesis is to be successful in attributing fine-tuning to chance alone, then the mechanism that generates the many worlds had better not be fine-tuned itself! For if it is, then the problem arises all over again.

But the proposed mechanisms for generating a World Ensemble are so vague that it's far from evident that the physics governing the multiverse will be free of any fine-tuning. For example, if M-theory is the physics of the multiverse, then it remains unexplained, as we have seen, why exactly eleven dimensions exist. And the mechanism that actualizes all the possibilities in the cosmic landscape may involve fine-tuning. So the postulate of a World Ensemble is by itself not enough to justify the alternative of chance.

Second Response to the Many Worlds Hypothesis

Furthermore, many theorists are skeptical of the Many Worlds Hypothesis itself. Why think that a World Ensemble actually exists? The hypotheses suggested for generating the many universes remain mere conjectures. Moreover, the Borde-Guth-Vilenkin theorem requires that even an expanding multiverse must have a beginning. In that case the mechanism that generates the many universes has been chugging away for only a finite amount of time. So by now, there may well be only a finite number of universes in the World Ensemble, which may not be enough to guarantee the appearance of a finely tuned universe by chance alone. Moreover, there's no

A BACKHANDED COMPLIMENT TO DESIGN

The current debate over fine-tuning has now become a debate over the Many Worlds Hypothesis. In order to explain fine-tuning we're being asked to believe not merely that there are other unobservable universes, but that there is an infinite number of such worlds and that they randomly vary in their fundamental constants and quantities. All this is needed to guarantee that a life-permitting universe like ours will appear by chance in the ensemble. The Many Worlds Hypothesis is really a sort of back-handed compliment to the design hypothesis. For otherwise sober scientists would not be flocking to adopt so speculative and extravagant a view as the Many Worlds Hypothesis unless they felt absolutely compelled to. So if someone says to you, "The fine-tuning could have happened by chance!" or "The improbable happens!" or "It was just dumb luck!" ask him, "Then why do the detractors of design feel compelled to embrace an extravagance like the Many Worlds Hypothesis in order to avoid design?"

reason to think that these many universes will vary randomly in their constants and quantities. There's just no evidence that the sort of World Ensemble required by the Many Worlds Hypothesis actually exists.

By contrast, we have good independent reasons for believing in a Designer of the cosmos, as Leibniz and al-Ghazali's arguments show.

Third Response to the Many Worlds Hypothesis

Most importantly, however, the Many Worlds Hypothesis faces what may be a devastating objection. Remember Boltzmann's Many Worlds Hypothesis? What sank Boltzmann's hypothesis was the fact that if our world is just a random member of a World Ensemble, then it is vastly more probable that we should be observing a much-smaller universe. It turns out that a parallel problem faces the Many Worlds Hypothesis as an explanation of cosmic fine-tuning.

Roger Penrose of Oxford University has pressed this objection forcefully.[5] He points out that the odds of our universe's initial low entropy condition's existing by chance alone are

TALK ABOUT IT

Given the flaws in the Many Worlds Hypothesis, why do you think so many people prefer to believe in chance rather than in a Designer?

one chance out of $10^{10^{(123)}}$. By contrast the odds of our solar system's suddenly forming by the random collision of particles is one chance out of $10^{10^{(60)}}$. This number, says Penrose, is "utter chicken feed" in comparison with $10^{10^{(123)}}$. What that means is that it is *far* more likely that we should be observing an orderly region no larger than our solar system, since a universe like that is so unfathomably more probable than a fine-tuned universe like ours.

In fact, we wind up with the same sort of illusionism that saddled Boltzmann's hypothesis. A small world with the illusion of a wider universe is more probable than a fine-tuned, real universe. Carried to its logical extreme, this has led to what theorists have called "the invasion of the Boltzmann brains." For the most probable observable universe is one which consists of a single brain which pops into existence by a random fluctuation with illusory perceptions of the external world! So if you accept the Many Worlds Hypothesis, you're obligated to believe that you are all that exists and that this book, your body, the earth, and everything you perceive in the world are just illusions.

No sane person believes that he is a Boltzmann brain. On atheism, therefore, it is highly improbable that there exists a randomly ordered World Ensemble. Ironically, the best hope for partisans of the multiverse is to maintain that God created it and ordered its worlds, so that they are not randomly ordered. God could give preference to observable worlds which are cosmically fine-tuned. To be rationally acceptable, the Many Worlds Hypothesis needs God.

With the failure of the Many Worlds Hypothesis, the alternative of chance collapses. Neither physical necessity nor chance provides a good explanation of the fine-tuning of the universe.

The Design Hypothesis

So what about design? Is this explanation better than physical necessity or chance, or is it equally implausible?

Dawkins' Objection

Detractors of design sometimes object that on this hypothesis the Cosmic Designer himself remains unexplained. This objection is what Richard Dawkins calls "the central argument of my book" *The God Delusion*.[6] He summarizes his argument as follows:

> 1. One of the greatest challenges to the human intellect has been to explain how the complex, improbable appearance of design in the universe arises.

2. The natural temptation is to attribute the appearance of design to actual design itself.

3. The temptation is a false one because the designer hypothesis immediately raises the larger problem of who designed the designer.

4. The most ingenious and powerful explanation is Darwinian evolution by natural selection.

5. We don't have an equivalent explanation for physics.

6. We should not give up the hope of a better explanation arising in physics, something as powerful as Darwinism is for biology.

Therefore, God almost certainly does not exist.

Dawkins' argument is jarring because the atheistic conclusion, "Therefore, God almost certainly does not exist," doesn't follow from the six previous statements even if we concede that each of them is true! There are no rules of logic which would permit such an inference. Dawkins' argument is plainly invalid.

At most, all that follows from Dawkins' argument is that we should not infer God's existence on the basis of the appearance of design in the universe. But that conclusion is quite compatible with God's existence and even with our justifiably believing in God's existence. Maybe we should believe in God on the basis of the cosmological argument or the moral argument. Maybe our belief in God isn't based on arguments at all but is grounded in religious experience or in divine revelation. The point is that rejecting design arguments for God's existence does nothing to prove that God doesn't exist or even that belief in God is unjustified. Dawkins' lack of philosophical depth is plainly on display here.

But does Dawkins' argument succeed even in undermining the argument for design? No, for some of the steps of Dawkins' argument are plausibly false. Step 5 refers to the cosmic fine-tuning which has been the focus of our discussion. Dawkins admittedly has nothing by way of explanation for it, and therefore the hope expressed in step 6 represents nothing more than the faith of a naturalist.

Moreover, consider step 3. Dawkins' claim here is that one is not justified in inferring design as the best explanation of the complex order of the universe because then a new problem arises: Who designed the Designer?

First Problem with Step 3

This claim is flawed on at least two counts. First, in order to recognize an explanation as the best, you don't need to have an explanation of the explanation. This is an elementary point in the philosophy of science. If archaeologists digging in the earth were to discover things looking like arrowheads and pottery shards, they would be justified in inferring that these artifacts are not the chance result of sedimentation and meta-morphosis, but products of some unknown group of people, even though they had no explanation of who these people were or where they came from. Similarly, if astronauts were to come upon a pile of machinery on the back side of the moon, they would be justified in inferring that it was the product of intelligent agents, even if they had no idea whatsoever who these agents were or how they got there.

In order to recognize an explanation as the best, you don't need to be able to explain the explanation. In fact, such a requirement would lead to an infinite regress of explanations, so that nothing could ever be explained and science would be destroyed! For before any explanation could be acceptable, you'd need an

NATURALISM

Naturalism is the belief that only natural explanations (as opposed to supernatural ones) should be considered. Because a designer is defined as supernatural— beyond nature—naturalism rules out this explanation, regardless of evidence.

explanation of the explanation, and then an explanation of the explanation of the explanation, and then…. Nothing could ever be explained.

So in the case at hand, in order to recognize that design is the best explanation of the appearance of design in the universe, one needn't be able to explain the Designer. Whether the Designer has an explanation can simply be left an open question for future inquiry.

Second Problem with Step 3

Second, Dawkins thinks that in the case of a divine Designer of the universe, the Designer is just as complex as the thing to be explained, so that no explanatory advance is made. This objection raises all sorts of interesting questions about the role played by simplicity in assessing competing explanations. For example, what weight is to be assigned to simplicity in comparison with other explanatory virtues? There are many other factors besides simplicity that scientists weigh in determining which explanation is the best, such as explanatory power, explanatory scope, and so forth. An explanation which has broader explanatory scope may be less simple than a rival explanation but still be preferred because it explains more things. Simplicity is not the only, or even most important, criterion for assessing theories.

But leave those questions aside. Dawkins' fundamental mistake lies in his assumption that a divine Designer is just as complex as the universe. That is plainly false. As a pure mind without a body, God is a remarkably simple entity. A mind (or soul) is not a physical object composed of parts. In contrast to the contingent and varied universe with all its inexplicable constants and quantities, a divine mind is startlingly simple, being a spiritual entity not in any way composite.

TALK ABOUT IT

Given the flaws in Dawkins' reasoning, how do you account for the huge popularity of his book (more than three million copies sold)? What, other than logic, might explain its popular appeal?

Certainly such a mind may have complex *ideas*—it may be thinking, for example, of the infinitesimal calculus—but the mind *itself* is a remarkably simple, spiritual entity. Dawkins

has evidently confused a mind's ideas, which may, indeed, be complex, with a mind itself, which is an incredibly simple entity not in any way composed of parts. Therefore, postulating a divine mind behind the universe most definitely does represent an advance in simplicity, for whatever that's worth.

Conclusion

Therefore it seems to me that of the three alternatives before us—physical necessity, chance, or design—the most plausible explanation of the fine-tuning of the universe is design. That gives us a transcendent, super-intelligent Designer of the cosmos who has fixed the values of nature's laws. Incredible! So now we have a third argument contributing to a cumulative case for the existence of God.

1. Plato, *Laws* 12.966e.
2. Plato, *Laws* 10.893b–899c.
3. John Horgan, "Physicist George Ellis Knocks Physicists for Knocking Philosophy, Falsification, Free Will," *Scientific American*, July 22, 2014, http://blogs.scientificamerican.com. See also George F. R. Ellis, "Does the Multiverse Really Exist?," *Scientific American* 305/2 (August 2011): 38–43. The laudatory cosmologist was Tony Rothman, himself no slouch!
4. Ellis, "Does the Multiverse Really Exist?," 43.
5. Roger Penrose, *The Road to Reality* (New York: Alfred E. Knopf, 2005), 762–65.
6. Richard Dawkins, *The God Delusion* (New York: Houghton Mifflin, 2006), 157–58.

THE DESIGN ARGUMENT

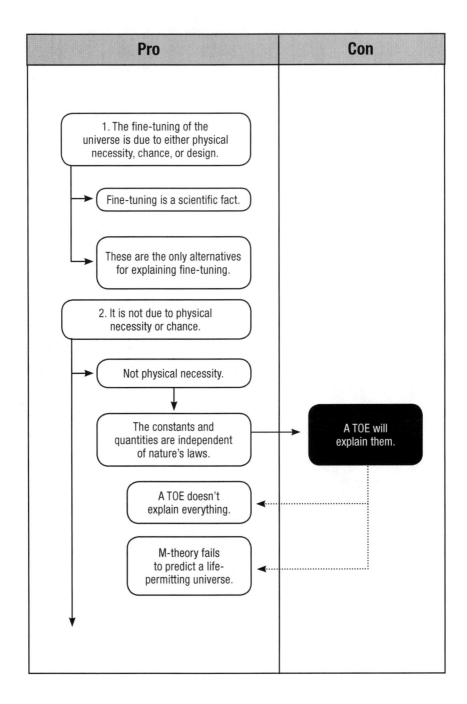

THE DESIGN ARGUMENT (cont.)

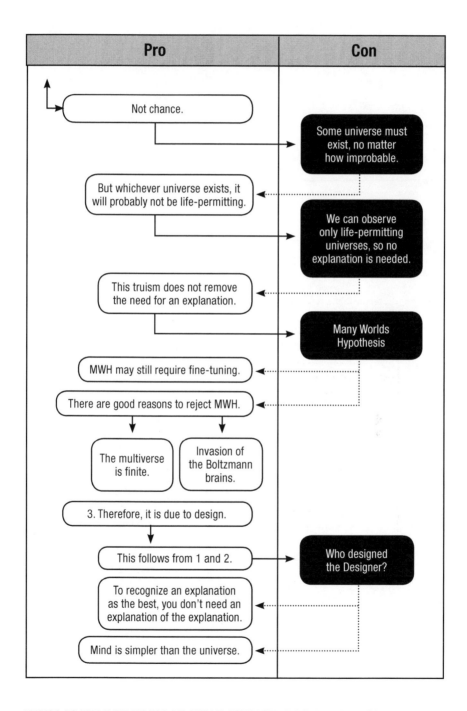

Pro	Con
Not chance.	Some universe must exist, no matter how improbable.
But whichever universe exists, it will probably not be life-permitting.	We can observe only life-permitting universes, so no explanation is needed.
This truism does not remove the need for an explanation.	Many Worlds Hypothesis
MWH may still require fine-tuning.	
There are good reasons to reject MWH.	
The multiverse is finite.	Invasion of the Boltzmann brains.
3. Therefore, it is due to design.	Who designed the Designer?
This follows from 1 and 2.	
To recognize an explanation as the best, you don't need an explanation of the explanation.	
Mind is simpler than the universe.	

CHAPTER 5

CAN WE BE GOOD WITHOUT GOD?

The central question about moral and ethical principles concerns their ontological foundation. If they are neither derived from God nor anchored in some transcendent ground, are they purely ephemeral?

Paul Kurtz, *Forbidden Fruit*

Can we be good without God?

At first the answer to this question might seem so obvious that even to ask it is apt to make people angry. For while religious believers doubtless find in God a source of moral strength that helps them lead better lives than they would have led without him, still it would be arrogant and ignorant to claim that unbelievers don't often lead good moral lives—in fact, sometimes, lives that put believers' lives to shame.

But wait! It would, indeed, be arrogant and ignorant to claim that people cannot be good without *belief* in God. But that wasn't the question. The question was: Can we be good *without God*? When we ask that question, we're posing in a provocative way a question about the nature of moral values. Are the values we hold dear and guide our lives by just social conventions, like driving on the right-hand versus left-hand side of the road? Or are they merely expressions of

WHAT IS THE
BASIS OF OUR
VALUES?

Are they based on:
1. Social convention?
2. Personal preference?
3. Evolution?
4. God?

personal preference, like having a taste for certain foods? Or are they somehow valid and binding independent of our opinion, and if they are objective in this way, what is their foundation?

A Moral Argument for God's Existence

Many philosophers have thought that morality provides a good argument for God's existence. One of the finest was William Sorley, who was a professor of moral philosophy at Cambridge University. In his *Moral Values and the Idea of God* (1918) Sorely argues that the best hope for a rational, unified view of reality is to postulate God as the ground of both the natural and the moral orders.

Sorely maintains that there is an objective moral order, which is as real and independent of our recognition of it as is the natural order of things. He recognizes that in one sense we can't prove that objective moral values exist, but he points out that in this same sense we can't prove that the natural world of physical objects exists either! The moral order and the natural order are thus on a similar footing. Just as we assume the reality of the world of objects on the basis of our sense experience, so we assume the reality of the moral order on the basis of our moral experience.

William Sorley

On Sorley's view, then, both the natural order and the moral order are part of reality. The question, then, is: What worldview can combine these two orders into the most coherent explanatory form? Sorely argues that the best explanation is God. There must be an infinite, eternal

> ### TALK ABOUT IT
>
> How do you respond to the idea that the objective moral order is just as real as the objective physical world? Why?

Mind who is the architect of nature and whose moral purpose man and the universe are gradually fulfilling.

I myself stumbled into the moral argument through the back door. Remember our discussion in chapter 1 of the absurdity of life without God? We saw that one aspect of the human predicament is that if there is no God, then there is no foundation for objective moral values. Everything becomes relative. To my surprise, the response of some students to this claim was to insist that objective moral values do exist. Certain things really are right or wrong!

Now what the students said didn't in any way refute the claim that without God there would be no objective values. Instead, they had unwittingly supplied the missing premise in a moral argument for God's existence! For now one may argue:

1. If God does not exist, objective moral values and duties do not exist.
2. Objective moral values and duties do exist.
3. Therefore, God exists.

This simple little argument is logically ironclad. I had argued for the truth of the first premise and the students had insisted on the second. Together the two premises imply the existence of God.

What makes this argument so powerful is that people generally believe both premises. In a pluralistic age, students are scared to death of imposing their values on someone else. They therefore give at least lip service to relativism. So premise 1 seems correct to them. At the same time, certain values have been deeply instilled into them, such as tolerance, open-mindedness, and love. In particular, they think it is objectively *wrong* to impose your values on someone

> ### TALK ABOUT IT
>
> Have you ever had a conversation with someone who said there are no objective moral values that apply to everyone? If so, how did that person deal with values like tolerance and love?

else! So they're deeply committed to premise 2 as well. They've just never connected the dots.

Let's examine more closely each of the argument's two premises in order to see what defense might be offered on their behalf and what objections might be raised against them.

PREMISE 1

If God does not exist, objective moral values and duties do not exist.

Two Important Distinctions

Before we look at reasons for accepting premise 1, we need to clarify a couple of important distinctions.

Values and Duties

VALUES AND
DUTIES

Moral value refers to the worth of a person or action, whether it is good or bad. *Moral duty* refers to our obligation to act in a certain way, whether that action is right or wrong.

First, the distinction between *values* and *duties*. Values have to do with whether something is good or bad. Duties have to do with whether something is right or wrong. Now you might think at first that this is a distinction without a difference: "good" and "right" mean the same thing, and the same goes for "bad" and "wrong." But if you think about it, you can see that this isn't the case.

Duty has to do with moral obligation, what you ought or ought not to do. But obviously you're not morally obligated to do something just because it would be good for you to do it. For example, it would be good for you to become a doctor, but you're not morally obligated to become a doctor. After all, it would also be good for you to become a firefighter or a farmer or a homemaker, but you can't do them all. Furthermore, sometimes all you have is bad choices (think of the movie *Sophie's Choice*), but it's not wrong for you to choose one, since you must choose.

So there's a difference between good/bad and right/wrong. Good/bad has to do with something's *worth*, while right/wrong has to do with something's being *obligatory*.

Objective and Subjective

Second, there's the distinction between being *objective* or *subjective*. By "objective" I mean "independent of people's opinions." By "subjective" I mean "dependent on people's opinions." So to say that there are objective moral values is to say that something is good or bad independent of whatever people think about it. Similarly, to say that we have objective moral duties is to say that certain actions are right or wrong for us regardless of what people think about it.

So, for example, to say that the Holocaust was objectively wrong is to say that it was wrong even though the Nazis who carried it out thought that it was right, and it would still have been wrong even if the Nazis had won World War II and succeeded in exterminating or brainwashing everybody who disagreed with them, so that everyone believed the Holocaust

Objective means independent of human opinion. For example, the laws of nature hold whether we acknowledge them or not, so they are objective. *Subjective* means dependent on human opinion. For example, matters of taste, like whether coffee tastes good, are person-relative and so are subjective.

was right. Premise 1 asserts that if there is no God, then moral values and duties are not objective in that sense.

Defense of Premise 1

So consider, first, moral values. Traditionally moral values have been based in God, who is the highest Good. But if God does not exist, what is the basis of moral values? In particular, why think that human beings have moral worth? The most popular form of atheism is naturalism, which holds that the only things that exist are the things postulated by our best scientific theories. But science is morally neutral; you can't find moral values in a test tube. It follows immediately that moral values don't really exist; they're just illusions of human beings.

Even if the atheist is willing to go beyond the bounds of science, why think that on atheism human beings are morally valuable? On a naturalistic view moral values are just the by-product of biological evolution and social conditioning. Just as a troupe of baboons exhibit cooperative and even self-sacrificial behavior because natural selection has determined it to be advantageous in the struggle for survival, so their primate cousins *homo sapiens* exhibit similar behavior for the same reason. As a result of sociobiological pressures there has evolved among *homo sapiens* a sort of "herd morality" which functions well in the perpetuation of our species. But on the atheistic view there doesn't seem to be anything about *homo sapiens* that makes this morality objectively true. If we were to rewind the film of human evolution back to the beginning and start anew, people with a very different set of moral values might well have evolved. As Darwin himself wrote in *The Descent of Man*:

> If ... men were reared under precisely the same conditions
> as hive-bees, there can hardly be a doubt that our unmarried
> females would, like the worker-bees, think it a sacred duty

to kill their brothers, and mothers would strive to kill their fertile daughters, and no one would think of interfering.[1]

For us to think that human beings are special and our morality objectively true is to succumb to the temptation to speciesism, an unjustified bias toward one's own species.

Charles Darwin

So if there is no God, any basis for regarding the herd morality evolved by *homo sapiens* as objectively true seems to have been removed. Take God out of the picture, and all you're left with is an ape-like creature on a speck of solar dust beset with delusions of moral grandeur.

Second, now consider moral duties. Traditionally our moral duties were thought to spring from God's commandments, such as the Ten Commandments. But if there is no God, what basis remains for objective moral duties? On the atheistic view, human beings are just animals, and animals have no moral obligations to one another. When a lion kills a zebra, it kills the zebra, but it does not *murder* the zebra. When a great white shark forcibly copulates with a female, it forcibly copulates with her but it does not *rape* her—for there is no moral dimension to these actions. They are neither prohibited nor obligatory.

"I'm sorry, officer. I just don't like tofu."

So if God does not exist, why think that we have any moral obligations to do anything? Who or what imposes these moral duties upon us? Where do they come from? It's hard to see why they would be anything more than a subjective impression resulting from societal and parental conditioning.

Certain actions such as incest and rape may not be biologically and socially advantageous and so in the course of human development have become taboo. But that does absolutely nothing to show that rape or incest is really *wrong*. Such behavior goes on all the time in the animal kingdom. The rapist who goes against the herd morality is doing nothing more serious than acting unfashionably, the moral equivalent, if you will, of Lady Gaga. If there is no moral lawgiver, then there is no objective moral law which we must obey.

> ### TALK ABOUT IT
>
> Try to come up with an atheist's argument to defend the idea that forcible copulation is morally wrong for humans but not for sharks. How would you reply?

Getting Clear about the Argument

Now it's extremely important that we clearly understand the issue before us. I can just hear someone saying indignantly, "Are you claiming that all atheists are bad people?" Such a person has completely misunderstood the argument.

The question before us is *not*: Must we believe in God in order to live moral lives? There's no reason to think that nonbelievers cannot live what we normally characterize as good and decent lives.

Again, the question is *not*: Can we recognize objective moral values and duties without believing in God? There's no reason to think that you have to believe in God in order to recognize that, for example, we ought to love our children.

Or again, the question is *not*: Can we formulate a system of ethics without referring to God? If the nonbeliever recognizes the intrinsic value of human beings, there's no reason to think he can't work out an ethical code of conduct which the believer will generally agree with. (Of course, the question will remain of how he can ground the intrinsic value of human beings in a naturalistic world.)

Rather the question is: If God does not exist, do objective moral values and duties exist? The question is not about the necessity of *belief* in God for objective morality but about the necessity of the existence of God for objective morality.

I've been shocked at how often even professional philosophers, who should know better, confuse these

IT'S ABOUT GOD'S EXISTENCE

The moral argument asserts not that *belief* in God is necessary for objective morality, but that the *existence* of God is necessary.

two questions. For example, I debated the humanist philosopher Paul Kurtz at Franklin and Marshall College on the topic "Goodness without God Is Good Enough." I argued that if God does not exist, there are no objective moral values, duties, or accountability for one's actions.

Prof. Kurtz, to my astonishment, completely missed the point. He replied:

> If God is essential, then how is it possible for the millions and millions of people who don't believe in God to none-theless behave morally and ethically? On your view, they could not. And so, God just is not essential … many people, indeed millions of people, have been optimistic about life, have lived a full life, and find life exciting and significant. Yet, they don't wring their hands about whether or not there is an afterlife. It's living life here and now that counts.[2]

Kurtz's point only shows that *belief* in God isn't essential to living a moral, optimistic life. It does nothing to refute the claim that if there is no God, then morality is just a human illusion.

To repeat: *belief* in God is not necessary for objective morality; *God* is.

TALK ABOUT IT

How would you explain the fact that atheists just know that harming an innocent human being is wrong, and can live good lives, without believing that God is the ultimate source of values and duties?

The Euthyphro Dilemma

The other response to the argument that one can count on hearing is the so-called Euthyphro dilemma, named after a character in one of Plato's dialogues. It basically goes like this: Is something good because God wills it? Or does God will something because it is good? If you say that something is good because God wills it, then what is good becomes arbitrary. God could have willed that hatred is good, and then we would have been morally obligated to hate one another. That seems crazy. Some moral values, at least, seem to be necessary. But if you say that God wills something because it is good, then what is good or bad is independent of God. In that case, moral values and duties exist independently of God, which contradicts premise 1.

Fortunately, we don't need to refute either horn of the Euthyphro dilemma because the dilemma it presents is a false one. There's a third alternative, namely, God wills something because he is good. What do I mean by that? I mean that God himself is the standard of goodness, and his commandments to us are expressions of his nature. In short, our moral duties are determined by the commands of a just and loving God.

So moral values are not independent of God because God's own character determines what is good. God is essentially compassionate, fair, kind, impartial, and so on. It is impossible for him to lack those essential properties, just as it is impossible for him to lack the properties of omnipotence, omniscience, and eternity. So he himself is the moral standard determining good and bad. He is the paradigm for goodness, just as the sound of a live orchestra is the paradigm for high-fidelity recording. God's commands in turn reflect his moral character. Therefore, they are not arbitrary. When the atheist demands, "If God were to command child abuse, would we be obligated to abuse our children?" he's asking a question like "If there were

THE EUTHYPHRO DILEMMA

1. Is something good because God wills it? Then the good is arbitrary.
2. Does God will something because it is good? Then it is a moral value independent of God.
Solution: God wills something because he is good.

a square circle, would its area be the square of one of its sides?" There is no answer because what it supposes is logically impossible.

Someone might persist, "But why is God the standard of moral value?" The question is in a certain sense misconceived. Anyone has the right to present his moral theory and to explain its parameters. The relevant question will be whether that moral theory is plausible, in particular whether its moral ultimate is a non-arbitrary and adequate stopping point. In contrast to humanism, theism has a non-arbitrary and adequate stopping point. For God is by definition the greatest conceivable being, a being which is worthy of worship. Nothing higher could be imagined. Thus, identifying the Good with God himself supplies a foundation for a plausible moral theory.

So the Euthyphro dilemma presents us with a false choice, and we shouldn't be tricked by it. The morally good/bad is determined by God's essential character, and the morally right/wrong is determined by his will. God wills something because he is good, and something is right because God wills it. This view of morality has been eloquently defended in our day by such eminent philosophers as Robert Adams, William Alston, and Philip Quinn. Yet atheists continue to attack the straw men erected by the Euthyphro dilemma. In the *Cambridge Companion to Atheism* (2007), for example, the article on God and morality, written by a prominent ethicist, refers neither to the work of these scholars nor to the alternative I've just explained, but attacks only the view that God arbitrarily made up moral values—a straw man which virtually nobody defends!

A STRAW MAN

The view of moral values and duties explained in the text has been eloquently defended in our day by such eminent philosophers as Robert Adams, William Alston, and Philip Quinn. Yet atheists continue to put forward the same old Euthyphro dilemma. In the recent *Cambridge Companion to Atheism* (2007), for example, the article on God and morality, written by a prominent ethicist, refers neither to the work of these scholars nor to the solution explained here, but attacks only the view that God arbitrarily made up moral values—a straw man that virtually nobody defends!

Atheistic Moral Platonism

The mention of Plato brings to mind another possible atheistic response to premise 1. Plato thought that the Good just exists on its own as a sort of self-existent Idea. (If you find this difficult to grasp, join the company!) Later Christian thinkers equated Plato's Good with God's moral nature; but Plato thought the Good just existed by itself. So some atheists might say that moral values like *Justice, Mercy, Love,* and so on, just exist without any foundation. We can call this view Atheistic Moral Platonism. It holds that objective moral values exist but are not grounded in God.

What might we say about this view? Three problems present themselves.

First, Atheistic Moral Platonism seems unintelligible. What does it mean to say, for example, that the moral value *Justice* just exists? It's hard to make sense of this. It's easy to understand what it means to say that some person is just, but it's bewildering when someone says that in the absence of any people *Justice* itself exists. Moral values seem to be properties of persons, and it's hard to understand how *Justice* can exist as an abstraction.

Second, this view provides no basis for moral duties. Let's suppose for the sake of argument that moral values like *Justice, Loyalty, Mercy, Forbearance,* and the like just exist. How does that result in any moral obligations for me? Why would I have a moral duty to be, say, merciful? Who or what lays such an obligation on me? Notice that on this view moral vices like *Greed, Hatred, Sloth,* and *Selfishness* also presumably exist on their own as abstractions. So why are we obligated to align our lives with one set of these abstractly existing objects rather than any other? Atheistic Moral Platonism, lacking a moral lawgiver, has no grounds for moral obligation.

Finally, third, it's fantastically improbable that the blind evolutionary process should spit forth precisely the sort of creatures who correspond to the abstractly existing realm of moral values. This seems to be an utterly incredible coincidence when you think about it. It's almost as if the moral realm *knew* that we were coming. As Sorley argues, it's far more plausible to think that both the natural realm and the moral realm are under the authority of a God who gave us both the laws of nature and the moral law than to think that these two independent realms just happened to mesh.

Humanism

So what's the atheist to do at this point? Most atheists want to affirm the objective reality of moral values and duties. So they simply embrace some sort of humanism and stop there. For example, new atheist Sam Harris

Humanism is the view that man is the measure of all things. In particular, man takes the place of God as the anchor of moral values, and moral duties are determined by what promotes human flourishing.

❧ ON GUARD FOR STUDENTS

says that whatever contributes to human flourishing is good, and whatever detracts from it is bad, and our obligation is bring about the greatest human flourishing.

Now Harris' brand of ethical consequentialism has sinister implications. Suppose that through some fluke of history the rape and murder of a little girl would bring about the greatest flourishing for future human beings. Then, not only would her rape and murder be good, but you would be morally obligated to commit such an atrocity, which seems unthinkable.

But humanism's problems lie much deeper than that. For, why, given atheism, would human flourishing be good? Just taking human flourishing as your ultimate stopping point seems to be a premature halt to inquiry, because of the arbitrariness and implausibility of such a stopping point.

First, given atheism, why think that what is conducive to human flourishing is any more valuable than what is conducive to the flourishing of ants or mice? Why think that inflicting harm on another member of our species is wrong? When I put this question to the Dartmouth ethicist Walter Sinnott-Armstrong in our debate on the existence of God, he replied, "It simply is. Objectively. Don't you agree?"[3] Of course, I agree that it *is* wrong to harm another human being, but I pointed out that this is not the question. The question is: Why *would it be* wrong if atheism were true? When I put this question to University of Massachusetts philosopher Louise Antony in our debate on "Is God Necessary for Morality?" she shot back, "I wonder if you have any friends!" I just smiled— but the point remains that, like it or not, given an atheistic worldview, picking out human flourishing as morally special seems to be arbitrary.

Moreover, it seems implausible as well. Atheists will sometimes say that moral properties like goodness and badness necessarily attach to certain natural states of affairs. For example, the property of badness necessarily attaches to a man's beating his wife. The property of goodness necessarily attaches to a mother's nursing her infant. Atheists will say that once all the purely natural properties are in place, then the moral properties necessarily come along with them. Now on atheism this seems extraordinarily implausible.

Why think that these strange, non-natural moral properties like "goodness" and "badness" even exist, much less somehow get necessarily attached to various natural states of affairs? I can't see any reason to think that on atheism a full description of the natural properties involved in some situation would determine or fix any moral properties of that situation at all.

These humanistic philosophers have simply taken a "shopping list" approach to ethical questions. Because they hold to humanism, they just help themselves to the moral properties they need to do the job. What is needed to make their view plausible is some sort of explanation for *why* moral properties attach to certain natural states of affairs. Again, it's inadequate for the humanist to assert that we do, in fact, see that human beings have intrinsic moral value, for that's not in dispute. Indeed, that's the second premise of the moral argument! What we want from the humanist is some reason to think that human beings would be morally significant if atheism were true. As it is, their humanism is just a stubborn moral faith.

PREMISE 2

Objective moral values and duties exist.

Defense of Premise 2

That brings us to the second premise, that *objective moral values and duties exist.* I initially thought that this would be the most controversial premise in the argument. In my debates with atheist philosophers, however, I find that almost nobody denies it. It might surprise you to learn that surveys taken at universities reveal, perhaps contrary to impression, that professors are more apt to believe in objective moral values than students, and that philosophy professors are more apt to believe in objective moral values than professors in general!

And even among students, I've found that although they give lip service to relativism, 95 percent can be very quickly convinced that objective moral values do exist after all. Just ask what they think of the Hindu practice of *sati* (burning widows alive on the funeral pyres of their husbands) or the ancient Chinese custom of crippling women for life by tightly binding their feet from childhood to resemble lotus blossoms. Ask them what they think of the Crusades or the Inquisition. Ask

TALK ABOUT IT

What do you make of the fact that professors are more apt to believe in objective moral values than students, and that philosophy professors are more apt to believe in objective moral values than professors in general? What might this say about these three groups of people? How might age be a factor? Education? Popular culture?

them if they think it's all right for Catholic priests to sexually abuse little boys and for the church to try to cover it up by moving the priest to another diocese. If you're dealing with someone who's an honest inquirer, almost every time that person will agree that there are at least some objective moral values and duties.

Moral Experience

Like William Sorley, contemporary philosophers who reflect on our moral experience see no more reason to distrust that experience than the experience of our five senses. I believe what my five senses tell me, that there is a world of physical objects out there. Sure, it's possible that I am a brain in vat of chemicals wired up with electrodes or a body lying in the Matrix programmed to inhabit a virtual reality. But in the absence of any reason to think that I am, I'm perfectly rational to accept the deliverances of my five senses. Similarly, in the absence of some reason to distrust my moral experience, I should accept what it tells me, that some things are objectively good or evil, right or wrong.

Most of us would agree that in moral experience we do apprehend objective values and duties. When I was speaking several years ago on a Canadian university campus, I noticed a poster put up by the Sexual Assault & Information Center. It read: "Sexual Assault: No One Has the Right to Abuse a Child, Woman, or Man." Most of us recognize that sexual abuse of another person is wrong. Actions like rape, torture, and child abuse aren't just socially unacceptable behavior—they're moral abominations. By the same token, love, generosity, and self-sacrifice are really good. People who fail to see this are just handicapped, the moral equivalent of someone who is blind, and there's no reason to let their impairment call into question what we see clearly.

So in the absence of some defeater of our moral experience, we are rational in believing in objective moral values and duties.

Sociobiological Objections to Moral Experience

The question, then, is: Do we have any overriding reason to discount completely our moral experience? It is not enough to show that sometimes we are wrong in our moral judgments, for the claim is not that our moral apprehension is infallible, any more than our five senses are infallible. We'd need some good reason to think that our moral apprehensions are utterly illusory.

Some people have claimed that the sociobiological account of the origins of morality undermines our moral experience. According to that account, you'll remember, our moral beliefs have been ingrained into us by evolution and social conditioning. Does that give us reason to deny our moral experience?

The sociobiological account clearly does nothing to undermine the *truth* of our moral beliefs. For the truth of a belief is independent of *how you came to hold* that belief. You may have acquired your moral beliefs through a fortune cookie or by reading tea leaves, and they could still happen to be true. In particular, if God exists, then objective moral values and duties exist, regardless of how we come to learn about them. The sociobiological account at best proves that our *perception* of moral values and duties has evolved. But if moral values are gradually discovered, not invented, then our gradual and fallible perception of those values no more undermines their objective reality than our gradual, fallible perception of the physical world undermines its objective reality.

But perhaps the sociobiological account undermines, not the *truth* of our moral beliefs, but our *justification* for holding such beliefs. If your moral beliefs were based on reading tea leaves, they might accidentally turn out to be true, but you wouldn't have any justification for thinking that they are true. So you wouldn't have a good reason for accepting premise 2.

Similarly, the objection is that if our moral beliefs have been shaped by evolution, then we can't have any confidence in them because evolution aims, not at truth, but at survival. Our moral beliefs have been selected for their survival value, not for their truth. So we can't trust our moral experience and so have no reason to think that premise 2 is true.

There are two problems with this objection to our knowledge of premise 2. First, it is question-begging because it assumes that atheism is true. If there is no God, then our moral beliefs are selected by evolution solely for their survival value, not for their truth. I myself pressed this point in defending premise 1. If God doesn't exist, then the sociobiological account is true, and our moral beliefs are illusory. But, you see, that's no reason to think that the sociobiological account *is* true. If God exists, then it's likely that he would want us to have fundamentally correct moral beliefs and so would either guide the evolutionary process to produce such beliefs or else instill them in us. Apart from the assumption of atheism, we have no reason to deny what our moral experience tells us. But to assume atheism is to beg the question.

Second, the objection is self-defeating. On naturalism, *all* our beliefs, not just our moral beliefs, are the result of evolution and social conditioning. Thus, the evolutionary account leads to skepticism about knowledge in general. But this is self-defeating because then we should be skeptical of the evolutionary account itself,

THE GENETIC FALLACY

This informal fallacy attempts to invalidate a view by showing how a person came to believe that view. For example, "The only reason you believe in democracy is that you were raised in a democratic country. Therefore, your view that democracy is the best form of government is false." As an objection to the truth of moral judgments, the sociobiological account is guilty of the genetic fallacy.

since it, too, is the product of evolution and social conditioning! The objection therefore undermines itself.

So given the warrant provided for premise 2 by our moral experience, we are justified in thinking that objective moral values and duties exist. Atheist philosopher Louise Antony summed it up beautifully when she remarked in our debate, "Any argument for moral skepticism is going to be based on premises which are less obvious than the existence of objective moral values themselves." Therefore, moral skepticism could never be justified.

Conclusion

From the two premises, it follows logically that God exists. The moral argument complements the cosmological and design arguments by telling us about the moral nature of the Creator and Designer of the universe. It gives us a personal, necessarily existent being not only who is perfectly good, but whose very nature is the standard of goodness and whose commands constitute our moral duties.

So, to answer the question that opened this chapter: no, we cannot truly be good without God; but if we can in some measure be good, then it follows that God exists.

Even Gentiles, who do not have God's written law, show that they know his law when they instinctively obey it, even without having heard it. They demonstrate that God's law is written in their hearts, for their own conscience and thoughts either accuse them or tell them they are doing right. (Romans 2:14–15 NLT)

1. Charles Darwin, *The Descent of Man and Selection in Relation to Sex*, 2nd ed. (New York: D. Appleton, 1909), 100.
2. William Lane Craig and Paul Kurtz, *God and Ethics: A Contemporary Debate*, ed. Nathan King and Robert Garcia (Lanham, MD: Rowman & Littlefield, 2008).
3. William Lane Craig and Walter Sinnott-Armstrong, *God? A Debate between a Christian and an Atheist* (New York: Oxford University Press, 2003).

ON GUARD FOR STUDENTS

THE MORAL ARGUMENT

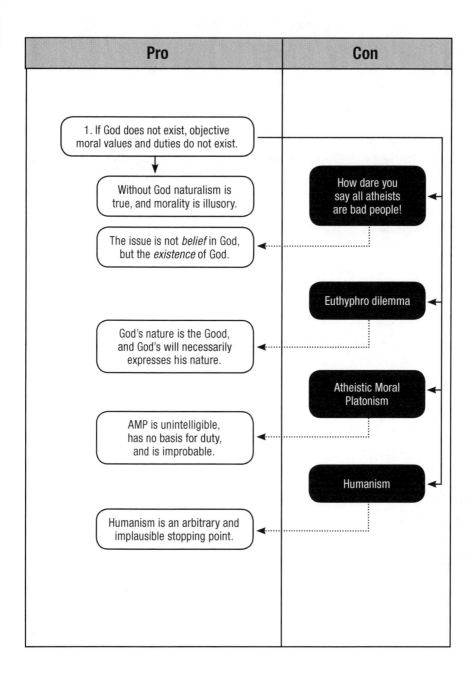

Pro	Con
1. If God does not exist, objective moral values and duties do not exist.	
Without God naturalism is true, and morality is illusory.	How dare you say all atheists are bad people!
The issue is not *belief* in God, but the *existence* of God.	
	Euthyphro dilemma
God's nature is the Good, and God's will necessarily expresses his nature.	
	Atheistic Moral Platonism
AMP is unintelligible, has no basis for duty, and is improbable.	
	Humanism
Humanism is an arbitrary and implausible stopping point.	

THE MORAL ARGUMENT (cont.)

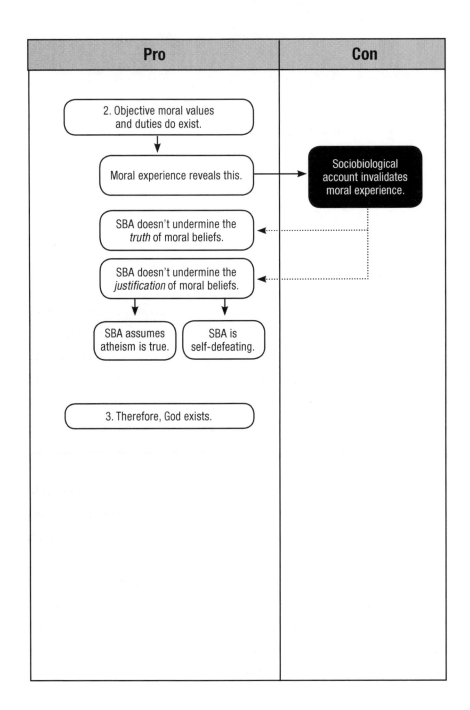

Pro	Con
2. Objective moral values and duties do exist.	
Moral experience reveals this.	Sociobiological account invalidates moral experience.
SBA doesn't undermine the *truth* of moral beliefs.	
SBA doesn't undermine the *justification* of moral beliefs.	
SBA assumes atheism is true. SBA is self-defeating.	
3. Therefore, God exists.	

CHAPTER 6

WHAT ABOUT ALL THE SUFFERING?

Is God willing to prevent evil, but not able? Then he is not
omnipotent. Is he able, but not willing? Then he is malevolent.
Is he both able and willing? Then whence cometh evil?

Epicurus

In the previous four chapters we've examined four arguments for the existence of God based on philosophical, scientific, and moral considerations. Together they seem to make up a pretty strong case for belief in God. But, of course, we need to consider the evidence on the other side of the scale, too. Can the atheist offer equally powerful arguments to show that God does *not* exist?

"There's No Evidence That God Exists!"

As a matter of fact, when you survey the literature, you find that there really aren't very many arguments against God's existence. The atheist's main complaint is that there isn't any evidence *for* God's existence. But in light of the four arguments we've just run through, that complaint falls flat.

In my experience I've found that nonbelievers are often so ill-prepared to discuss these arguments that when they do confront an argument, all they can do in response is just repeat themselves, "That's no evidence that God exists!" One blogger characterized my debate with the British atheist Lewis Wolpert in Central Hall, Westminster, London, in this way:

Wolpert: "There's no evidence for God's existence!"

Craig: "There *is* evidence for God's existence, and here it is:
…"

Wolpert: "There's no evidence for God's existence!"

Craig: "There *is* evidence for God's existence, and here it is:
…"

Wolpert: "There's no evidence for God's existence!"

Sadly, this characterization is not far from the truth! Sometimes it seems as if many nonbelievers have just learned the slogan, "There's no evidence for God's existence!" It becomes a cover for intellectual laziness and lack of engagement. It's just a way of saying, "I'm not convinced by your arguments."

Now if this is to be more than just an autobiographical comment on the unbeliever's part, he must think that some of the arguments' premises are false. So the next question to ask him is, "Which premise do you reject, and why?"

One atheist I was talking with exclaimed at that point, "I reject all of them!" To which I replied, "Surely you don't reject *all* of them. Do you reject that 'The universe exists' or that 'The fine-tuning of the universe is due to physical necessity, chance, or design'?" He recognized that his remark had been careless. From that point on we were able to have a fruitful conversation about which premises he actually found problematic.

TALK ABOUT IT

Do you think it's ever helpful to engage with statements like, "I think religion is all just in your head," or, "Religion has done more harm to society than anything else"? If so, under what circumstances, and how? If not, why not?

Staying focused on the premises will help us to keep on track. It's so easy in discussions about these emotionally charged issues to get distracted by assertions like "Religion poisons everything!" or "Religion is all just in your head!" I understand that's how many people feel. But the claim we're considering is that there's no evidence for God's existence. Since we've already surveyed some arguments for God's existence, it's now incumbent upon the person who rejects the conclusions of those arguments to explain which premises in the argument he rejects, and why.

Of course, even if it were the case that there's no evidence for God's existence, that's no reason to believe that God does *not* exist. An Australian forensic scientist I met in Sydney

TALK ABOUT IT

What are some of the emotional reasons why a person might reject God and have no interest in logical arguments?

told me that there is a saying beloved of criminologists: *absence of evidence is not evidence of absence.* A suspect might still be the murderer even if there is no evidence that he is. To rule him out, you need an alibi, that is, positive evidence that he did not commit the crime. To rule out God's existence, we need more than just absence of evidence; we need some positive evidence of absence.

Atheism Redefined

Very often atheists themselves admit that they have no evidence of God's absence, but they try to put a different spin on it. They'll tell you, "No one can prove a universal negative" (like "There is no God"). They think this somehow excuses them from needing evidence against God's existence.

But not only is it false that you can't prove a universal negative (all you have to do is show something is self-contradictory), but more importantly, this claim is really an admission that it's impossible to prove atheism! Atheism involves a universal negative; you can't prove a universal negative; therefore, atheism is unprovable. It turns out that it is the atheist who is believing a view for which there is and can be no evidence. This argument ought to be part of the Christian's apologetic arsenal!

Unfortunately, what many atheists do at this point is to revise the definition of atheism, so that atheism is no longer the view that God does not exist, but becomes merely the absence of belief in God. Anyone who lacks a belief in God counts as an atheist.

This is not only contrary to the traditional meaning of the word, but it is really hopeless as a definition. For on this new definition, atheism is no longer a viewpoint or position, like "There is no God." Rather it's just a description of someone's psychological state, namely, the state of lacking a belief in God. As such, atheism is neither true nor false, and even babies turn out to be atheists! But can you imagine the following conversation between two young mothers?

> Brooke: "Julie, I heard that you just had twins! Congratulations!"
> Julie: "Yes, thank you! But, you know, it's so sad …"
> Brooke: "What is?"
> Julie: "Well, they're both atheists!"

On this redefinition even my cat Muff (who, I'm sure, has never even thought about the question) turns out to be an atheist!

Is Muff an atheist?

KEY TERMS

Theism: "God exists."
Atheism: "God does not exist."
Agnosticism: "God may or may not exist."

All of this trivializes atheism and still leaves us wondering whether or not God exists. Call it "atheism" or "shmatheism," what we want to know is if God exists, and anyone who says that he does not needs to have some evidence or arguments for his position.

The Argument from Suffering

Thoughtful atheists do try to provide arguments against God's existence. Undoubtedly, the most important of these is the problem of suffering. When you consider the extent and depth of suffering in the world, whether due to natural disasters or to man's own inhumanity to man, then you have to admit that it's hard to believe in God. The horrible suffering in the world certainly seems to be evidence of God's absence.

In 1985, when Jan and I were living just outside Paris, the problem of suffering was brought home to me in a powerful way by two incidents shown on French television. In Mexico City a terrible earthquake had devastated blocks of high-rise apartment buildings. As rescue teams in the aftermath of the quake searched the rubble for survivors, they came across a ten-year-old boy who was trapped alive somewhere in the recesses of a collapsed building. During the next several days, the whole world watched in agony as the teams tried to remove the rubble to get to the boy. They could communicate with him but could not reach him. His grandfather, who had been trapped with him, was already dead. "I'm scared!" he cried. After about eleven days, there was silence. Alone in the darkness, trapped without food and water, afraid, the little boy died before the rescue teams could free him.

That same year a mudslide swept over a village in Colombia. As rescuers came to help survivors, they came across a little girl who was pinned up to her chin in muddy water. For some reason or other, they could not free her or remove the water. All they could do was stand by helplessly and watch her die. Every night on the news we saw film of the little girl's decline. It was the most pathetic sight I have ever seen. She stood there, unable to move, spitting out the water that continually flowed into her mouth. As the days went by, she became more exhausted, and deep, black circles formed under her eyes. She was dying before our very eyes, as we watched on television. Finally, the evening newscaster reported that she was gone.

Those two incidents rent my heart. I'll be honest with you. When I see these sorts of things going on, it makes it hard for me to believe in God.

But as a philosopher I'm called upon to say what I *think* about some question, not how I *feel* about it. And as difficult as the problem of suffering may be emotionally, that's not a reason in and of itself to think that God does not exist. We need an argument.

Versions of the Problem of Suffering

So in dealing with this emotionally loaded topic, I think it's crucial that we make a number of distinctions to keep our thinking clear (Fig. 1).

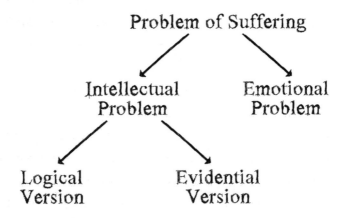

Fig. 1. Various versions of the problem of suffering. Answers to one version may not be appropriate to another version.

First and foremost, we must distinguish between the *intellectual* problem posed by suffering and the *emotional* problem posed by suffering. The intellectual problem concerns whether it's plausible to think that God and suffering can coexist. The emotional problem concerns people's dislike of a God who would permit suffering.

It's vital that we keep these problems distinct because any answer to the intellectual problem will doubtless seem dry and unmoving to the person who's struggling with the emotional problem, and the answer to the emotional problem will probably seem superficial and weak to anyone who is contemplating suffering as an abstract, philosophical question.

I suspect that for most people the terrible suffering in the world is really an emotional, not an intellectual, problem. They've never really thought about it deeply. Their unbelief is born, not out of *refutation*,

TALK ABOUT IT

Have you experienced serious suffering? How does your experience of suffering (or relative lack of experience with it) affect the way you think about the problem of suffering?

but out of *rejection*. People just want nothing to do with a God who would allow them or others to suffer terribly. But in order to support my claim that suffering poses mainly an emotional problem, we need to examine in detail the intellectual problem to see if it succeeds as a proof of atheism.

Intellectual Problem of Suffering

Now in discussing the intellectual problem of suffering, it's important that we keep in mind who has the burden of proof here. In the previous chapters we were considering arguments for God, and so it was the believer who had to bear the burden of proof. But now it's the atheist's turn. We're considering arguments *for* atheism. We want to hear from the atheist some arguments against God. So now it's the atheist who must shoulder the burden of proof. It's up to him to give us an argument leading to the conclusion "Therefore, God does not exist."

Too often unbelievers shift the burden of proof to the believer's shoulders. "Give me some good explanation for why God permits suffering," the unbeliever will demand, and then he sits back and plays the skeptic at all the believer's attempted explanations. The atheist winds up having to prove nothing. This may be good debating strategy on the atheist's part, but it's philosophically illegitimate and intellectually dishonest.

The atheist mustn't shirk his intellectual responsibilities. He's the one who claims that the coexistence of God and suffering is impossible or improbable. So it's up to him to give us his argument and to support his premises. It's the theist's turn to play the skeptic and question whether the atheist has shown that God cannot or does not have a good reason for permitting the suffering in the world. The atheist has to bear his share of the burden of proof when it's his turn to present his case against God.

The intellectual problem of suffering comes in two versions. The *logical version* tries to show that the coexistence of God and suffering is logically impossible. The *evidential version* tries to show that the coexistence of God and suffering is highly improbable. Let's look at each.

Logical Version

According to the logical version of the problem it's *logically impossible* for God and suffering to both exist. They're like the irresistible force and the immovable object. Necessarily, if one exists, then the other does not. Since suffering obviously exists, it follows that God does not exist.

The key to this argument is the atheist's claim that it's impossible that God and suffering both exist. The atheist is claiming that the following two statements are logically inconsistent:

1. An all-loving, all-powerful God exists.
2. Suffering exists.

Now the obvious question is, why think that these two statements are logically inconsistent? There's no *explicit* contradiction between them (one statement is not the opposite of the other). So if the atheist thinks there's some hidden, *implicit* contradiction between them, he must be making some hidden assumptions which would serve to bring out the contradiction and make it explicit. So the question is, what are those hidden assumptions?

There seem to be two hidden assumptions made by the atheist. They are:

3. If God is all-powerful, he can create any world that he wants.

4. If God is all-loving, he prefers a world without suffering.

The argument here is that God is all-loving and all-powerful. Therefore, he both *can* and *wants* to create a world without suffering. Therefore, it follows that the world has no suffering. But that contradicts 2, that *Suffering exists*. Therefore, God must not exist.

In order for this argument to show that it is logically impossible for God and suffering to coexist, both of the hidden assumptions made by the atheist have to be *necessarily true*. But are they?

Consider 3, that *If God is all-powerful, he can create any world that he wants*. Is that necessarily true? Well, not if it's possible that people have free will! It's logically impossible to *make* someone do something *freely*. That is as logically impossible as making a round square or a married bachelor. God's being all-powerful does not mean that he can bring about the logically impossible—indeed, there is no such "thing" as the logically impossible. It's just an inconsistent combination of words.

(Notice that if you do think that an all-powerful being *can* do the logically impossible, then the problem of suffering evaporates immediately, for then God can bring it about that he and suffering both exist, even though this is logically impossible!)

Since it's possible that people have free will, it turns out that 3 is not necessarily true. For if people have free will, they may refuse to do what God desires. So there will be any number of possible worlds which God cannot

THE FREEDOM OF THE WILL

The notion of freedom under discussion here is called *libertarian freedom*. Some philosophers would say that the essence of libertarian freedom is the ability to choose between action A or not-A in the same circumstances. An arguably better analysis of libertarian freedom sees its essence in the absence of causal determination of a person's choice apart from the person's own causal activity. That is to say, causes other than the person himself do not determine how that person chooses in some set of circumstances; it is up to him how he chooses. This conception of freedom is very different from the voluntarist or compatibilist view, which defines *freedom* in terms of voluntary (or noncoerced) action, so that an action's being causally determined is compatible with its being "free." The notion of freedom operative in this chapter is libertarian freedom, which precludes God's determining how we shall freely choose.

create because the people in them wouldn't cooperate with God's desires.

In fact, for all we know, it's possible that in any world of free persons with as much good as this world, there would also be as much suffering. This conjecture need not be true or even probable, but so long as it's even *logically possible*, it shows that it is not necessarily true that God can create any world that he wants. So assumption 3 is just not necessarily true. On this basis alone, the atheist's argument is fallacious.

But what about 4, that *If God is all-loving, he prefers a world without suffering?* Is that necessarily true? It doesn't seem like it. For God could have overriding reasons for allowing the suffering in the world. We all know cases in which we permit suffering in order to bring about a greater good. The atheist might insist that an all-powerful being would not be so limited. He could bring about the greater good directly, without allowing any suffering. But clearly, given human freedom of the will, that may not be possible. Some goods, for example, moral virtues, can be achieved only through the free cooperation of people. It may well be the case that God has good reasons for permitting suffering. In any case, it is at least *possible*, and that is sufficient to defeat the atheist's claim that assumption 4 is necessarily true.

The point is that the atheist, in assuming the necessary truth of 3 and 4, has taken on a burden of proof so heavy that it's unsustainable. He would have to show that free will is impossible and that it's impossible that God have good reasons for permitting suffering.

We can push the argument a notch further. We can make it plausible that God and suffering *are* logically consistent. All we have to do is come up with a statement that is consistent with God's existence and entails that suffering exists. Here is such a statement:

> 5. God could not have created another world with as much good as this world but with less suffering, and God has good reasons for permitting the suffering that exists.

The idea here is that given human freedom, God's options are restricted, and it may be that a world with as much good as the actual world, but with less suffering, wasn't an option. Nevertheless, God has good reasons for the suffering he allows. If 5 is even *possibly* true, it shows that it's possible that God and suffering both exist. And it surely is plausible that 5 is possibly true.

I'm therefore pleased to be able to report that after centuries of discussion, the books on the logical version of the problem of suffering have been closed. It's widely admitted by both atheist and theist philosophers alike that the logical version of the problem of suffering is bankrupt. The burden of proof that it lays on the atheist's shoulders, namely, trying to show that the coexistence of God and suffering is impossible, is just too heavy to bear.

Evidential Version

But we're not out of the woods yet! For now we come to the evidential problem of suffering, which is still very much a live issue. The atheistic claim here is that the suffering in the world renders it *improbable* that God exists. In particular, it seems highly improbable that God could have good reasons for permitting the suffering in the world. So much of that suffering appears to be utterly pointless and unnecessary. Surely God could have reduced the suffering in the world without reducing the world's overall goodness. So the suffering in the world provides evidence that there is no God.

This is a much more powerful version of the argument than the logical version. Since its conclusion is more modest (namely, that it's improbable that God exists), the atheist's burden of proof is much lighter. So is this a good argument? Let me raise three points by way of assessment.

1. *We're not in a good position to say with confidence that it's improbable that God lacks good reasons for permitting the suffering in the world.*

The key to the evidential argument is the atheist's claim that God doesn't have good reasons for permitting the suffering that occurs. Now we all recognize that much of the suffering in the world looks unjustified. We see neither its point nor its necessity. The success of the atheist's argument will depend on whether we're warranted in inferring that because the suffering *looks* unjustified it really *is* unjustified. My first point is that we're just not in a position to make that kind of judgment with any confidence.

As finite persons, we're limited in space and time, in intelligence and insight. But God sees the end of history from its beginning and providentially orders history to his ends through people's free decisions and actions. In order to achieve his purposes, God may have to allow a great deal of suffering along the way. Suffering which appears pointless within our limited framework may be seen to have been justly permitted by God within his wider framework.

Two illustrations of this point come to mind, one from contemporary science and one from popular culture.

First illustration: In so-called Chaos Theory scientists have discovered that certain large-scale systems, for example, the weather or insect populations, are extraordinarily sensitive to the smallest disturbances. A butterfly fluttering on a twig in West Africa may set in motion forces which will eventually issue in a hurricane over the Atlantic Ocean. Yet it's impossible for anyone observing that butterfly fluttering on that branch to predict such an outcome. We have no way of knowing how the alteration of some seemingly insignificant event can radically alter the world.

Second illustration: The movie *Sliding Doors*, starring Gwyneth Paltrow, tells the story of a young woman who is rushing down the stairs to the subway to catch a train. As she nears the train, the movie splits into two paths her life might take. In the one life the doors to the train slide shut just before she can board. In the other life she makes it through the doors just before they close. Based on this seemingly trivial event, the two paths of her life increasingly diverge. In the one she is enormously successful, prosperous, and happy. In the other life she encounters failure, misery, and unhappiness. And all because of a split-second difference in getting through the sliding doors!

Moreover, that difference is due to whether a little girl playing with her dolly on the stair railing is snatched away by her father or momentarily blocks the young woman's path as she hurries down the stairs to catch the train. We can't help but wonder about the innumerable other trivialities that led up to that event: whether the father and his daughter were delayed leaving the house that morning because she didn't like the cereal her mother gave her for break- fast, whether the man had been inattentive to his daughter because his thoughts were preoccupied with something he had read in the paper, and so on.

But the most interesting part is the film's ending: in the happy, successful life the young woman is suddenly killed in an accident, while the other life turns around, and the life of hardship and suffering turns out to be the truly good life after all! My point is obviously not that things always turn out for the best in this earthly life. No, my point is much more modest: given the dizzying complexity of life, we are simply in no position at all to judge that God has no good reason for permitting some instance of suffering to afflict our lives.

Every event that occurs sends a ripple effect through history, such that God's reason for permitting it might not emerge until centuries later and perhaps in another country. Only an all-knowing God could grasp the complexities of directing a world of free people toward his envisioned goals. Just think of the innumerable, incalculable events involved in arriving at a single historical event, say, the Allied victory on D-Day! We have no idea of what suffering might be involved in order for God to achieve some intended purpose through the freely chosen actions of human persons. Nor should we expect to discern God's reasons for permitting suffering. It's hardly surprising that much suffering seems pointless and unnecessary to us, for we are overwhelmed by such complexity.

This is not to appeal to mystery but rather to point to our inherent limitations, which make it impossible for us to say, when confronted with some example of suffering, that God probably has no good reason for permitting it to occur. Unbelievers themselves recognize these limitations in other contexts. For example, one of the decisive objections to utilitarianism (the theory of ethics which says that we should do whatever will bring about the greatest happiness for the greatest number of people) is that we have no idea of the ultimate outcome of our actions. Some short-term good might actually lead to untold misery, while some action that looks disastrous in the short term may bring about the greatest good. We don't have a clue.

Once we contemplate God's providence over the whole of human history, I think we can see how hopeless it is for finite, limited observers to speculate about the probability of God's having a good reason for the suffering we observe. We're simply not in a position to assess such probabilities with any confidence.

2. *Relative to the full scope of the evidence, God's existence may well be probable.* Probabilities are always relative to some background information. For example, suppose we're given the information that Joe is a college student and that 80 percent of college students ski. Relative to that information it's highly probable that Joe is a skier. But now suppose we're given the additional information that Joe is an amputee, and that 95 percent of college students who are amputees do not ski. Relative to this new information, it now becomes highly improbable that Joe is a skier. To repeat: probabilities are relative to background information.

Now the atheist claims that God's existence is improbable. We should immediately ask, "*Improbable relative to what?*" What is the background information? The suffering in the world? If that's all the background information you're considering, then it's no wonder God's existence looks improbable relative to that! (Though, as I've just argued, appearances can be deceiving!) But that's not the really interesting question. The interesting question is whether God's existence is probable relative to the *full* scope of the evidence. It may be the case that whatever improbability suffering is thought to cast upon God's existence, it's outweighed by the arguments for the existence of God.

Consider, in particular, the moral argument. Much of the suffering in the world consists of evil acts which people perpetrate against one another. But then we may argue as follows:

1. If God does not exist, objective moral values do not exist.
2. Evil exists.
3. Therefore, objective moral values exist (some things are evil!).
4. Therefore, God exists.

Although at a superficial level suffering calls into question God's existence, at a deeper level suffering actually *proves* God's existence. For apart from God, suffering is not really bad. If the atheist believes that suffering is bad or *ought not to be*, then he's making moral judgments that are possible only if God exists.

Most people who write about the problem of suffering are tacitly assuming that there are no good arguments for the existence of God.

So, for them, the question is whether suffering makes atheism probable given that *there's nothing on the other side of the scale.* But I think there are very weighty arguments for God on the other side of the scale. Therefore, I could concede that God's existence is improbable relative to the suffering in the world alone but point out that this is just outweighed by the arguments for God's existence.

TALK ABOUT IT

If God doesn't exist, then suffering may be painful, but it isn't bad in a moral sense. Why, then, are even atheists aware that tragic events are bad?

3. *Christianity entails doctrines that increase the probability of the coexistence of God and suffering.* If the Christian God exists, then it's not so improbable that

suffering should also exist. It actually turns out that the problem of suffering is *easier* to deal with given the Christian God than on some bare-boned concept of God. For Christianity entails certain doctrines which increase the probability of suffering. What are these doctrines? Let me mention four:

TALK ABOUT IT

Which do you tend to value more: temporal happiness or knowledge of God? How does that affect your actions and reactions?

(a) *The chief purpose of life is not happiness, but the knowledge of God.* One reason that the problem of suffering seems so difficult is that we naturally tend to assume that if God exists, then his purpose for human life is happiness in this life. God's role is to provide a comfortable environment for his human pets.

But on the Christian view, this is false. We are not God's pets, and the goal of human life is not happiness *per se*, but the knowledge of God—which in the end will bring true and everlasting human fulfillment. Much of the suffering in life may be utterly pointless with respect to the goal of producing human happiness; but it may *not* be pointless with respect to producing a deeper knowledge of God.

Innocent human suffering provides an occasion for deeper dependency on and trust in God, either on the part of the sufferer or those around him. Of course, whether God's purpose is achieved through our suffering will depend on our response. Do we respond with anger and bitterness toward God, or do we turn to him in faith for strength to endure?

Because God's ultimate goal for humanity is the knowledge of himself—which alone can bring eternal

HEALTH AND WEALTH?

The "health and wealth" gospel and the gospel of positive thinking that are being proclaimed in various megachurches and denominations are false gospels that are setting people up for a fall. That kind of gospel won't preach in Darfur or in Iraq or in a thousand other places. And if it won't preach there, it isn't the true gospel. We need to understand that God's plan for human history may involve terrible suffering for us, whose point or reason we can't expect to see. Our hope lies not in worldly happiness but in that day when God will wipe away every tear.

happiness to people—history cannot be seen in its true perspective apart from the Kingdom of God. On the Christian view, the purpose of human history is the Kingdom of God. God's desire is to draw freely as many people as he can into his everlasting Kingdom. It may well be the case that suffering is part of the means God uses to draw people freely into his Kingdom.

A reading of a missions handbook such as Patrick Johnstone's *Operation World* reveals that it is precisely in countries that have endured severe hardship that Christianity is growing at its greatest rates, while growth curves in the indulgent West are nearly flat. Consider, for example, the following reports:[1]

> **China:** It is estimated that 20 million Chinese lost their lives during Mao's Cultural Revolution. Christians stood firm in what was probably the most widespread and harsh persecution the Church has ever experienced. The persecution purified and indigenized the Church. Since 1977 the growth of the Church in China has no parallels in history. Researchers estimate that there were 30–75 million Christians by 1990. Mao Zedong unwittingly became the greatest evangelist in history.

> **El Salvador:** The 12-year civil war, earthquakes, and the collapse of the price of coffee, the nation's main export, impoverished the nation. Over 80% live in dire poverty. An astonishing spiritual harvest has been gathered from all strata of society in the midst of the hate and bitterness of war. In 1960 evangelicals were 2.3% of the population, but today are around 20%.

> **Ethiopia:** Ethiopia is in a state of shock. Her population struggles with the trauma of millions of deaths through repression, famine, and war. Two great waves of violent persecution refined

and purified the Church, but there were many martyrs. There have been millions coming to Christ. Protestants were fewer than 0.8% of the population in 1960, but by 1990 this may have become 13% of the population.

Examples like these could be multiplied.[2] The history of mankind has been a history of suffering and war. Yet it has also been a history of the advance of the Kingdom of God. Fig. 2 is a chart released in 1990 by the U.S. Center for World Mission documenting the growth in the number of committed Christians over the centuries.

THE DIMINISHING TASK

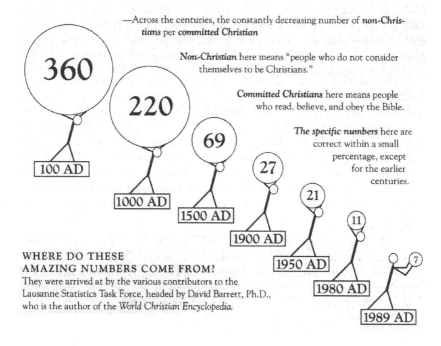

—Across the centuries, the constantly decreasing number of *non-Christians* per *committed Christian*

Non-Christian here means "people who do not consider themselves to be Christians."

Committed Christians here means people who read, believe, and obey the Bible.

The specific numbers here are correct within a small percentage, except for the earlier centuries.

360
100 AD

220
1000 AD

69
1500 AD

27
1900 AD

21
1950 AD

11
1980 AD

7
1989 AD

WHERE DO THESE
AMAZING NUMBERS COME FROM?
They were arrived at by the various contributors to the Lausanne Statistics Task Force, headed by David Barrett, Ph.D., who is the author of the *World Christian Encyclopedia.*

Fig. 2. Ratio of committed Christians to non-Christians over history. Neither category includes merely nominal Christians. Even if all of them were included with the non-Christians, there would still today be only about nine nonbelievers for every committed believer in the world.

So God abandoned them to do whatever shameful things their hearts desired. As a result, they did vile and degrading things with each other's bodies. They traded the truth about God for a lie. So they worshiped and served the things God created instead of the Creator himself, who is worthy of eternal praise! Amen. That is why God abandoned them to their shameful desires.... Since they thought it foolish to acknowledge God, he abandoned them to their foolish thinking and let them do things that should never be done. (Romans 1:24–26, 28 NLT)

According to Johnstone, "We are living in the time of the largest ingathering of people into the Kingdom of God that the world has ever seen."[3] It's not at all improbable that this astonishing growth in God's Kingdom is due in part to the presence of suffering in the world.

(b) *Mankind is in a state of rebellion against God and his purpose.* Rather than submit to and worship God, people rebel against God and go their own way and so find themselves alienated from God, morally guilty before him, groping in spiritual darkness, and pursuing false gods of their own making. The terrible human evils in the world are testimony to man's depravity in his state of spiritual alienation from God. The Christian isn't surprised at the moral evil in the world; on the contrary, he *expects* it. The Bible states that God has given mankind up to the sin it has freely chosen; he doesn't interfere to stop it but lets human depravity run its course (Romans 1:24, 26, 28). This only serves to heighten mankind's moral responsibility before God, as well as our wickedness and our need of forgiveness and moral cleansing.

(c) *God's purpose is not restricted to this life but spills over beyond the grave into eternal life.* According to Christianity, this life is but the cramped and narrow foyer opening up into the great hall of God's eternity. God promises eternal life to all who place their trust in Christ as Savior and Lord. When God asks his children to bear horrible suffering in this life, it is only with the prospect of a heavenly joy and recompense that is beyond all comprehension.

The apostle Paul, who wrote much of the New Testament, underwent a life of incredible suffering. His life as an apostle was punctuated by "afflictions, hardships, calamities, beatings, imprisonments, tumults, labors, watching, hunger" (2 Corinthians 6:4–5). Yet he wrote:

> We do not lose heart.... For this slight momentary afflic-
> tion is preparing for us an eternal weight of glory beyond
> all comparison, because we look not to the things that are
> seen but to the things that are unseen; for the things that are
> seen are transient, but the things that are unseen are eternal.
> (2 Corinthians 4:16–18)

Paul lived life in the perspective of eternity. He understood that the length of this life, being finite, is literally infinitesimal in comparison with the eternal life he would spend with God. The longer we spend in eternity, the more the sufferings of this life will shrink by comparison toward an infinitesimal moment. That's why Paul called the sufferings of this life a "slight, momentary affliction": he wasn't being insensitive to the plight of those who suffer horribly in this life—on the contrary, he was one of them—but he saw that those sufferings were simply overwhelmed by the ocean of everlasting joy and glory which God will give to those who trust him.

Here's a provocative thought: it may well be that there is suffering in the world that serves no earthly good at all, that is entirely pointless from a human point of view, but which God permits simply that he might over-whelmingly reward in the afterlife those who undergo such suffering in faith and confidence in God. People in heaven, looking back, will say, "I would go through it a million, million times over to know this happiness!"

(d) *The knowledge of God is an incommensurable good.* The passage cited from Paul also serves to make this point. Paul imagines, as it were, a scale, in which all the suffering of this life is placed on one side, while on the other side is placed the glory which God will bestow upon his children in heaven. And the weight of glory is so great that it is beyond comparison with the suffering. For to know God, the locus of infinite goodness and love, is an incomparable good, the fulfillment of human existence. The sufferings of this life cannot even be compared to it. Thus, the person who knows God, no matter what he suffers, no matter how awful his pain, can still truly say, "God is good to me!" simply in virtue of the fact that he knows God, an incommensurable good.

These four Christian doctrines increase the probability of the coexistence of God and the suffering in the world. They in turn decrease any improbability which suffering might seem to cast upon the existence of the Christian God.

The atheist may respond at this point that we have no reason to think that the Christian God exists or that these four Christian doctrines are true. Whoa! He's trying to shift the burden of proof again! It's the atheist who claims that suffering makes God's existence improbable. It's entirely legitimate for the Christian to say, "Not the Christian God!" The atheist needs to show that the Christian God is improbable relative to the suffering in the world. So he needs to show either that these doctrines are probably *false* or else show that God's existence is improbable even given these doctrines. He has the burden of proof in either case.

Reasons for Suffering

Let's return now to the two incidents that so powerfully portrayed to me the problem of suffering: the Mexican boy who slowly died from the collapse of a building and the Colombian girl who drowned in the aftermath of the mudslide. In the first place, both incidents concerned natural disasters intertwined with human moral sin. The whole of Latin America has been victimized by an unjust and uncaring upper class, which has, in its lust for power and wealth, exploited the masses, leaving them poor and underprivileged. The suffering of those two children is indirectly attributable to this corrupt and unchristian system, for if the societies in which the children lived were following Christian principles, their families would not have been forced to live in unsafe housing that was improperly located or so poorly built that it disintegrated under the stress of earthquake or rain. In a world free from sin, it's possible that neither of the tragedies would have taken place. Hence, given a Christian doctrine of sin and mankind's fallen state, such tragedies are not surprising.

Why did God permit these children to suffer so? We're in no position to know. Perhaps through the tragic death of this boy, God knew Mexican authorities would be shocked into requiring new construction standards for earthquake-proof buildings, thereby saving many future lives. Maybe he let it happen because the authorities *should* be so shocked. Maybe he permitted it so that some other person, facing death or illness in a hospital and seeing the reports on television, would be inspired by the boy's courage to face his own challenge with faith and bravery. Maybe God permitted the Colombian girl to slowly drown because he knew that only then would her family—or somebody else—turn to him in faith for eternal life. Or perhaps he knew that only through such a terrible incident would her family move away to another place where they, or even their descendants, might in turn come to be influenced or to influence someone else for Christ. Given our inherent limitations, we can only guess. We're not in a position to judge that it is either impossible or improbable that God had good reasons for permitting these events to occur.

Indeed, perhaps there wasn't any *earthly* reason at all why God permitted those catastrophes. Maybe they served no earthly good whatsoever. Perhaps the

DOCTRINES ABOUT GOD AND SUFFERING

These four doctrines increase the probability of the coexistence of God and suffering:

1. The chief purpose of life is not happiness, but the knowledge of God.

2. Mankind is in a state of rebellion against God and his purpose.

3. God's purpose is not restricted to this life but spills over beyond the grave into eternal life.

4. The knowledge of God is an incommensurable good.

RESPONSE TO
THE EVIDENTIAL
ARGUMENT

1. We're not in a good position to say with confidence
that it's improbable that
God lacks good reasons for
permitting the suffering in
the world.
2. Relative to the full scope
of the evidence, God's existence may well be probable.
3. Christianity entails
doctrines that increase the
probability of the coexistence
of God and suffering.

catastrophes were simply the unfortunate by-product of natural geological and meteorological laws and the children their unlucky victims. But when that little girl and boy finally left this life and stepped into the next, Jesus enfolded them in his loving arms, wiped away their tears, and filled them with a glorious happiness beyond all expression, saying, "Well done, my child; enter into the joy of your Master." In that eternity of joy, they will know a weight of glory beyond all comparison with what he asked them to suffer here.

In summary, the evidential version of the problem of suffering just can't be put through successfully. It requires probability judgments way beyond our ability, it fails to take into account the full scope of the evidence, which includes the arguments for God, and it is diminished in force when it comes to the Christian God. Since neither the logical nor the evidential version of the problem goes through, the intellectual problem of suffering fails as a disproof of God.

Emotional Problem of Suffering

But when I say "fails," I mean "fails intellectually." The anguish of the problem of suffering and the gnawing doubt may still remain. That brings us back to the emotional problem of suffering. I've already said that for most people, suffering is not really an intellectual problem but an emotional problem.

You might be thinking, "Then why go through all this intellectual material if it's not really the problem?" Two reasons: First, people *think* their problem is intellectual, so by working through it we can help them to see the real problem. Second, what I've shared can be of tremendous help when we have to go through suffering. We need to understand that God's plan for human history may involve terrible suffering for us, whose point or reason we can't expect to see. Our hope lies not in worldly happiness but in that day when God will wipe away every tear.

So what can be said to those who are struggling with the emotional problem of suffering? In one sense, the most important thing may not be what one says at all. The most important thing may be just to be there as a loving friend and sympathetic listener. But some people may need counsel, and we ourselves may need to deal with this problem when we suffer. Does the Christian faith also have the resources to deal with this problem as well?

It certainly does! For it tells us that God is not a distant Creator or impersonal ground of being, but a loving Father who shares our sufferings and hurts with us.

It tells us that Christ endured a suffering beyond all understanding: on the cross he bore the punishment for the sins of the whole world. None of us can comprehend that suffering. Though he was innocent, he voluntarily underwent incomprehensible suffering for us. And why?—because he loves us so much!

When God asks us to undergo suffering that seems unmerited, pointless, and unnecessary, meditation upon the cross of Christ can help to give us the moral strength and courage needed to bear the cross that we are asked to carry.

I mentioned earlier that knowing God is an incommensurable good to which our suffering cannot even be compared. Few of us really understand this truth. But a former colleague of mine got to know a woman who did. He used to make it his habit to visit shut-ins in nursing homes in an attempt to bring a bit of cheer and love into their lives. One day he met a woman whom he could never forget:

> As I neared the end of [the] hallway, I saw an old woman strapped up in a wheelchair. Her face was an absolute horror.

The empty stare and white pupils of her eyes told me that she was blind. The large hearing aid over one ear told me that she was almost deaf. One side of her face was being eaten by cancer. There was a discolored and running sore covering part of one cheek, and it had pushed her nose to one side, dropped one eye, and distorted her jaw so that what should have been the corner of her mouth was the bottom of her mouth. As a consequence, she drooled constantly.... I also learned later that this woman was eighty-nine years old and that she had been bedridden, blind, nearly deaf, and alone, for twenty-five years. This was Mabel.

I don't know why I spoke to her—she looked less likely to respond than most of the people I saw in that hallway. But I put a flower in her hand and said, "Here is a flower for you. Happy Mother's Day." She held the flower up to her face and tried to smell it, and then she spoke. And much to my surprise, her words, although somewhat garbled because of her deformity, were obviously produced by a clear mind. She said, "Thank you. It's lovely. But can I give it to someone else? I can't see it, you know, I'm blind."

I said, "Of course," and I pushed her in her chair back down the hallway to a place where I thought I could find some alert patients. I found one, and I stopped the chair. Mabel held out the flower and said, "Here, this is from Jesus."

Tom and Mabel became friends over the next few years, and Tom began to realize that he was no longer helping Mabel, but she was helping him. He began to take notes on what she said. After a stressful week, Tom went to Mabel and asked her, "Mabel, what do you think about as you lie here all day?" She replied:

"I think about my Jesus."

I sat there and thought for a moment about the difficulty, for me, of thinking about Jesus for even five minutes, and I asked, "*What* do you think about Jesus?" She replied slowly and deliberately as I wrote. And this is what she said:

"I think how good He's been to me. He's been awfully good to me in my life, you know … I'm one of those kind who's mostly satisfied … Lots of folks would think I'm kind of old-fashioned. But I don't care. I'd rather have Jesus. He's all the world to me."

And then Mabel began to sing an old hymn:

"Jesus is all the world to me,

My life, my joy, my all.

He is my strength from day to day,

Without him I would fall.

When I am sad, to him I go,

No other one can cheer me so.

When I am sad, He makes me glad.

He's my friend."

This is not fiction. Incredible as it may seem, a human being really lived like this. I know. I knew her. *How could she do it?* Seconds ticked and minutes crawled, and so did days and weeks and months and years of pain without human company and without an explanation of why it was all happening—and she lay there and sang hymns. *How could she do it?*

The answer, I think, is that Mabel had something that you and I don't have much of. She had power. Lying there in that bed, unable to move, unable to see, unable to hear, unable to talk to anyone, she had incredible power.[4]

TALK ABOUT IT

How does Mabel's story affect you? What does
Tom mean when he says, "She had power"?

Paradoxically, then, even though the problem of suffering is the greatest objection to the existence of God, at the end of the day God is the only solution to the problem of suffering. If God does not exist, then we are locked without hope in a world filled with pointless and unredeemed suffering. But if the Christian God exists, then we have hope. For God redeems us from evil and takes us into the everlasting joy of an incommensurable good—fellowship with himself.

It becomes urgent, then, to discover, not just whether God exists, but whether the Christian God exists.

1. Patrick Johnstone, *Operation World* (Grand Rapids, MI: Zondervan, 1993), 164, 207–8, 214.
2. For example, the 7.0 magnitude earthquake that devastated Haiti in 2010 has led to unprecedented revival in that island nation. Missionary Seth Barnes of Adventures in Missions reported, "'Revival' is too small a word for what we saw in Haiti ... everywhere there were prayer meetings—groups as small as 20 or as large as 60,000.... The spiritual atmosphere of the country is completely different now. Voodoo priests by the hundreds have given their lives to Christ" (personal communication to Johnson Ferry Global Ministries staff).
3. Johnstone, *Operation World*, 25.
4. Thomas E. Schmidt, *Trying to Be Good: A Book of Doing for Thinking People* (Grand Rapids, MI: Zondervan, 1990).

THE PROBLEM OF SUFFERING

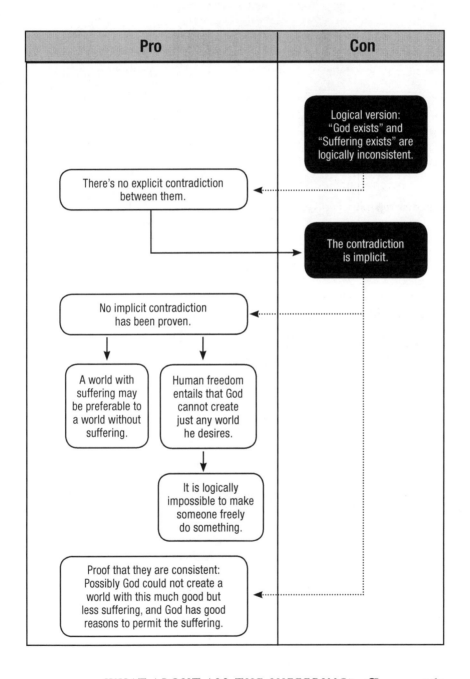

Pro	Con
	Logical version: "God exists" and "Suffering exists" are logically inconsistent.
There's no explicit contradiction between them.	
	The contradiction is implicit.
No implicit contradiction has been proven.	
A world with suffering may be preferable to a world without suffering.	Human freedom entails that God cannot create just any world he desires.
	It is logically impossible to make someone freely do something.
Proof that they are consistent: Possibly God could not create a world with this much good but less suffering, and God has good reasons to permit the suffering.	

THE PROBLEM OF SUFFERING (cont.)

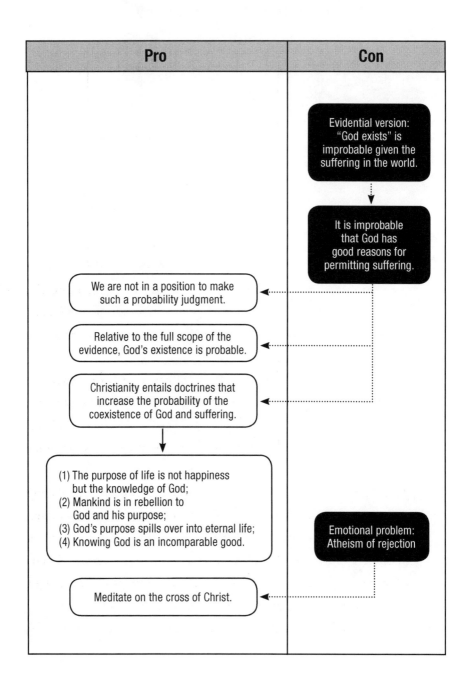

Pro	Con
	Evidential version: "God exists" is improbable given the suffering in the world.
	It is improbable that God has good reasons for permitting suffering.
We are not in a position to make such a probability judgment.	
Relative to the full scope of the evidence, God's existence is probable.	
Christianity entails doctrines that increase the probability of the coexistence of God and suffering.	
(1) The purpose of life is not happiness but the knowledge of God; (2) Mankind is in rebellion to God and his purpose; (3) God's purpose spills over into eternal life; (4) Knowing God is an incomparable good.	Emotional problem: Atheism of rejection
Meditate on the cross of Christ.	

CHAPTER 7

WHO WAS JESUS?

He asked them, "But who do you say that I am?"
Mark 8:29 NRSV

The theologian George Ladd has said that the scandal and the greatness of the Christian religion is its claim that God has revealed himself through the medium of historical events. This is scandalous to some because it means that the truth of Christianity stands or falls with the historicity of certain events. But at the same time this makes Christianity great because it affords us a means of verifying its truth.

The centerpiece of the Christian faith is, of course, Jesus of Nazareth, and the centerpiece of Christian beliefs about Jesus is belief in his resurrection from the dead. The earliest Christians were convinced that despite Jesus' public execution, God had raised him from the dead as a vindication of his radical personal claims.

What shall we make of this? An event without a context is inherently ambiguous. That's especially true for an alleged miracle. Considered in isolation, an alleged miracle, even if it occurred, might be nothing more than a freak of nature. Thus, an event like Jesus' resurrection must be explored in its historical context. What is the proper context for understanding Jesus' alleged resurrection? It is Jesus' own unparalleled life and claims. So before we look at the historical credibility of Jesus' resurrection, let's set the stage by asking who Jesus thought himself to be.

Primacy of the New Testament Documents

Now immediately we confront a problem. Since Jesus himself didn't leave behind any writings of his own, we're dependent upon the records of others for knowing what Jesus said and did. Now this situation isn't unusual for figures of antiquity. For example, the famous Greek philosopher Socrates also left behind no writings of his own. We're dependent upon his disciple Plato for most of our knowledge of Socrates' life and teaching. In the same way, we're dependent upon the records of Jesus' followers for his life and teaching.

But while this situation isn't unusual, it does raise the question, how do we know that these records are accurate? Maybe Jesus' followers *said* that he said and did certain things which he really didn't. In particular, since the early Christians believed that Jesus was God, maybe they made up sayings and stories about how Jesus claimed to be divine. So we shouldn't be surprised that Jesus in the Gospels makes claims and does things implying his divinity. Maybe the historical Jesus who really lived was very different from the divine figure we read about in the Gospels. How can we tell if these records are historically accurate?

Up until the modern era these sorts of questions were basically unanswerable. But with the rise of textual criticism and the modern study of history, historians began to develop the tools to unlock these questions. Today Jesus is no longer just a figure in a stained glass window, but a real, flesh-and-blood person of history, just like Julius Caesar or Alexander the Great, whose life can be investigated by the standard methods of history. The writings contained in the New Testament can be scrutinized using the same historical criteria that we use in investigating other sources of ancient history like Thucydides' *Peloponnesian War* or the *Annals* of Tacitus.

Now the first thing we need to do in order to conduct a historical investigation of Jesus is to assemble our sources. Jesus of Nazareth is referred to in a range of ancient sources inside and outside the New Testament, including Christian, Roman, and Jewish sources.[1] This is really quite extraordinary when you reflect on how obscure a figure Jesus was, having had at most a three-year public life as an itinerant Galilean preacher. Despite his relative obscurity, we have far more information about Jesus than we do for most *major* figures of antiquity.

The most important of these historical sources have been collected into the New Testament. References to Jesus outside the New Testament tend to *confirm* what we read in the Gospels, but they don't really tell us anything *new*. Therefore, the focus of our investigation must be upon the documents found in the New Testament.

Now many students don't understand this procedure. They think that if you examine the New Testament writings themselves rather than look at sources outside the New Testament, then somehow you're reasoning in a circle, using the Bible to prove the Bible. If you even quote a passage out of the New Testament, they think you're somehow begging the question, presupposing that the New Testament is reliable.

But that attitude displays an ignorance of what historians are doing when they examine the writings in the New Testament. They're not treating the Bible as a holy, inspired book and trying to prove it's true by quoting it. Rather they're treating the New Testament just like any other collection of ancient documents and investigating the degree to which these documents are historically reliable.

It's important to understand that originally there wasn't any such book called "The New Testament." There were just these separate documents handed down from the first century, things like the Gospel of Luke, the Gospel of John, the Acts of the Apostles, Paul's letter to the church in Corinth, Greece, and so on. It wasn't until a couple centuries later that the church officially collected all these documents under one cover, which came to be known as the New Testament.

The church included in the New Testament only the earliest sources which were closest to Jesus and the original disciples and left out the later, secondary accounts like the forged apocryphal gospels, which everyone knew were fakes. So from the very nature of the case, the best historical sources were included in the New Testament. People who insist on evidence taken only from writings *outside* the New Testament don't understand what they're asking historians to do. They're demanding that we ignore the earliest, primary sources about Jesus in favor of sources which are later, secondary, and less reliable, which is just crazy as historical methodology.

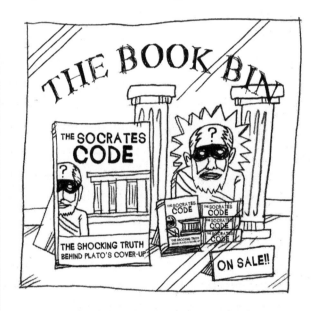

This is important because all of the radical reconstructions of the historical Jesus in the news today are based on later writings outside the New Testament, in particular the so-called apocryphal gospels. What are the apocryphal gospels? They are gospels forged under the apostles' names, like the Gospel of Thomas, the Gospel of Peter, the Gospel of Philip, and so forth. They first began to appear in the second half of the

APOCRYPHAL GOSPELS

The so-called apocryphal gospels are gospels forged under the apostles' names during the centuries after Christ. None is earlier than the second half of the second century after Christ. While not very valuable as sources for the life of Jesus, they are significant to the church historian who wants to learn about the various competing movements, often deeply influenced by pagan gnostic philosophy, that the Christian church contended with during the first few centuries after Christ. Some of the apocryphal gospels include:
 Gospel of Peter
 Gospel of Thomas
 Gospel of the Hebrews
 Infancy Gospel of Thomas
 Gospel of Judas
 Gospel of Philip

ON GUARD FOR STUDENTS

second century after Christ. Revisionists claim that these extra-biblical writings are the key to correctly reconstructing the historical Jesus.

Professor Luke Johnson, a distinguished New Testament scholar at Emory University, points out that all of the recent flood of books claiming to uncover the real Jesus follow the same, predictable pattern:

> 1. The book begins by trumpeting the scholarly credentials of the author and his prodigious research.
> 2. The author claims to offer some new, and maybe even suppressed, interpretation of who Jesus *really* was.
> 3. The truth about Jesus is said to be discovered by means of sources outside the Bible which enable us to read the Gospels in a new way which is at odds with their face value meaning.
> 4. This new interpretation is provocative and even titillating, for example, that Jesus married Mary Magdalene or was the leader of a hallucinogenic cult or a peasant cynic philosopher.
> 5. It is implied that traditional Christian beliefs are therefore undermined and need to be revised.

If you hear of books following this familiar pattern, your critical antennae should automatically go up! You are about to be duped. For the fact is that there is no historically credible source outside the New Testament which calls into question the portrait of Jesus painted in the Gospels. The apocryphal gospels are later, derivative writings shaped by the theology of the second century and later. What this means is that despite all the hoopla, the documents contained in the New Testament are our primary sources for the life of Jesus.

Ironically, there *are,* in fact, sources outside the New Testament which are vitally important to the study of the historical Jesus, but they are not the later, derivative sources mentioned above. Rather they are the *earlier,* often oral, sources that are quoted by the New Testament writers. These sources take us back even closer to the events of Jesus' life and are therefore less likely to be colored by legendary accretions. As we shall see, some of these early sources identified by New Testament historians reach back to within the first five years after Jesus' crucifixion and are therefore a valuable source of historical information.

So try not to think of the New Testament as a single book; think of it as what it originally was: a bunch of separate documents coming to us out of the first century telling this remarkable story about Jesus of Nazareth. The question then must be: How historically reliable are these documents?

Burden of Proof

Here we confront the very crucial question of the burden of proof. Should we assume that the Gospels are reliable unless they are proven to be unreliable? Or should we assume that the Gospels are unreliable unless they are proven to be reliable? Are they innocent until proven guilty or guilty until proven innocent?

Skeptical scholars almost always assume that the Gospels are guilty until proven innocent, that is, they assume that the Gospels are unreliable unless and until they are proven to be correct concerning some particular fact. I want to list, however, five reasons why I think this skeptical assumption is wrong.

1. *There was insufficient time for legendary influences to expunge the core historical facts.* Sometimes students say, "How can you know anything that happened two thousand years ago?" What they fail to understand is that the crucial time gap is not the gap between the evidence and today; rather what's important is the gap between the evidence and the original events that the evidence is about. If the gap between the events and the evidence is short, then it doesn't matter how far the event and the evidence have both receded into the past. Good evidence doesn't become poor evidence just because of the passage of time! So long as the time gap between the event and the evidence for that event is short, it's just irrelevant how long it has been to the present day. The question then is how close the sources for Jesus' life are to the time he lived. I'll say something about that in a minute.

Fig. 1. Our primary sources for Jesus' life all come from the first century AD, most of them within sixty years of Jesus' crucifixion. By contrast, the apocryphal gospels were written at least over one hundred years after the crucifixion.

2. *The Gospels are not comparable to folk tales or contemporary "urban legends."* Tales like those of Paul Bunyan and Pecos Bill or contemporary urban legends like the "vanishing hitchhiker" rarely concern actual historical individuals and are thus not like the Gospel narratives, which are about real people who actually lived, real events that actually occurred, and real places that actually existed. You can read about people like John the Baptist, Pontius Pilate, and Joseph Caiaphas in sources outside the New Testament.

3. *The Jewish transmission of sacred traditions was highly developed and reliable.* In an oral culture like that of first-century Palestine, the ability to memorize and retain large tracts of oral tradition was a highly prized and highly developed skill. From the earliest age children in the home, the elementary school, and the synagogue were taught to memorize faithfully sacred tradition. The disciples would have exercised similar care with the teachings of Jesus. To compare the Jewish transmission of traditions to the child's game of "telephone" is a misrepresentation.

4. *There were significant restraints on the embellishment of traditions about Jesus, such as the presence of eyewitnesses and the apostles' supervision.* Since those who had seen and heard Jesus continued to live and the tradition about Jesus remained under the supervision of the original apostles, these factors would act as a natural check on tendencies to elaborate the facts in a direction contrary to that preserved by those who had known Jesus. In fact, in the case of the Gospels, it would be more accurate to speak of "oral history" rather than "oral tradition," since the living eyewitnesses and apostles were still about.

5. *The Gospel writers have a proven track record of historical reliability.* Where the Gospel writers can be checked, they are usually shown to be reliable. Discrepancies are the exception, not the norm.

Now we don't have space to discuss all five of these points. But let me elaborate a bit on the first and the fifth points.

1. *There was insufficient time for legendary influences to expunge the core historical facts.* No modern scholar thinks of the Gospels as bald-faced lies, the result of a massive conspiracy. The only places you find such conspiracy theories is on atheist websites and in sensationalist books and movies. When you read the pages of the New Testament, there's no doubt that these people sincerely believed in the truth of what they proclaimed. Rather ever since the nineteenth century, skeptical scholars have explained away the Gospels as *legends*. Like stories of Robin Hood or King Arthur and the Knights of the Round Table, as the stories about Jesus were passed on over the decades, they got muddled and exaggerated and mythologized until the original facts were all but lost. The Jewish teacher was transformed into the divine Son of God.

One of the major problems with the legend hypothesis, however, which is almost never addressed by skeptical critics, is that the time gap between Jesus' death and the writing of the Gospels is just too short for this to have happened.

This point has been well explained by the late A. N. Sherwin-White in his book *Roman Society and Roman Law in the New Testament.* Professor Sherwin-White was *not* a theologian; he was a professional Greco-Roman historian of times prior to and contemporaneous with Jesus. According to Sherwin-White, the sources for Roman and Greek history are usually biased and removed one or two generations or even centuries from the events they record. Yet, he says, historians reconstruct with confidence the course of Roman and Greek history.

For example, the two earliest biographies of Alexander the Great were written by Arrian and Plutarch more than four hundred years after Alexander's death, and yet classical historians still consider them to be trustworthy. The fabulous legends about Alexander the Great did not develop until the centuries *after* these two writers. According to Sherwin-White, the writings of Herodotus enable us to determine the rate at which legend accumulates, and the tests show that even two generations is too short a time span to allow legendary tendencies to wipe out the hard core of historical facts.

When Professor Sherwin-White turns to the Gospels, he states that for the Gospels to be in their core legends, the rate of legendary accumulation would have to be unbelievable. All historians agree that the Gospels were written down and circulated during the first generation after the events, while the eyewitnesses were still alive. In order for the Gospels to be legendary at their core, more generations would be needed.

In fact, adding a time gap of two generations to Jesus' death in AD 30 lands you in the second century, when the apocryphal gospels first begin to appear. These do contain all sorts of fabulous stories about Jesus, trying to fill in the years between his boyhood and the commencement of his ministry, for example. These are better candidates for the legends sought by the skeptical critics, not the biblical Gospels.

This point becomes even more difficult for skepticism when we remember that the Gospels themselves use *sources* that go back even closer to the events of Jesus' life. For example, the story of Jesus' suffering and death, commonly called the Passion Story, was probably not originally written by Mark. Rather Mark used a source for this narrative. Since Mark is the earliest Gospel, his source must be even earlier still. In fact,

HERODOTUS

Herodotus (fifth century BC) was a Greek who wrote a long work he called *Istoriai*. This Greek word meant "Inquiries" or "Researches," but we generally call it *The Histories*, and our word *history* comes from this title. He was the first writer who tried to collect historical information systematically— information about the war between the Greeks and Persians that was fought in his parents' day. He claimed to have traveled and inter- viewed eyewitnesses from Babylon to Sicily, although he also liked to include stories that are more colorful than credible, and we don't know if he really went to all the places he described. While far from 100 percent reliable, Herodotus's work is full of clues for the careful modern historian. Legendary influences did not erase the core historical facts of the Greco-Persian war.

Rudolf Pesch, a German expert on Mark, says the Passion source must go back to at least AD 37. That's just seven years after Jesus' death.

Or again, Paul in his letters hands on information concerning Jesus' teaching, last supper, betrayal, crucifixion, burial, and resurrection appearances. Paul's letters were written even before the Gospels, and some of his sources, for example, the material he quotes in his first letter to the Corinthian church about Jesus' resurrection appearances, has been dated to within five years after Jesus' death. It just becomes irresponsible to speak of legends in such cases.

5. *The Gospel writers have a proven track record of historical reliability.* Again let me look at just one example: Luke. Luke was the author of a two-part work: the Gospel of Luke and the Acts of the Apostles. These are really one work and are separated in the Bible only because the church grouped the Gospels together in the New Testament.

Luke is the Gospel author who writes most self-consciously as a historian. In the preface to his work he writes:

> Inasmuch as many have undertaken to compile a narrative of the things that have been accomplished among us, just as those who from the beginning were eyewitnesses and ministers of the word have delivered them to us, it seemed good to me also, having followed all things closely for some time past, to write an orderly account for you, most excellent Theophilus, that you may have certainty concerning the things you have been taught. (Luke 1:1–4 ESV)

This preface is written in classical Greek such as the great Greek historians used; after this Luke switches to a more common Greek. But he has put his reader on alert that he can write, if he wants to, like the learned Greek historian. He speaks of his lengthy investigation of the story he is about to tell and assures us that it is based on eyewitness information and is accordingly trustworthy.

Now who was this author we call Luke? From what he says, he was clearly not an eyewitness to Jesus' life. But we discover an important fact about him from the book of Acts. Beginning in the 16th chapter of Acts, when Paul reaches Troas in modern-day Turkey, the author suddenly starts using the first-person plural: "*We* set sail from Troas to Samothrace," "*We* remained in Philippi some days," "As *we* were going to the place of prayer," etc. The most obvious explanation is that the author had joined Paul on his evangelistic tour of the Mediterranean cities. Eventually he accompanies Paul back to Israel and finally to Jerusalem. What this means is that the author of Luke-Acts was, in fact, in firsthand contact with the eyewitnesses of Jesus' life and ministry in Jerusalem.

Skeptical critics have done backflips to try to avoid this conclusion. They say that the use of the first-person plural in Acts should not be taken literally; it was just a literary device which was common in ancient sea voyage stories. Never mind that many of the passages in Acts are not about Paul's sea voyage, but take place on land! The more important point is that this theory, when you check it out, turns out to be sheer fantasy. There just was no literary device in the ancient world of sea voyages in the first-person plural—the whole thing has been shown to be a scholarly fiction! There's no avoiding the conclusion that Luke-Acts was written by a traveling companion of Paul who had the opportunity to inter-view eyewitnesses to Jesus' life while in Jerusalem.

So who were some of these eyewitnesses? Perhaps we can get some clue by subtracting from the Gospel of Luke everything found in the other Gospels and seeing

LUKE'S UNIQUE
NARRATIVES

A few of the narratives that are unique to Luke are:
The birth narratives that focus on Mary and her cousins (Luke 1:5–2:40)
The account of Jesus as a boy (Luke 2:41–52)
Jesus' rejection in his hometown, Nazareth (Luke 4:14–30)
The account of the women who traveled with Jesus and funded his ministry (Luke 8:1–3)

what is unique to Luke. When you do this, what you discover is that many of Luke's unique narratives are connected to *women* who followed Jesus: people like Joanna and Susanna, and, significantly, Mary, Jesus' mother.

Was the author reliable in getting the facts straight? The book of Acts enables us to answer that question decisively. The book of Acts overlaps significantly with the secular history of the ancient world, and the historical accuracy of Acts is indisputable. This has recently been demonstrated anew by Colin Hemer, a classical scholar who turned to New Testament studies in his book *The Book of Acts in the Setting of Hellenistic History.* Hemer goes through the book of Acts with a fine-tooth comb, pulling out a wealth of historical detail, ranging from what would have been common knowledge down to details which only a local person would know. Again and again Luke's accuracy is demonstrated: from the sailings of the Alexandrian corn fleet to the coastal terrain of the islands to the peculiar and shifting titles of local officials, Luke gets it right.

According to Professor Sherwin-White, "The confirmation of historicity in Acts is overwhelming. Any attempt to reject its historicity even in matters of detail must now appear absurd."[2] The judgment of Sir William Ramsey, a world-famous archaeologist, still stands: "Luke is a historian of the first rank.... This author should be placed among the very greatest of historians."[3]

Given Luke's care and demonstrated reliability, as well as his contact with eyewitnesses within the first generation after the events, this author is trustworthy.

On the basis of the five reasons listed above, I personally think that we would be justified in assuming the historical reliability of what the Gospels say about Jesus unless they are proven to be wrong on some point. But in any case, at the very least, we cannot assume they are wrong until proven right. In investigating them we should at least adopt a position of neutrality.

Criteria of Authenticity

Now if we do adopt a position of neutrality when approaching the Gospels, how do we move beyond neutrality to the affirmation that some event is actually historical? Scholars have developed a number of so-called "criteria of authenticity" to enable us to do that.

It's vital that these criteria be properly stated and understood, for they've often been grossly misused. The criteria are really signs of historical credibility. A story in the Gospels exhibiting one of these signs is, all things being equal, more likely to be historical than it would have been without it. In other words, the presence of one of these signs increases the probability that the recorded incident is historical.

What are some of these signs of historical authenticity? Here's a list of some of the most important:

1. *Historical fit*: the incident fits in with known historical facts of the time and place.
2. *Independent, early sources*: the incident is related in multiple sources which are near to the time when the incident is said to have occurred and which don't rely on each other or on a common source.
3. *Embarrassment*: the incident is awkward or counter-productive for the early Christian church.
4. *Dissimilarity*: the incident is unlike earlier Jewish ideas and/or unlike later Christian ideas.

5. *Semitisms*: traces of Hebrew or Aramaic language (spoken by Jesus' countrymen) appear in the story.

6. *Coherence*: the incident fits in with facts already established about Jesus.

TALK ABOUT IT

Why would embarrassment be a sign of historical authenticity? Can you think of any passages in the Gospels that an editor would have left out if he were interested in making the Gospels' heroes look as good as possible?

Notice a couple of things about these "criteria." First, they're all *positive* signs of historical credibility. Therefore, they can only be used to *establish* the historicity of some incident, not to *deny* it. If a story is *not* embarrassing or dissimilar or found in independent early sources, that obviously doesn't mean that the incident isn't historical.

The only way you could justifiably use the criteria to deny historical credibility would be by presupposing that the Gospels are unreliable until they are proven to be reliable. We're right back to the burden of proof issue again! If we adopt a position of neutrality in approaching the Gospels, then the failure to prove an incident is historical just leaves you in a position of neutrality. You just don't know whether it's historical or not.

Second, the criteria don't presuppose the general reliability of the Gospels. The criteria apply to specific incidents, not to a whole book. So they can be used to detect historical nuggets of information in any source, even the apocryphal gospels or the Koran. That means that in order to defend the historical credibility of some event in the life of Jesus, say, his burial, a historian needn't accept or defend the historical credibility of other events like his birth in Bethlehem, his feeding the five thousand, his triumphal entry into Jerusalem, and so on. Specific incidents can be evaluated on their own by these criteria.

Before we apply these criteria to events and sayings of Jesus in the Gospels, it's worth noting a general problem facing those who deny that Jesus made any radical personal claims at all. We know from Paul's letters that within twenty years of Jesus' death, Jesus was regarded and worshipped by his contemporaries as God incarnate (Philippians 2:5–7). It's inexplicable how monotheistic Jews could have attributed divinity to a man they had accompanied during his lifetime if he never claimed any such things himself. Monotheism is the heart of the Jewish religion, and it would have been blasphemous to say that a human being was God. Yet this is precisely what the earliest Christians did proclaim and believe about Jesus! Such a claim must have been rooted in Jesus' own teaching. And, in fact, we do find in Jesus' teachings and activities both *explicit* and *implicit* personal claims which imply his divinity.

Explicit Claims

In the Gospels there are a number of explicit self-descriptions used by Jesus which provide insight into his self-understanding. Until recently, critical scholars have been quite skeptical of the authenticity of such claims. In 1977 a group of seven British theologians headed by Professor John Hick caused a great stir in the press and among laymen by publishing a book provocatively entitled *The Myth of God Incarnate*. In it he asserted that today the majority of New Testament scholars agree that Jesus never claimed to be the Messiah or the Son of God or, indeed, any of the divine titles that are attributed to him in the Gospels. Rather, these titles developed later in the Christian church and were written back into the stories handed down about

> Have the same mindset as Christ Jesus: Who, being in very nature God, did not consider equality with God something to be used to his own advantage; rather, he made himself nothing by taking the very nature of a servant, being made in human likeness. (Philippians 2:5–7 NIV)

Jesus, so that in the Gospels he *appears* to claim these titles for himself. Thus, the divine Christ of the Gospels who appears as God incarnate is a myth and ought to be rejected.

Today no such skeptical consensus exists. On the contrary, the balance of scholarly opinion on Jesus' use of personal titles may have actually tipped in the opposite direction. Let's take a look at the authenticity of three of Jesus' explicit claims: his claims to be the Messiah, the unique Son of God, and the Son of Man. As we look at each title, I'll first show by means of the criteria of authenticity that Jesus did make such a claim, and then, second, I'll discuss the significance of that claim for who Jesus held himself to be.

Messiah

Israel's ancient hope for a Messiah, or Anointed One, sent from God had revived during the century prior to Jesus' birth. The most important messianic concept was the idea of a descendant of King David who would become king over Israel and the nations. More than just a warrior king, he would also be a spiritual shepherd of Israel.

The Greek word for Messiah is *"Christos"* or Christ. Early Christians connected this title so closely to Jesus that it became practically a proper name: "Jesus Christ." The very term used to describe his followers, "Christians," shows how central their belief was that Jesus was the promised Messiah.

What Did Jesus Claim?

The question is: Where did they come up with this idea? If Jesus himself never claimed to be the Messiah, what would prompt his followers to call him that? After all, he did not reestablish David's throne in Jerusalem; instead, he was crucified by his enemies. Even the belief that God had raised him from the dead would not have led his followers to see him as the Messiah, for there just was no connection between resurrection and Messiahship. Only if Jesus' crucifixion was the direct result of his claim to be the Messiah would his resurrection lead his followers to see him as the risen Messiah.

Moreover, there's good evidence that Jesus did, in fact, think that he was the Messiah. For example, there's the story of Peter's famous confession:

> And Jesus went on with his disciples, to the villages of Caesarea Philippi. And on the way he asked his disciples, "Who do people say that I am?" And they told him, "John the Baptist; and others say, Elijah; and others, one of the prophets." And he asked them, "But who do you say that I am?" Peter answered him, "You are the Messiah." (Mark 8:27–29)

Is this a historical incident? It would be natural for people of that time to be interested in who Jesus claimed to be. Independent accounts tell us that John the Baptist was confronted with a similar question (Luke 3:15–16; John 1:19–27). No doubt the disciples, who had left their families and jobs to follow Jesus, would have asked themselves whom they were following. Peter's reply to Jesus' question is independently confirmed in John 6:69, where Peter says, "We have believed, and have come to know, that you are the Holy One of God."

FROM A DEAD SEA SCROLL

"[For the hea]vens and the earth shall listen to his Messiah [and all t]hat is in them shall not turn away from the commandments of the holy ones.... He will honor the pious upon the th[ro]ne of the eternal kingdom, setting prisoners free, opening the eyes of the blind, raising up those who are bo[wed down.] ... And the Lord shall do glorious things which have not been done, just as he said. For he will heal the injured, he shall make alive the dead, he shall proclaim good news to the afflicted." (4Q521; brackets indicate gaps in the document)

"You're a Cynic philosopher with political ambitions! . . . No, wait! You're . . ."

Another story illustrating Jesus' messianic self-consciousness is the story of Jesus' answer to John the Baptist in prison (Matthew 11:2–6; Luke 7:19–23). Many scholars think this story comes from a very old source shared by Matthew and Luke. John asks Jesus, "Are you the one who is to come, or shall we look for another?" The criterion of embarrassment supports the historicity of this incident, since John the Baptist seems to be doubting Jesus. The phrase "the one who is to come" harks back to John's prophecy of "him who comes after me," which is independently recorded in Mark and John (Mark 1:7; John 1:27). Jesus' answer to John is a blend of prophecies from Isaiah 35:5–6; 26:19; 61:1, the last of which explicitly mentions being God's Anointed One. "Go and tell John what you hear and see: the blind receive their sight and the lame walk, lepers are cleansed and the deaf hear, and the dead are raised up, and the poor have good news preached to them. And blessed is the one who is not offended by me" (Matthew 11:4–6 ESV). Perhaps most remarkably of all, these very signs are listed as signs of the Messiah's coming in one of the Dead Sea scrolls from the Jewish sect that lived at Qumran at the time of Jesus

(4Q521). In sum, the criteria of embarrassment, historical fit, and coherence with other authentic material, coupled with its presence in a very early source, give good grounds for seeing this incident as historical.

But even more convincing than Jesus' *words* are Jesus' *actions*, which disclose his sense of being the Messiah. His triumphal entry into Jerusalem seated on a donkey was a dramatic, provocative assertion of his messianic status. The story is independently told by Mark and John (Mark 11:1–11; John 12:12–19). They agree on the core of the story: one week before his death Jesus rode into Jerusalem seated on a colt and was hailed by the Passover festival crowds with shouts of "Hosanna! Blessed is he who comes in the name of the Lord!" in anticipation of the coming of David's kingdom.

In mounting a colt and riding into Jerusalem, Jesus is deliberately fulfilling the prophecy of Zechariah 9:9:

> Rejoice greatly, O daughter of Zion!
> Shout aloud, O daughter of
> Jerusalem!
> Behold, your king is coming to you;
> righteous and having salvation
> is he,
> humble and mounted on a donkey,
> on a colt, the foal of a donkey. (ESV)

ENTRY INTO JERUSALEM

As they approached Jerusalem and came to Bethphage and Bethany at the Mount of Olives, Jesus sent two of his disciples, saying to them, "Go to the village ahead of you, and just as you enter it, you will find a colt tied there, which no one has ever ridden. Untie it and bring it here. If anyone asks you, 'Why are you doing this?' say, 'The Lord needs it and will send it back here shortly.'"

They went and found a colt outside in the street, tied at a doorway. As they untied it, some people standing there asked, "What are you doing, untying that colt?" They answered as Jesus had told them to, and the people let them go. When they brought the colt to Jesus and threw their cloaks over it, he sat on it. Many people spread their cloaks on the road, while others spread branches they had cut in the fields. Those who went ahead and those who followed shouted,

"Hosanna!"

"Blessed is he who comes in the name of the Lord!"

"Blessed is the coming kingdom of our father David!"

"Hosanna in the highest heaven!"

Jesus entered Jerusalem and went into the temple courts. He looked around at everything, but since it was already late, he went out to Bethany with the Twelve. (Mark 11:1–11 NIV)

Jesus is deliberately and provocatively claiming to be the promised king of Israel.

Skeptical scholars have sometimes questioned the historicity of Jesus' triumphal entry because such a public demonstration would have led to Jesus' immediate arrest by the Romans. But this is a very weak objection. A man on a slowly moving donkey with no show of arms would hardly have looked menacing. His triumphal entry was not something the Romans would have understood or were expecting, and his procession probably just melted into the crowd once it got to Jerusalem. According to Mark 11:11, upon his arrival Jesus just looks around and then leaves. He does nothing to provoke arrest by the Roman authorities.

Virtually all critics acknowledge that during the following week Jesus did cause some sort of disruption in the Jerusalem Temple, which resulted in a temporary halt to commercial activities there. Significantly, the last sentence of Zechariah's prophecy is "There shall no longer be a trader in the house of the LORD of hosts on that day" (Zechariah 14:21). Jesus is deliberating fulfilling these prophecies, asserting his authority in the holiest precincts of Judaism.

The Temple comes up again at Jesus' trial. We have independent reports that Jesus had made a prophecy about the Temple's destruction (Mark 14:58; John 2:19), which the Jewish authorities sought to turn against him. In Jewish literature of Jesus' day God is identified as the one who built the Temple and who threatens to destroy it. In the Dead Sea scrolls the Messiah is called the Son of God, who will build the Temple (4Q174). At the trial Jesus is accused of claiming to do the same thing. His refusal to answer these charges provokes the high priest to demand, "Are you the Messiah, the Son of the Blessed?" (Mark 14:61). This accusation shows that Jesus was on trial for his messianic claims.

The Roman authorities at that time reserved for themselves the right to capital punishment, so the Jewish authorities could not execute Jesus. But Jesus' claim to be the Messiah could be represented to the Roman authorities as treasonous, so that they would execute Jesus. Independent sources testify that the plaque nailed to the cross over Jesus' head recording the charge against him read, "The King of the Jews" (Mark 15:26; John 19:19). The criterion of dissimilarity also supports the authenticity of the charge, for "the King of the Jews" was never a title used for Jesus by the early church. Historical scholars see this charge against Jesus as so firmly established that it is historical bedrock.

The overlapping of so many factors, each ratified by criteria such as independent sources, historical fit, dissimilarity, and so on, makes for a powerful cumulative case that Jesus did, indeed, see himself as the Jewish Messiah.

What Did Jesus Mean?

In claiming to be the Messiah, Jesus has not necessarily said anything superhuman. Scholars typically take the Messiah to be just a human figure. But it must be said that the picture of the Messiah in several pre-Christian Jewish documents is of an extraordinarily exalted figure. In the extra-biblical *Psalms of Solomon* he is called "the Lord Messiah," who "will strike the earth with the word of his mouth forever ... And he himself (will be) free from sin ... and he will not weaken in his days" (17:32–37). In Isaiah we read:

> For to us a child is born,
>> to us a son is given;
> and the government shall be upon his shoulder,
>> and his name shall be called
> Wonderful Counselor, Mighty God,
>> Everlasting Father, Prince of Peace. (Isaiah 9:6 ESV)

Here the title "Mighty God" is given to the Messiah, whose reign, Isaiah goes on to say, will be without end. In the first-century extra-biblical *Similitudes of*

TALK ABOUT IT

What are you learning about Jesus from this chapter that is helpful for you personally? What have you learned that you could share with a non-Christian whom you know?

Enoch the Messiah is portrayed as a God-like figure who has existed with the Lord "prior to the creation of the world and for eternity" (I Enoch 48:6). So the idea of Messiah as a heavenly, divine figure was afoot in Jesus' day.

When we come to Jesus' self-understanding, notice that John the Baptist is described as the fulfillment of Malachi and Isaiah's prophecies of a messenger crying in the wilderness:

> Behold, I send my messenger, and he will prepare the way before me. And the Lord whom you seek will suddenly come to his temple. (Malachi 3:1 ESV)

> A voice cries: "In the wilderness prepare the way of the LORD, make straight in the desert a highway for our God." (Isaiah 40:3)

In Matthew 11:10 and Luke 7:27 Jesus himself identifies John the Baptist as the messenger of Malachi 3:1. So who is to come after the messenger, according to these prophecies? It is the Lord, God himself! Jesus goes on to speak of himself as the Son of Man who has come after John the Baptist (Matthew 11:19; Luke 7:34). As we'll see, the Son of Man is a divine-human figure who could fulfill both the divine and human aspects of John's prediction.

The Son of God
What Did Jesus Claim?

We've already seen that at Jesus' trial the high priest challenged him about being the Son of God. This is a claim that Jesus often makes in the Gospels. We'll look at just three examples.

First, consider Jesus' parable of the wicked tenants of the vineyard:

A man planted a vineyard, and set a hedge around it, and dug a pit for the wine press, and built a tower, and let it out to tenants, and went into another country. When the time came, he sent a servant to the tenants, to get from them some of the fruit of the vineyard. And they took him and beat him, and sent him away empty-handed. Again he sent to them another servant, and they wounded him in the head, and treated him shamefully. And he sent another, and him they killed; and so with many others, some they beat and some they killed. He had still one other, a beloved son; finally he sent him to them, saying, "They will respect my son." But those tenants said to one another, "This is the heir; come, let us kill him, and the inheritance will be ours." And they took him and killed him, and cast him out of the vineyard. What will the owner of the vineyard do? He will come and destroy the tenants, and give the vineyard to others. (Mark 12:1–9)

In this parable, the vineyard symbolizes Israel (see Isaiah 5:1–7), the owner is God, the tenants are the Jewish religious leaders, and the servants are prophets sent by God. The tenants beat and reject the owner's servants. Finally, the owner decides that he has one left to send: his only, beloved son. "They will respect my son," he says. But instead, the tenants kill the son because he is the heir to the vineyard.

Even skeptical scholars recognize the authenticity of this parable, since it's also found in one of their favorite sources, the Gospel of Thomas (65), and so is by their reckoning independently confirmed. Moreover, the parable not only reflects the actual experience of absentee landowners in the ancient world but also employs typical images and themes found in Jewish parables: Israel as a vineyard, God as the owner, unworthy rebellious tenants, the figure of a son, and so on, so that it fits well within a Jewish context. The parable also contains interpretative nuances rooted in the Aramaic paraphrases of Isaiah 5, which were in use in Jesus' day. There are, furthermore, aspects of the parable which make it unlikely that the parable originated later in the Christian church. For example, the concern in the parable over who should possess the vineyard after it is taken from the present tenants was a nonissue for the early Christians, since Rome destroyed Jerusalem in AD 70. And the absence of the resurrection of the slain son in the parable doesn't fit well with the early Christians' belief in Jesus' resurrection.

Now what does this parable tell us about Jesus' self-understanding? It tells us that he thought of himself as God's only Son, distinct from all the prophets, God's final messenger, and even the heir of Israel itself! Notice that you cannot delete the figure of the son from the parable as an inauthentic, later addition, for then the parable lacks any climax and point. Moreover, the uniqueness of the son is not only explicitly stated in the parable but is inherently implied by the tenants' plan to murder the heir in order to claim possession of the vineyard. So this parable discloses to us that Jesus believed and taught that he was the only Son of God.

Jesus explicitly claims to be God's Son in Matthew 11:27 (compare Luke 10:22): "All things have been delivered to me by my Father; and no one knows the Son except the Father, and no one knows the Father except the Son and any one to whom the Son chooses to reveal him."

Again there's good reason to regard this as an authentic saying of Jesus. It is a saying of Jesus from

JEWISH PSEUDEPIGRAPHA

There are a number of Jewish writings that date from just before or around the time of Christ, and that were written under the names of famous prophets and kings. These works are not included in the Old Testament but are valuable to the historian for the glimpse they provide into Jewish religious life and thinking at the time of Christ. Some of the pseudepigrapha are:

Testament of the Twelve Patriarchs: second century BC

1 Enoch: second century BC

Psalms of Solomon: first century BC

4 Ezra: first century AD

2 Baruch: second century AD

ON GUARD FOR STUDENTS

a source shared by Matthew and Luke and is therefore very early. The saying has also been shown to go back to an original Aramaic version, which counts in favor of its authenticity. Moreover, it is unlikely that early Christians invented this saying because it says that the Son is unknowable—"no one knows the Son except the Father"—which would exclude even Jesus' followers from knowing him. But the conviction of the post-Easter church is that one *can* know the Son (Philippians 3:8–11). So this saying is unlikely to be the product of later church theology.

So what does this saying tell us about Jesus' self-concept? It tells us that he thought of himself as the exclusive Son of God and the *only* revelation of God the Father to mankind! Think of it! Jesus thought of himself as God's Son in an absolute and unique sense and as invested with the exclusive authority to reveal his Father God to men.

Finally, another fascinating saying revealing Jesus' sense of being God's Son is his saying concerning the date of his return at history's end: "But of that day or that hour no one knows, not even the angels in heaven, nor the Son, but only the Father" (Mark 13:32). It seems highly unlikely that this saying could be the later product of Christian theology, because it ascribes ignorance to the Son. The criterion of embarrassment requires the authenticity of the reference to the Son's ignorance. Just how embarrassing the saying was is evident in the fact that although Matthew reproduces it (Matthew 24:36), Luke omits it, and most copyists of Matthew's Gospel also chose to drop the verse

> More than that, I regard everything as loss because of the surpassing value of knowing Christ Jesus my Lord. For his sake I have suffered the loss of all things, and I regard them as rubbish, in order that I may gain Christ and be found in him, not having a righteousness of my own that comes from the law, but one that comes through faith in Christ, the righteousness from God based on faith. I want to know Christ and the power of his resurrection and the sharing of his sufferings by becoming like him in his death, if somehow I may attain the resurrection from the dead. (Philippians 3:8–11 NRSV)

(though it is preserved in the best manuscripts). That Mark preserves this saying, despite his emphasis on Jesus' predictive power and foreknowledge, is testimony to his faithfulness in handing on the traditions about Jesus. Here once more we see Jesus' consciousness of being God's unique Son.

What Did Jesus Mean?

On the basis of these three sayings of Jesus, we have good evidence that Jesus thought of himself as the unique Son of God. Once again, however, we mustn't jump the gun. For although Gentile readers of the Gospels would be apt to interpret the expression "Son of God" in terms of divine status, in a Jewish context this was not the customary sense of the title. Jewish kings were referred to as God's sons, and in Jewish literature a righteous man could be characterized as God's child, having God as his father.

Still, given the uniqueness and exclusivity of Jesus' claim, such generic usage is really irrelevant to Jesus' claim. We've seen that Jesus thought of himself as God's Son in a singular sense that set him apart from even the prophets who had gone before. But what was that sense?

The answer may be, once more, that Jesus thought of himself as God's unique Son merely in the sense that he was the promised Messiah. The nonbiblical book IV Ezra 7:28–29 speaks of Messiah as God's Son but nonetheless as mortal: "My son the Messiah shall be revealed ..., and those who remain shall rejoice four hundred years. And after these years my son the Messiah shall die, and all who have human breath." The Dead Sea scrolls also show that the Messiah was thought to be God's Son. The uniqueness of Jesus' Sonship could be a function of the uniqueness of the Messiah.

On the other hand, it must be said in all honesty that these Jewish texts do not even approach the sort of absoluteness and exclusivity claimed by Jesus in the sayings we've examined. There's nothing in the Dead Sea scrolls to suggest that the Messiah is the *only* Son of God. Being the Messiah might set Jesus apart from all the prophets who had come before him and make him the heir of Israel, as claimed in his parable of the vineyard, but being a merely human Messiah would not give him exclusive knowledge of the Father or make him the absolute revelation of God, as claimed in Matthew 11:27. Moreover, the saying in Mark 13:32 not only discloses Jesus' sense of unique Sonship but also presents us with an ascending scale from men to angels to the Son to the Father. Jesus' sense of being God's Son involved a sense of proximity to the Father which transcended that of any human being (such as a king or prophet) or even any angelic being.

Such an exalted conception of God's Son is not foreign to first-century Judaism. The New Testament itself bears witness to this fact (Colossians 1:13–20; Hebrews 1:1–12). Similarly, in IV Ezra 13 Ezra sees a vision of a man arising out of the sea who is identified by God as "my Son" (13:32, 37) and who proceeds to subdue all the nations. The Son is portrayed in this book as a pre-existent, heavenly figure who is revealed on earth at the proper time.

So we have here the same ambiguity with the title "the Son of God" that we encountered in considering the title "Messiah." These titles have many different meanings and are therefore ambiguous when taken out of context. In order to understand the meaning that Jesus invested in such self-descriptions we need to look at Jesus' teaching and actions. But before we do so, there's one more title, the most significant of all, which demands our attention.

The Son of Man
What Did Jesus Claim?

It's very likely that Jesus claimed to be the Son of Man. This was Jesus' favorite self-description and is the title found most frequently in the Gospels (over eighty times). Yet remarkably, this title is found only once outside the Gospels in the rest of the New Testament (Acts 7:56). That shows that the designation of Jesus as "the Son of Man" was not a title that arose in later Christianity and was then written back into the traditions about Jesus. On the basis of the criteria of independent sources and of dissimilarity we can say with confidence that Jesus called himself "the Son of Man."

What Did Jesus Mean?

The key question then becomes the *meaning* of the phrase. Some critics maintain that in calling himself "Son of Man," Jesus merely meant "a human person," just as the Old Testament prophet Ezekiel referred to himself as "a son of man." But with Jesus there's a crucial difference. For Jesus did not refer to himself as "a son of man," but as "*the* Son of Man." Jesus' use of the phrase with the definite article "the" is consistent throughout the Gospels.

By using the definite article Jesus was directing attention to the divine-human figure prophesied in Daniel 7:13–14. Daniel describes his vision in the following way:

> I saw in the night visions,
> and behold, with the clouds of heaven
>   there came one like a son of man,
> and he came to the Ancient of Days
>   and was presented before him.
> And to him was given dominion
>   and glory and kingdom,
> that all peoples, nations, and languages
>   should serve him;
> his dominion is an everlasting dominion,
>   which shall not pass away,
> and his kingdom one
>   that shall not be destroyed.

That Jesus believed in the appearance of the figure described in Daniel's vision is reported in independent sources (Mark 8:38; 13:26–27; Matthew

10:32–33; Luke 12:8–9; Matthew 24:27, 37, 39; Luke 17:24, 26, 30). In Daniel's vision the figure looks like a human being (a son of man), but he comes on the clouds of heaven, and to him is given a dominion and glory which belongs properly to God alone.

Other Jewish writings outside the Bible speak similarly of the Son of Man. The *Similitudes of Enoch* describe the pre-existent Son of Man (I Enoch 48:3–6; compare 62:7), who "shall depose the kings from their thrones and kingdoms" (I Enoch 46:5) and shall sit "upon the throne of his glory" (I Enoch 69:29). I've also mentioned the similar vision of IV Ezra 13, in which Ezra sees "something like the figure of a man come up out of the heart of the sea," whom the Most High identifies as "my son" (IV Ezra 13:37) and who pre-exists with the Most High.

The point in mentioning these passages is not that people listening to Jesus would have recognized his allusions to such works or ideas—they evidently did not—but rather that the understanding of Daniel's Son of Man as a divine-human figure fits with first-century Jewish ideas. By using the indirect expression "the Son of Man" to refer to himself, Jesus prevented a premature revelation of his super-human and messianic status.

Some scholars recognize that Jesus believed in a coming, end-time figure called the Son of Man, but they claim that Jesus was talking about someone else! Such an interpretation is sheer fancy. It would require us to say that all of the Son of Man sayings used by Jesus to refer either to himself or to an earthly, suffering figure are inauthentic. If even one of these sayings is authentic, then this interpretation is invalid. For example, Matthew 8:20 (ESV), "Foxes have holes, and birds of the air have nests, but the Son of Man has nowhere to lay his head," is generally taken to be authentic, but it obviously doesn't refer to some end-time, cosmic figure.

Moreover, this interpretation can't make sense of Jesus' claim to ultimate authority. There's something of a scholarly consensus, as we'll see, that Jesus had a sense of unsurpassed authority. He put himself in God's place by his words and actions. But then it makes no sense to suppose that he thought someone else was coming to judge the world, someone who would, in fact, judge Jesus himself. Jesus' consciousness of unsurpassed authority is incompatible with the view that he thought someone else was the coming Son of Man.

All three of the titles we've examined so far come together in a remarkable way at Jesus' trial. Mark records:

> And the high priest stood up in the midst, and asked Jesus, "Have you no answer to make? What is it that these men testify against you?" But he was silent and made no answer. Again the high priest asked him, "Are you the Messiah, the Son of the Blessed?" And Jesus said, "I am; and you will see the Son of man seated at the right hand of Power, and coming with the clouds of heaven." And the high priest tore his garments, and said, "Why do we still need witnesses? You have heard his blasphemy. What is your decision?" And they all condemned him as deserving death. (Mark 14:60–64)

Here in one fell swoop Jesus affirms that he is the Messiah, the Son of God, and the coming Son of Man. He compounds his crime by adding that he is to be seated at God's right hand, a claim that is truly blasphemous in Jewish ears. The trial scene beautifully illustrates how in Jesus' self-understanding all the diverse claims blend together, thereby taking on connotations that outstrip any single title taken out of context.

Implicit Claims

So the skepticism of earlier scholars concerning Jesus' explicit claims has greatly receded as we've gained insight into first century Palestinian Judaism. Moreover, we can gain additional insight into Jesus' self-understanding by examining his teaching and behavior.

Most scholars believe that Jesus, in what he taught and by the way he acted, made claims that imply the same thing as the titles "Messiah," "the Son of God," and "the Son of Man." In other words, the titles only serve to express *explicitly* what Jesus in his teaching and behavior had already expressed about himself *implicitly*. Let's therefore review some of the implicit personal claims of Jesus widely accepted in New Testament scholarship, wholly apart from the question of the titles.

Jesus' Preaching of the Kingdom

One of the undisputed facts about Jesus is that the centerpiece of his preaching was the coming of the Kingdom of God. As we'll see, Jesus carried out a ministry of miraculous healings and exorcisms as signs to the people of the inbreaking of God's Kingdom.

The question then arises as to Jesus' role in that Kingdom. Was he merely a herald of that Kingdom or did he have a more significant role to play? Here we encounter the very interesting saying of Jesus concerning his twelve disciples' role in the coming Kingdom: "Truly, I say to you, in the new world … you who have followed me will also sit on twelve thrones, judging the twelve tribes of Israel" (Matthew 19:28; compare Luke 22:28–30). The saying is likely to be authentic, not only because it seems to envision an earthly kingdom which did not immediately materialize, but also because of the awkwardness of envisioning a throne for Judas Iscariot, who was known to have fallen away. Jesus' calling *twelve* disciples is no accident: the number twelve corresponds to the twelve tribes of Israel.

Now if the twelve disciples are to sit on thrones judging the twelve tribes of Israel, who will be the king over all of Israel? The clear answer is Jesus himself. He will certainly not be beneath one of the disciples or outside of Israel; rather he will be over the disciples as the King of Israel. In short, Jesus thought of himself as Israel's royal Messiah. Thus Jesus' messianic self-understanding is implicit in his proclamation of the inbreaking of God's Kingdom in his person and ministry, wholly apart from his explicit claims.

Jesus' Authority

Jesus' personal sense of acting and speaking with divine authority is evident in a number of ways.

His Teaching

First, his authority comes to expression in the *content* and *style* of his teaching. These two aspects of his teaching are especially evident in the Sermon on the Mount. A Jewish rabbi's typical style of teaching was to quote extensively from other learned teachers, who provided the basis of authority for his own teaching. But Jesus did exactly the opposite. He began, "You have heard that it was said to the men of old …" and quoted the Law of Moses. Then he continued, "But I say to you …" and gave his own teaching. Jesus thus equated his own authority with that of the divinely given Law. It's no wonder that Matthew comments, "When Jesus finished these sayings, the crowds were astonished at his teaching, for he taught them as one who had authority, and not as their scribes" (Matthew 7:28–29).

But it's not just that Jesus placed his personal authority on a par with that of the divine Law. More than that, he *adjusted* the Law on his own authority. Although modern Jewish scholars have tried to assimilate Jesus' teachings to the tradition of Judaism, Jesus' placing his own personal authority over against the divine Law given through Moses is the rock upon which all such attempts are finally broken. Take, for example, Jesus' teaching on divorce in Matthew 5:31–32 (compare Mark 10:2–12). Here Jesus explicitly quotes the teaching of the Law (Deuteronomy 24:1–4) and opposes to it, on the basis of his own authority, his own teaching on the matter. In Mark's Gospel, he declares that Moses does not represent the perfect will of God on this matter and presumes to correct the Law on his own authority as to what is really the will of God. But no human being, no prophet or teacher or charismatic, had that kind of authority.

His Use of "Truly, Truly, I Say to You"

Second, Jesus' use of the words "Truly, truly I say to you" expresses his authority. This expression is historically unique and is recognized on all hands to have been the way Jesus marked off his authoritative word on some subject. The Orthodox Jewish writer Ahad Ha'am protests, "Israel cannot accept with religious enthusiasm, as the Word of God, the utterances of a man who speaks in his own name—not 'thus saith the Lord,' but '*I* say unto you.' This 'I' is in itself sufficient to drive Judaism away from the Gentiles forever."[4]

His Exorcisms

Third, Jesus' authority is especially evident in his role as an exorcist. Embarrassing as it may be to many modern theologians, it's historically certain that Jesus believed he had the power to cast out demons. This was a sign to people of his divine authority. He declared, "But if it is by the finger of God that I cast out demons, then the kingdom of God has come upon you" (Luke 11:20). This saying, which is recognized by New Testament scholars as authentic, is remarkable for two reasons. First, it shows that Jesus claimed divine authority over the spiritual forces of evil. Second, it

> You have heard the law that says, "A man can divorce his wife by merely giving her a written notice of divorce." But I say that a man who divorces his wife, unless she has been unfaithful, causes her to commit adultery. And anyone who marries a divorced woman also commits adultery. (Matthew 5:31–32 NLT)

shows that Jesus believed that in himself the Kingdom of God had come. Jesus is saying, "My ability to rule the spiritual forces of darkness shows that in me the Kingdom of God is already present among you." In claiming that in himself the Kingdom of God had already arrived, as visibly demonstrated by his exorcisms, Jesus was, in effect, putting himself in God's place.

His Claim to Forgive Sins

Finally, Jesus' sense of divine authority comes clearly to expression in his claim to forgive sins. Several of Jesus' parables, which are acknowledged on all hands to have been uttered by the historical Jesus, show that he assumed the prerogative to forgive sins. In parables like the prodigal son, the lost sheep, and so forth, Jesus describes persons who have wandered away from God and are lost in sin. In Jewish thought such a person was irretrievably lost and therefore given up as dead. But Jesus extended forgiveness to such persons and welcomed them back into the fold. The problem is that no one but God had the authority to make such a proclamation. No mere prophet could presume to speak for God on this matter. As New Testament scholar Royce Gruenler puts it, Jesus "is consciously speaking as the voice of God on matters that belong only to God."[5]

What Jesus taught in his parables, he acted out in real life. One of the most radical features of the historical Jesus was his practice of inviting prostitutes, toll collectors, and other outcasts into fellowship with him around the dinner table. This was a living illustration of God's forgiveness of them and his invitation to them to fellowship in the Kingdom of God. In table fellowship with the immoral and unclean, Jesus is acting in the place of God to welcome them into God's Kingdom. It's no wonder that the religious authorities saw this presumptuous activity as blasphemous (compare the reaction to Jesus' claim in Mark 2:1–12 that he has authority as the Son of Man to forgive sins)!

Thus, most New Testament critics acknowledge that the historical Jesus acted and spoke with a self-consciousness of divine authority and that furthermore, he saw in his own person the coming of the long-awaited Kingdom of God and invited people into its fellowship.

"This guy acts like he thinks he's a god."

Jesus' Miracles

Jesus believed himself to be not only an exorcist but a miracle worker. Recall his reply to the disciples of John the Baptist, "Go and tell John what you hear and see: the blind receive their sight and the lame walk, lepers are cleansed and the deaf hear, and the dead are raised up, and the poor have good news preached to them" (Matthew 11:4–5). Jesus evidently believed that he had the power to heal people and even to raise the dead.

Moreover, the miracle stories are so widely represented in all the Gospel sources that it would be implausible to think that they are not rooted in the life of Jesus. Therefore, the consensus of New Testament scholarship today is that Jesus did perform "miracles"—however you might want to explain these. At the end of his long and detailed study of Jesus' miracles the preeminent historical Jesus scholar John Meier concludes that Jesus' role as a miracle healer "has as much historical corroboration as almost any other statement we can make about the Jesus of history."[6]

The miracles of Jesus take on a deeper significance in that they, like his exorcisms, were taken to be signs of the inbreaking of the Kingdom of God. As such, Jesus' miracles were fundamentally different from the wonders performed by pagan magicians or Jewish holy men. Moreover, Jesus' miracles differed from those of Jewish holy men in that Jesus never prays for a miracle to be done. He may first express thanks to God the Father, but then he does the miracle himself. And he does so in his own name, not God's. Moreover, none of the other Jewish miracle workers carried out a prophetic ministry, made messianic claims, or brought any new teaching in conjunction with their miracles. Thus, Jesus' self-understanding cannot be reduced simply to that of another charismatic Jewish holy man.

Jesus' Role as Judge

Jesus held that people's attitudes toward himself would be the determining factor in how God will judge them on the Judgment Day. He proclaimed, "I tell you, every one who acknowledges me before men, the Son of man also will acknowledge before the angels of God; but he who denies me before men will be denied before the angels of God" (Luke 12:8–9). I have no doubt that Jesus is referring here to himself as the Son of Man, not to somebody else. But be that as it may, the point is that whoever the Son of Man may be, Jesus is claiming that people will be judged before him on the basis of their response to Jesus. Think of it: people's eternal destiny is fixed by how they respond to Jesus! Make no mistake: if Jesus were *not* divine, then this claim could only be regarded as the most narrow and objectionable dogmatism. For Jesus is saying that people's salvation depends on their confession to Jesus himself.

Conclusion

A discussion of Jesus' claims could go on and on. But I think enough has been said to indicate the radical self-concept of Jesus. Here is a man who thought of himself as the promised Messiah, God's only Son, Daniel's Son of Man to whom all dominion and authority would be given, who claimed to act and speak with divine authority, who held himself to be a worker of miracles, and who believed that people's eternal destiny hinged on whether or not they believed in him. Today there is virtually a consensus that Jesus came on the scene with an unheard-of authority, namely with the authority of God, with the claim of the authority to stand in God's place.

Jesus' radical personal claims and activities, culminating in his trial and crucifixion, constitute the proper historical context for evaluating the evidence for Jesus' resurrection. Historians are unanimous that Jesus of Nazareth, having been condemned by the Jewish authorities for blasphemy and delivered to the Roman authorities on the pretext of treason, met his death by crucifixion. But what happened next?

1. For citation and examination of these texts, see Robert E. Van Voorst, *Jesus Outside the New Testament: An Introduction to the Ancient Evidence* (Grand Rapids, MI: William B. Eerdmans, 2000).
2. A. N. Sherwin-White, *Roman Society and Roman Law in the New Testament* (Oxford: Clarendon, 1963), 189.
3. William M. Ramsay, *The Bearing of Recent Discovery on the Trustworthiness of the New Testament* (London: Hodder & Stoughton, 1915), 222.
4. Ahad Ha'am, "Judaism and the Gospels," in *Nationalism and the Jewish Ethic*, ed. H. Kohn (New York: Schocken Books, 1962), 298.
5. Royce Gordon Gruenler, *New Approaches to Jesus and the Gospels* (Grand Rapids, MI: Baker, 1982), 46.
6. John P. Meier, *A Marginal Jew, Volume 2: Mentor, Message, and Miracles*, Anchor Bible Reference Library (New York: Doubleday, 1994), 969–70.

I. Jesus had a divine-human self-understanding.

    A. The worship of Jesus by monotheistic Jews as God incarnate within twenty years of His death requires an adequate cause to be found in Jesus' own claims.

    B. Explicit claims

        1. Messiah

            a. The belief in the early church that Jesus was the Messiah requires an adequate cause.

            b. Peter's confession (Mark 8:27–29)

            c. Jesus' answer to John the Baptist (Matthew 11:2–6; Luke 7:19–23)

            d. Jesus' triumphal entry (Mark 11:1–11; John 12:12–19)

            e. Jesus' action in the temple (Mark 11:15–17)

            f. Jesus' condemnation by the Sanhedrin (Mark 14:61–65)

            g. Jesus' crucifixion as "King of the Jews" (Mark 15:26)

        2. The Son of God

            a. Parable of the vineyard (Mark 12:1–9)

            b. "No one knows the Father except the Son" (Matthew 11:27)

            c. "No one knows ... not even ... the Son" (Mark 13:32)

            d. Jesus' trial confession (Mark 14:60–64)

        3. The Son of Man

            a. Jesus' favorite title

            b. Reference to the divine-human figure of Daniel 7 (Daniel 7:13–14)

            c. Jesus' trial confession (Mark 14:60–64)

    C. Implicit claims

        1. Jesus' preaching of the Kingdom of God (Matthew 19:28)

        2. Jesus' authority

            a. The content and style of Jesus' teaching (Matthew 5:31–32)

      b. "Truly, I say to you" (Mark 8:12; 9:1; etc.)

      c. Jesus' role as an exorcist (Luke 11:20)

      d. Jesus' claim to forgive sins (Mark 2:1–12)

3. Jesus' miracles (Matthew 11:4–5)

4. Jesus' role as Judge (Luke 12:8–9)

CHAPTER 8

DID JESUS RISE FROM THE DEAD?

*If Jesus rose from the dead, then you have to accept all that he said; if he
didn't rise from the dead, then why worry about any of what he said?*
Timothy Keller, *Reason for God*

You wouldn't expect that an alleged event like Jesus' resurrection from the
dead would have much, if anything, by way of historical evidence in its favor.
It is all the more remarkable, then, just how good a historical case can be
made for the historicity of this event.

We need to look, first, at the evidence to be explained and then, second,
at the various explanations of that evidence. The evidence to be explained can
be summed up under three independently established facts: (1) Jesus' empty
tomb, (2) Jesus' appearances alive after his death, and (3) the origin of the
disciples' belief in his resurrection. If these three facts can be shown to be
historically credible, then the next question to be asked is, "What is the best
explanation of these facts?" The explanation given by the earliest followers
of Jesus was: "God raised Jesus from the dead." I'll call this the Resurrection
Hypothesis. We'll want to know how this hypothesis compares with rival
explanations of the facts.

The Evidence to Be Explained

If the three facts mentioned above—the empty tomb, the post-mortem appearances, and the origin of the belief in Jesus' resurrection—can be established

and if no plausible, natural explanation can account for them as well as the Resurrection Hypothesis, then one would be justified in inferring Jesus' resurrection as the best explanation of the facts. So let's examine the evidence supporting each of these three facts.

The Fact of Jesus' Empty Tomb

Here we'll examine five lines of evidence supporting the fact that Jesus' tomb was found empty by a group of his women followers on the Sunday after his crucifixion.

1. *The historical reliability of the story of Jesus' burial supports the empty tomb.* Now you might ask, how does the fact of Jesus' burial prove that his tomb was found empty? The answer is this: if the burial story is basically accurate, then the location of Jesus' tomb was known in Jerusalem to both Jew and Christian alike, since both were present when Jesus was laid in the tomb. But in that case, the tomb must have been empty when the disciples began to preach that Jesus was risen.

Why? *First,* the disciples could not have believed in Jesus' resurrection if his corpse still lay in the tomb. It would have been wholly un-Jewish, not to say stupid, to believe that a man was raised from the dead when his body was known to be still in the grave. *Second,* even if the disciples had preached Jesus' resurrection despite his occupied tomb, scarcely anybody else would have believed them. One of the most remarkable facts about the early Christian belief in Jesus' resurrection was that it flourished in the very city where Jesus had

RESURRECTION

In Jesus' day it was clear what the various Greek, Aramaic, etc. words for *resurrection* did *not* mean.

Resurrection did *not* mean life after death in some disembodied form, it did *not* mean the immortality of the soul in either torment or paradise, and it did *not* mean reincarnation. It meant the reversal of death, restoration to some kind of bodily immortality.

Many pagans believed in disembodied life after death, but they considered resurrection impossible. Some (not all) Jews expected resurrection for the righteous at the end of days—but not for anybody before then. A resurrected body might differ from our bodies, but it had to be a body. Neither a ghost nor a disembodied soul nor a spirit on a higher plane of consciousness would have been called "resurrected."

ON GUARD FOR STUDENTS

been publicly crucified. So long as the people of Jerusalem thought that Jesus' body was in the tomb, few would have been prepared to believe the nonsense that Jesus had been raised from the dead. And *third*, even if they had so believed, the Jewish authorities would have exposed the whole affair simply by pointing to Jesus' tomb or perhaps even exhuming the body as decisive proof that Jesus had not been raised.

The suggestion of some skeptics that the Jewish authorities didn't take this business about Jesus' being risen as anything more than a minor nuisance not worth dealing with is highly implausible and contrary to the evidence. They were deeply concerned about squelching the budding Christian movement (think of their hiring Saul of Tarsus to persecute Jewish Christians!). They would certainly have checked the tomb to see if the corpse were gone.

Even if the remains in the tomb were no longer recognizable, the burden of proof would have been upon anyone who said that these were *not* Jesus' remains. But no such dispute over the identification of Jesus' corpse ever seems to have taken place. As we'll see, the dispute between Jewish non-Christians and Jewish Christians lay elsewhere.

Thus, if the story of Jesus' burial is historical, then it's a very short inference to the fact of the empty tomb as well. For that reason, critics who deny the empty tomb feel compelled to argue against the burial as well. Unfortunately for them, Jesus' burial in the tomb is one of the best-established facts about Jesus. Space doesn't permit me to go into all the details of the evidence for the burial. But let me just mention a couple points:

First, *Jesus' burial is reported in extremely early, independent sources.* The account of Jesus' burial in a tomb by Joseph of Arimathea is part of Mark's source material for the Passion Story (the story of Jesus' suffering and death). Here is Mark's story of the burial and empty tomb of Jesus (15:42–16:8):

> And when evening had come, since it was the day of Preparation, that is, the day before the sabbath, Joseph of Arimathea, a respected member of the council, who was also

himself looking for the kingdom of God, took courage and went to Pilate, and asked for the body of Jesus. And Pilate wondered if he were already dead; and summoning the centurion, he asked him whether he was already dead. And when he learned from the centurion that he was dead, he granted the body to Joseph. And he bought a linen shroud, and taking him down, wrapped him in the linen shroud, and laid him in a tomb which had been hewn out of the rock; and he rolled a stone against the door of the tomb. Mary Magdalene and Mary the mother of Joses saw where he was laid.

And when the sabbath was past, Mary Magdalene, and Mary the mother of James, and Salome, bought spices, so that they might go and anoint him. And very early on the first day of the week they went to the tomb when the sun had risen. And they were saying to one another, "Who will roll away the stone for us from the door of the tomb?" And looking up, they saw that the stone was rolled back—it was very large. And entering the tomb, they saw a young man sitting on the right side, dressed in a white robe; and they were amazed. And he said to them, "Do not be amazed; you seek Jesus of Nazareth, who was crucified. He has risen, he is not here; see the place where they laid him. But go, tell his disciples and Peter that he is going before you to Galilee; there you will see him, as he told you." And they went out and fled from the tomb; for trembling and astonishment had come upon them; and they said nothing to any one, for they were afraid.

Since Mark is the earliest of the four Gospels, this story derives from a very early source, which most scholars think is based on eyewitness testimony.

Moreover, Paul in 1 Corinthians 15:3–5 quotes an old Christian tradition that he had received from the earliest disciples. Paul probably received this tradition no later than his visit to Jerusalem in AD 36 (Galatians 1:18), if not earlier in Damascus. It therefore goes back to within the first five years after Jesus' death in AD 30. The tradition is a summary of the early Christian preaching and may have been used in Christian instruction. Its form would have made it suitable for memorization. Here's what it says:

> ... that Christ died for our sins in accordance with the
> Scriptures,
> and that he was buried,
> and that he was raised on the third day in accordance with
> the Scriptures,
> and that he appeared to Cephas, then to the Twelve.

Notice that the second line of this tradition refers to Jesus' burial.

But, we might wonder, was the burial mentioned in Paul's tradition the same event as the burial by Joseph of Arimathea? The answer to that question is made clear by a comparison of the four-line formula passed on by Paul with the Gospel narratives on the one hand and the sermons in the Acts of the Apostles on the other:

1 Cor. 15:3–5	Acts 13:28–31	Mark 15:37–16:7
Christ died ...	Though they found no cause for a sentence of death, they asked Pilate to have him killed.	And Jesus gave a loud cry and breathed his last.
he was buried ...	They took him down from the tree and laid him in a tomb.	Joseph bought a linen cloth, and taking down the body, wrapped it in the linen cloth and laid it in a tomb.
he was raised ...	But God raised him from the dead ...	"He has risen, he is not here; see the place where they laid him."
he appeared ...	... and for many days he appeared to those who came up with him from Galilee to Jerusalem, and they are now his witnesses to the people.	"But go, tell his disciples and Peter that he is going before you to Galilee; there you will see him."

This remarkable correspondence of independent traditions is convincing proof that Paul's four-line formula is a summary or outline of the basic events of Jesus' passion and resurrection, including his burial in the tomb. We thus have evidence from some of the earliest, independent sources in the New Testament for the burial of Jesus in the tomb.

But that's not all! For further independent testimony to Jesus' burial by Joseph is also found in the sources behind Matthew and Luke and in the Gospel of John. The differences between Mark's account of the burial and those of Matthew and Luke suggest that they had sources other than Mark alone. Moreover, we have another independent source for the burial in John's Gospel. Finally, we have the early sermons in the book of Acts, which probably preserve the early preaching of the apostles. These sermons also mention Jesus' interment in a tomb. Thus, we have the remarkable number of at least five independent sources for Jesus' burial, some of which are extraordinarily early.

Second, *as a member of the Jewish Sanhedrin that condemned Jesus, Joseph of Arimathea is unlikely to be a Christian invention.* Joseph is described as a rich man, a member of the Jewish Sanhedrin. The Sanhedrin was a sort of Jewish high court made up of seventy of the leading men of Judaism, which presided in Jerusalem. There was an understandable hostility in the early church toward the Jewish Sanhedrists. In Christian eyes, they had engineered a judicial murder of Jesus. The sermons in Acts, for example, go so far as to say that the Jewish leaders crucified Jesus (Acts 2:23, 36; 4:10)! Given his status as a Sanhedrist, Joseph is the last person you'd expect to care properly for Jesus. Thus, Jesus' burial by Joseph is very probable, since it would be almost inexplicable why Christians would make up a story about a Jewish Sanhedrist who does what is right by Jesus.

For these and other reasons, most New Testament critics agree that Jesus was buried by Joseph of Arimathea in a tomb. According to the late John A. T. Robinson of Cambridge University, the burial of Jesus in the tomb is "one of the earliest and best-attested facts about Jesus."[1] But if this conclusion is correct, then, as I've explained, it's very difficult to deny the fact of the empty tomb.

2. The discovery of Jesus' empty tomb is independently reported in very early sources. Mark's Passion source probably didn't end with Jesus' burial but with the women's discovery of Jesus' empty tomb. For the burial story and the empty tomb story are really one story, forming a smooth, continuous narrative. They're linked by grammatical and linguistic ties. Furthermore, it seems unlikely that the early Christians would have circulated a story of Jesus' Passion ending in his burial. The Passion Story is incomplete without victory at the end. Hence, Mark's source probably included and may have ended with the discovery of the empty tomb.

We've seen that in 1 Corinthians 15:3–5 Paul quotes from an extremely early tradition that refers to Christ's burial and resurrection. Although the empty tomb is not explicitly mentioned, a comparison of the four-line

MARK'S BURIAL ACCOUNT

It was Preparation Day (that is, the day before the Sabbath). So as evening approached, Joseph of Arimathea, a prominent member of the Council, who was himself waiting for the kingdom of God, went boldly to Pilate and asked for Jesus' body. Pilate was surprised to hear that he was already dead. Summoning the centurion, he asked him if Jesus had already died. When he learned from the centurion that it was so, he gave the body to Joseph. So Joseph bought some linen cloth, took down the body, wrapped it in the linen, and placed it in a tomb cut out of rock. Then he rolled a stone against the entrance of the tomb. Mary Magdalene and Mary the mother of Jesus saw where he was laid. (Mark 15:42–47 NIV)

MARK'S EMPTY TOMB ACCOUNT

When the Sabbath was over, Mary Magdalene, Mary the mother of James, and Salome bought spices so that they might go to anoint Jesus' body. Very early on the first day of the week, just after sunrise, they were on their way to the tomb and they asked each other, "Who will roll the stone away from the entrance of the tomb?"

But when they looked up, they saw that the stone, which was very large, had been rolled away. As they entered the tomb, they saw a young man dressed in a white robe sitting on the right side, and they were alarmed.

"Don't be alarmed," he said. "You are looking for Jesus the Nazarene, who was crucified. He has risen! He is not here. See the place where they laid him. But go, tell his disciples and Peter, 'He is going ahead of you into Galilee. There you will see him, just as he told you.'"

Trembling and bewildered, the women went out and fled from the tomb. They said nothing to anyone, because they were afraid. (Mark 16:1–8 NIV)

formula with the Gospel narratives on the one hand and the sermons in Acts on the other reveals that the third line is, in fact, a summary of the empty tomb story.

Moreover, two further features of Paul's tradition imply the empty tomb. First, the expression "he was buried" followed by the expression "he was raised" implies the empty tomb. The idea that a man could be buried and then be raised from the dead and yet his body still remain in the grave is a peculiarly modern notion! For first-century Jews there would have been no question but that the tomb of Jesus would have been empty. Therefore, when the tradition states that Christ "was buried and he was raised," it automatically implies that an empty tomb was left behind. Given the early date and origin of this tradition, its drafters could not have believed such a thing were the tomb not empty.

Second, the expression "on the third day" implies the empty tomb. Very briefly summarized, since no one actually saw Jesus rise from the dead, why did the early disciples proclaim that he had been raised "on the third day"? Why not the seventh day? The most likely answer is that it was on the third day that the women discovered the tomb of Jesus empty; and so naturally, the resurrection itself came to be dated on that day.

We have, then, extraordinarily early, independent evidence for the fact of Jesus' empty tomb. The discovery of Jesus' empty tomb cannot be written off as a later legendary development.

But there's more! For once again there are good reasons to discern independent sources for the empty tomb in the other Gospels and Acts. Matthew is clearly working with an independent source, for he includes the story of the guard at the tomb, which is unique to his Gospel. Moreover, his comment about how the rumor that the disciples had stolen Jesus' body "has been spread among the Jews to this day" (Matthew 28:15) shows that Matthew is responding to prior tradition. Luke also has an independent source, for he tells the story, not found in Mark, of two disciples visiting the tomb to verify the women's report that the tomb was vacant. The story can't be regarded as Luke's creation, since the incident is independently reported in John. And, again, given John's independence of the other three Gospels, we have yet another independent report of the empty tomb. Finally, in the sermons in the book of Acts, we again have indirect references to the empty tomb. For example, Peter draws the sharp contrast, "David died and was buried and his tomb is with us to this day," but "this Jesus God has raised up" (Acts 2:29–32; compare 13:36–37).

Historians think they've hit historical pay dirt when they have two independent accounts of the same event. But in the case of the empty tomb we have no fewer than six, and some of these are among the earliest materials to be found in the New Testament.

3. *Mark's story is simple and lacks legendary development.* Like the burial account, Mark's account of the empty tomb is remarkably simple and unembellished by theological motifs likely to

THE GOSPEL OF PETER'S ACCOUNT OF THE RESURRECTION

Early in the morning, as the Sabbath dawned, there came a large crowd from Jerusalem and the surrounding areas to see the sealed tomb. But during the night before the Lord's day dawned, as the soldiers were keeping guard two by two in every watch, there came a great sound in the sky, and they saw the heavens opened and two men descend shining with a great light, and they drew near to the tomb. The stone which had been set on the door rolled away by itself and moved to one side, and the tomb was opened and both of the young men went in.

Now when these soldiers saw that, they woke up the centurion and the elders (for they also were there keeping watch). While they were yet telling them the things which they had seen, they saw three men come out of the tomb, two of them sustaining the other one, and a cross following after them. The heads of the two they saw had heads that reached up to heaven, but the head of him that was led by them went beyond heaven. And they heard a voice out of the heavens saying, "Have you preached unto them that sleep?" The answer that was heard from the cross was, "Yes!" (Gospel of Peter 9:1–10:5) characterize a later legendary account. For example, the resurrection itself is not witnessed or described, and there's no reflection on Jesus' triumph over sin and death, no use of divine titles, no quotation of fulfilled prophecy, no description of the Risen Lord. It's very different than a Christian fictional creation—just compare how the resurrection is portrayed in modern Passion plays!

To appreciate how restrained Mark's narrative is, you only have to read the account in the apocryphal Gospel of Peter, which describes Jesus' triumphant exit from the tomb as a gigantic figure whose head reaches above the clouds, supported by giant angels, followed by a talking cross, heralded by a voice from heaven, and all witnessed by a Roman guard, the Jewish leaders, and a multitude of spectators! This is how real legends look: they're colored by theological and apologetical developments. By contrast, Mark's account is stark in its simplicity.

4. *The tomb was probably discovered empty by women.* In order to grasp this point, we need to understand two things about the place of women in Jewish society.

First, women were not regarded as credible witnesses. This attitude toward the testimony of women is evident in the Jewish historian Josephus'

FLAVIUS JOSEPHUS

Flavius Josephus (AD 37–100) was born into a Jewish priestly family as Joseph ben Mattathias. He became a military commander of Jewish forces in Galilee during the Jewish Revolt of AD 66, which ended in the destruction of Jerusalem in AD 70. Trapped in a cave by Roman forces, Josephus persuaded his men that they draw lots and kill each other successively, the last man committing suicide. But as the last one left alive, Josephus promptly surrendered to the Romans and joined their cause. After the war he became a Roman citizen and adopted his Roman name. His principal works are a history of the Jewish Revolt and a history of the Jewish people entitled *Antiquities of the Jews*. In this latter work he mentions Jesus of Nazareth twice, as well as Jesus' brother James, John the Baptist, Caiaphas, Pilate, and other persons mentioned in the Gospels.

description of the rules for admissible testimony: "Let not the testimony of women be admitted, on account of the levity and boldness of their sex" (*Antiquities* IV.8.15). No such regulation is to be found in the Bible. It is rather a reflection of the patriarchal society of first-century Judaism.

Second, women occupied a low rung on the Jewish social ladder. Compared to men, women were second-class citizens. Consider these rabbinical texts: "Sooner let the words of the Law be burnt than delivered to women!" (Sotah 19a) and again: "Happy is he whose children are male, but unhappy is he whose children are female!" (Kiddushin 82b). The daily prayer of every Jewish man included the blessing, "Blessed are you, Lord our God, ruler of the universe, who has not created me a Gentile, a slave, or a woman" (Berachos 60b).

So given their low social status and inability to serve as legal witnesses, it's quite amazing that it is *women* who are the discoverers of and principal witnesses to the empty tomb. If the empty tomb story were a legend, then the male disciples would have been made to be the ones who discover the empty tomb. The fact that women, whose testimony was deemed worthless, were the chief witnesses to the fact of the empty tomb can only be plausibly explained if, like it or not, they actually *were* the discoverers of the empty tomb, and the Gospels faithfully record what for them was a very embarrassing fact.

5. *The earliest Jewish response presupposes the empty tomb.* In Matthew 28:11–15 we find an attempt to refute the earliest Jewish response to the Christian proclamation of the resurrection. According to Matthew's account, the guard posted at Jesus' tomb returned to the chief priests:

> Behold, some of the guard went into the city and told the chief priests all that had taken place. And when they had assembled with the elders and taken counsel, they gave a sum of money to the soldiers and said, "Tell people, 'His disciples came by night and stole him away while we were asleep.' And if this comes to the governor's ears, we will

satisfy him and keep you out of trouble." So they took the money and did as they were directed; and this story has been spread among the Jews to this day.

Now our interest is not so much in Matthew's story of the guard at the tomb as in his incidental remark at the end, "This story has been spread among the Jews to this day." This remark reveals that the author was concerned to refute a widespread Jewish explanation of the resurrection.

Now what were unbelieving Jews saying in response to the disciples' proclamation that Jesus was risen? That these men were full of new wine? That Jesus' body still lay in the tomb in the garden? No. They were saying, "The disciples stole away his body." Think about that. "*The disciples stole away his body.*" The Jewish authorities did not deny the empty tomb but instead entangled themselves in a hopeless series of absurdities trying to explain it away. In other words, the Jewish claim that the disciples had stolen the body presupposes that the body was missing. This is evidence for the fact of the empty tomb which is really top-drawer because it comes, not from the followers of Jesus, but from the very opponents of the early Jesus movement.

Taken together these five lines of evidence constitute a powerful case that Jesus' tomb was, indeed, found empty on the first day of the week by a group of his women followers. As a historical fact, this seems to be well-established. According to Jacob Kremer, a New Testament critic who has specialized in the study of the resurrection: "By far most scholars hold firmly to the reliability of the biblical statements about the empty tomb."[2] In fact, in a survey of over 2,200 publications on the resurrection in English, French, and German since 1975, Gary Habermas found that 75 percent of scholars accepted the historicity of the discovery of Jesus' empty tomb.[3] The evidence

TALK ABOUT IT

If you were to talk with a non-Christian friend about this evidence for the empty tomb, how do you think he or she would respond?

is so compelling that even a number of Jewish scholars, such as Pinchas Lapide and Geza Vermes, have declared themselves convinced on the basis of the evidence that Jesus' tomb was found empty.

The Fact of Jesus' Post-Mortem Appearances

In 1 Corinthians 15:3–8, Paul writes:

> For I delivered to you ... what I also received,
>
>> that Christ died for our sins in accordance with the scriptures,
>>
>> that he was buried,
>>
>> that he was raised on the third day in accordance with the scriptures,
>>
>> and that he appeared to Cephas, then to the twelve.
>>
>> Then he appeared to more than five hundred brethren at one time, most of whom are still alive, though some have fallen asleep. Then he appeared to James, then to all the apostles. Last of all, as to one untimely born, he appeared also to me.

This is a truly remarkable claim. We have here an indisputably authentic letter of a man personally acquainted with the first disciples, and he reports that they actually saw Jesus alive after his death. More than that, he says that he himself also saw an appearance of Jesus. What are we to make of this claim? Did Jesus really appear to people alive after his death?

To answer this question, let's consider the evidence for the resurrection appearances of Jesus. Once again, space won't allow me to examine in detail all the evidence for Jesus' post-mortem appearances. But I'd like to look at three main lines of evidence.

1. *Paul's list of eyewitnesses to Jesus' resurrection appearances shows that such appearances occurred.* In 1 Corinthians 15 Paul gives a list of witnesses to Jesus'

resurrection appearances. Let's look briefly at each appearance to see whether it's plausible that such an event actually took place.

(a) *Appearance to Peter.* We have no story in the Gospels telling of Jesus' appearance to Peter. But the appearance is mentioned here in the old Christian tradition quoted by Paul, which originated in the Jerusalem church, and it's vouched for by the apostle Paul himself. As we know from Galatians 1:18, Paul spent about two weeks with Peter in Jerusalem three years after his conversion on the Damascus Road. So Paul knew personally whether Peter claimed to have had such an experience or not. In addition to this, the appearance to Peter is mentioned in another old Christian tradition found in Luke 24:34: "The Lord has really risen and has appeared to Simon" (NASB). That Luke is passing on a prior tradition here is evident from the awkward way in which it is inserted into his story of the appearance to the Emmaus disciples. So although we have no story of the appearance to Peter, it is quite well-founded historically. As a result, virtually all New Testament critics agree that Peter saw an appearance of Jesus alive from the dead.

(b) *Appearance to the Twelve.* Undoubtedly, the group referred to here is that original group of twelve disciples who had been chosen by Jesus during his ministry—minus, of course, Judas, whose absence didn't affect the formal title of the group. This is the best-attested resurrection appearance of Jesus. It, too, is included in the very early traditional formula that Paul cites, and Paul himself had contact with members of the Twelve. Moreover, we have independent stories of this appearance in Luke 24:36–42 and John 20:19–20. Undoubtedly, the most notable feature of these appearance stories is the physical demonstrations of Jesus' showing his wounds and eating before the disciples. The purpose of the physical demonstrations is to show two things: first, that Jesus was raised *physically*; and second, that he was the *same Jesus* who had been crucified. There can be little doubt that such an appearance occurred, for it is attested in the old Christian tradition, vouched for by Paul, who had personal contact with the Twelve, and is independently described by both Luke and John.

(c) *Appearance to five hundred brethren.* The third appearance comes as something of a shock: "Then he appeared to more than five hundred brethren at one time"! This is surprising, since we have no mention whatsoever of this appearance elsewhere in the New Testament. This might make us rather skeptical about this appearance. But Paul himself apparently had personal contact with these people, since he knew that some had died. This is seen in Paul's parenthetical comment, "most of whom are still alive, though some have fallen asleep." Why does Paul add this remark? A great New Testament scholar of Cambridge University, C. H. Dodd, replies, "There can hardly be any purpose in mentioning the fact that the most of the 500 are still alive, unless Paul is saying, in effect, 'The witnesses are there to be questioned.'"[4] Notice: Paul could never have said this if the event had not occurred. He could not have challenged people to talk to the witnesses if the event had never taken place and there were no witnesses. But evidently there were witnesses to this event, and Paul knew that some of them had died in the meantime. Therefore, the event must have taken place.

I suspect that this appearance is not related in the Gospels because it probably took place in Galilee. As one puts together the various appearances in the Gospels, it seems that they occurred first in Jerusalem, then in Galilee, and then in Jerusalem again. The appearance to the five hundred would have to be out of doors, perhaps on a hillside near a Galilean village. In Galilee thousands had gathered to hear Jesus teach during his ministry. Since the Gospels focus their attention on the appearances in Jerusalem, we don't have any story of this appearance to the five hundred. An intriguing possibility is that this was the appearance predicted by the angel at the tomb and described by Matthew (28:16–17).

(d) *Appearance to James.* The next appearance is one of the most amazing of all: Jesus appeared to James, his younger brother. What makes this amazing is that apparently neither James nor any of Jesus' younger brothers believed in Jesus during his lifetime (Mark 3:21, 31–35; John 7:1–10). They didn't believe he was the Messiah, or a prophet, or even anybody special. By the criterion of embarrassment, this is doubtless a historical fact of Jesus' life and ministry.

But after the resurrection, Jesus' brothers show up in the Christian fellowship in the upper room in Jerusalem (Acts 1:14). There's no further mention of them until Acts 12:17, the story of Peter's deliverance from prison by the angel. What are Peter's first words? "Report this to *James*." In Galatians 1:19 Paul tells of his two-week visit to Jerusalem about three years after his Damascus Road experience. He says that besides Peter, he saw none of the other apostles *except James* the Lord's brother. Paul at least implies that James was now being reckoned as an apostle. When Paul visited Jerusalem again fourteen years later, he says there were three "pillars" of the church in Jerusalem: Peter, John, and *James* (Galatians 2:9). Finally, in Acts 21:18 James is the sole head of the Jerusalem church and of the council of elders. We hear no more about James in the New Testament; but from Josephus, the Jewish historian, we learn that James was stoned to death illegally by the Sanhedrin sometime after AD 60 for his faith in Christ (*Antiquities* 20.200).

Not only James but also Jesus' other brothers became believers and were active in Christian preaching, as we see from 1 Corinthians 9:5: "Do we not have the right to be accompanied by a wife, as the other apostles and *the brothers of the Lord* and Cephas?"

Now, how is this to be explained? On the one hand, it seems certain that Jesus' brothers did not believe in him during his lifetime. On the other hand, it's equally certain that they became ardent Christians, active in ministry. Jesus' crucifixion would only confirm in James' mind that his elder brother's messianic pretensions were delusory, just as he had thought. Many of us have brothers. What would it take to make you believe that your brother is the Lord, so that you would die for this belief, as James did? Can there be any doubt that the reason for this remarkable transformation is to be found in the fact that "then he appeared to James"? Even the skeptical New Testament critic Hans Grass admits that the conversion of James is one of the surest proofs of the resurrection of Jesus Christ.[5]

(e) *Appearance to "all the apostles."* This appearance was probably to a limited circle of Christian missionaries somewhat wider than the Twelve. For such a group, see Acts 1:21–22. Once again, the fact of this appearance is guaranteed by Paul's personal contact with the apostles themselves.

Jesus appears to James.

(f) *Appearance to Saul of Tarsus.* The final appearance is just as amazing as the appearance to James: "Last of all," says Paul, "he appeared also to me." The story of Jesus' appearance to Saul of Tarsus (or Paul) just outside Damascus is related in Acts 9:1–9 and is later told again twice. That this event actually occurred is established beyond doubt by Paul's references to it in his own letters.

This event changed Saul's whole life. He was a rabbi, a Pharisee, a respected

Jewish leader. He hated the Christian heresy and did everything in his power to stamp it out. He tells us that he was even responsible for the *execution* of Christian believers. Then suddenly he gave up everything. He left his position as a respected Jewish leader and became

a Christian missionary: he entered a life of poverty, labor, and suffering. He was whipped, beaten, stoned and left for dead, shipwrecked three times, in constant danger, deprivation, and anxiety. Finally, he made the ultimate sacrifice and was martyred for his faith at Rome. And it was all because on that day outside Damascus, he saw "Jesus our Lord" (1 Corinthians 9:1).

In summary, Paul's testimony makes it historically certain that various individuals and groups of people experienced appearances of Jesus after his death and burial, however we might want to explain these.

2. *The Gospel accounts provide multiple independent reports of post-mortem appearances of Jesus.* The Gospels independently report post-mortem appearances of Jesus, even some of the same appearances found in Paul's list. The appearance to Peter is independently mentioned by Paul and Luke (1 Corinthians 15:5; Luke 24:34) and is universally acknowledged by critics. The appearance to the Twelve is independently reported by Paul, Luke, and John (1 Corinthians 15:5; Luke 24:36–43; John 20:19–20) and is again not in dispute. The appearance to the women disciples is independently reported by Matthew and John (Matthew 28:9–10; John 20:11–17) and enjoys, as well, ratification by the criterion of embarrassment, given the low credibility accorded to the testimony of women. It's generally agreed that the absence of this appearance from the list of appearances in the tradition quoted by Paul is a reflection of the discomfort in citing female witnesses. Finally, that Jesus appeared to the disciples in Galilee is independently reported by Mark, Matthew, and John (Mark 16:7; Matthew 28:16–17; John 21).

Taken sequentially, the appearances follow the pattern of Jerusalem—Galilee—Jerusalem, matching the pilgrimages of the disciples as they returned to Galilee following the Passover/Feast of Unleavened Bread and then traveled again to Jerusalem two months later for Pentecost.

From this evidence what should we conclude? We can call these appearances hallucinations if we want to, but we cannot deny that they occurred. Even the skeptical critic Gerd Lüdemann is emphatic: "It may be taken as historically certain that Peter and the disciples had experiences after Jesus' death in which Jesus appeared to them as the risen Christ."[6] The evidence makes it certain that on separate occasions different individuals and groups had experiences of seeing Jesus alive from the dead. This conclusion is virtually indisputable.

3. *The resurrection appearances were physical, bodily appearances.* So far the evidence we've examined doesn't depend on the nature of the post-mortem appearances of Jesus. I've left it open whether they were visionary or physical in nature. It remains to be seen whether even visionary experiences of the risen Jesus can be plausibly explained on purely psychological grounds. But if the appearances were physical and bodily in nature, then a purely psychological explanation becomes next to impossible. So it is worth examining what we can know about the nature of these appearances.

(a) *Paul implies that the appearances were physical.* He does this in two ways.

First, he conceives of the resurrection body as physical. Everyone recognizes that Paul does not teach the immortality of the soul alone but the resurrection of the *body*. In 1 Corinthians 15:42–44 Paul describes the differences between the present, earthly body and our future, resurrection body, which will be like Christ's. He draws four essential contrasts between the earthly body and the resurrection body:

The earthly body is:	*But the resurrection body is:*
mortal	immortal
dishonorable	glorious
weak	powerful
natural	spiritual

Now only the last contrast could possibly make us think that Paul did not believe in a physical resurrection body. But what does he mean by the words translated here as "natural/spiritual"?

The word translated "natural" literally means "soul-ish." Now obviously, Paul doesn't mean that our present body is made out of soul. Rather by this word he means "dominated by or pertaining to human nature." Similarly, when he says the resurrection body will be "spiritual," he doesn't mean "made out of spirit." Rather, he means "dominated by or oriented toward the Spirit." It's the same sense of the word "spiritual" as when we say that someone is a spiritual person.

In fact, look at the way Paul uses exactly those same words in 1 Corinthians 2:14–15:

> The natural man does not receive the gifts of the Spirit of God, for they are folly to him, and he is not able to understand them, because they are spiritually discerned. The spiritual man judges all things but is himself to be judged by no one. (author translation)

Natural man does not mean "physical, visible man," but "man oriented toward human nature." And *spiritual man* does not mean "intangible, invisible man" but "man oriented toward the Spirit." The contrast is the same in 1 Corinthians 15. The present, earthly body will be freed from its slavery to sinful human nature and become instead fully empowered and directed by God's Spirit. Thus, Paul's doctrine of the resurrection body implies a physical resurrection.

Second, Paul, and indeed all the New Testament, makes a distinction between an *appearance* of Jesus and a *vision* of Jesus. The appearances of Jesus soon ceased, but visions of Jesus continued in the early church.

NATURAL AND SPIRITUAL

In 1 Corinthians 15:44, the Greek word translated as "natural" in NIV, NKJV, KJV, and NASB is *psychikos*, or "soul-ish," from the word *psyche*, or "soul." The word translated as "spiritual" is *pneumatikos*. Paul is not talking of physical vs. ethereal bodies, but of soul-led vs. Spirit-led bodies. This is clear when we look at 1 Corinthians 2:14, where Paul uses the same words, *psychikos* and *pneumatikos*, to describe different sorts of people in Corinth. The contrast is not one of materiality but of orientation.

ON GUARD FOR STUDENTS

Now the question is: What is the difference between an appearance and a vision? The answer of the New Testament seems to be clear: a vision, though caused by God, was purely in the mind, while an appearance took place "out there" in the external world.

Compare Stephen's vision of Jesus in Acts 7 with the resurrection appearances of Jesus. Though Stephen saw an identifiable, bodily image, what he saw was a vision of a man, not a man who was physically there, for no one else present experienced anything at all. By contrast the resurrection appearances took place in the world "out there" and could be experienced by anybody present. Paul could rightly regard his experience on the Damascus Road as an appearance, even though it took place after Jesus' ascension, because it involved manifestations in the external world like the light and the voice, which Paul's companions also experienced to varying degrees. Thus, the distinction between a vision and an appearance of Jesus also implies that the resurrection appearances were physical.

(b) *The Gospel accounts show that the appearances were physical and bodily.* Again, two points deserve to be made.

First, every resurrection appearance related in the Gospels is a physical, bodily appearance. The unanimous testimony of the Gospels in this regard is quite impressive. If *none* of the appearances was originally a physical, bodily appearance, then it's very strange that we have a completely unanimous testimony in the Gospels that *all* of them were physical, with no trace of the supposed original, nonphysical appearances. Such a thorough-going corruption of oral tradition in so short a time, while the original eyewitnesses were still about, is most unlikely.

Second, if all the appearances were originally nonphysical visions, then we're at a complete loss to explain the rise of the Gospel accounts. For physical, bodily appearances would be foolishness to Gentiles and a stumbling block to Jews, since neither could accept physical resurrection from the dead, but both would have been quite happy to accept visionary appearances of the deceased.

"But he's alive spiritually!
He appeared to me in a vision!
Mary saw him too — didn't you,
Mary — tell them!"

To be perfectly candid, the only grounds for denying the physical, bodily nature of the post-mortem appearances of Jesus is philosophical, not historical: such appearances would be miracles of the most stupendous proportions, and that many critics cannot swallow. But in that case we need to retrace our steps to think again about the evidence for the existence of God. If God exists, there's no good reason to be skeptical about miracles. As the agnostic Australian philosopher Peter Slezak nicely put it in our debate, for a God who is able to create the entire universe, the odd resurrection would be child's play! Most New Testament critics are unfortunately untrained in philosophy and are, hence, naïve when it comes to these issues.

So on the basis of these three lines of evidence, we can conclude that the fact of Jesus' post-mortem appearances to various individuals and groups under a variety of

TALK ABOUT IT

Why does Jesus' bodily resurrection matter to Christians? What difference would it make if Jesus simply lives on as a spirit and has no body?

circumstances is firmly established historically and, moreover, that these appearances were bodily and physical.

The Fact of the Origin of the Christian Faith

The third fact to be explained is the very origin of the Christian faith. We all know that Christianity sprang into being sometime midway through the first century after Christ. Why did it come into existence? What caused this movement to begin? Even skeptical New Testament scholars recognize that the Christian faith owes its origin to the belief of the earliest disciples that God had raised Jesus of Nazareth from the dead. In fact, they pinned nearly everything on this belief.

To take just one example: their belief that Jesus was the Messiah. Jews had no conception of a Messiah who, instead of triumphing over Israel's enemies, would be shamefully executed by them as a criminal. Messiah was supposed to be a triumphant figure who would command the respect of Jew and Gentile alike and who would establish the throne of David in Jerusalem.

A Messiah who failed to deliver and to reign, who was defeated, humiliated, and slain by his enemies, is a contradiction in terms. Nowhere do Jewish texts speak of such a "Messiah." Therefore, it's difficult to overemphasize what a disaster the crucifixion was for the disciples' faith. Jesus' death on the cross spelled the humiliating end for any hopes they had entertained that he was the Messiah.

TALK ABOUT IT

Which of the lines of evidence in this chapter do you find most convincing personally? How do you think non-Christians you know would respond to the various lines of evidence? Which would be most compelling for them?

But the belief in the resurrection of Jesus reversed the catastrophe of the crucifixion. Because God had raised Jesus from the dead, he was seen to be Messiah after all. Thus, Peter proclaims in Acts 2:23–24, 36: "This man ... God raised ... again ... let all the house of Israel know for certain that God has made him both Lord and Messiah—this Jesus whom you crucified" (author's adaptation of NASB). It was on the basis of belief in his resurrection that the disciples could believe that Jesus was the Messiah.

It's no surprise, therefore, that belief in Jesus' resurrection was universal in the early Christian church. The traditional formula quoted in 1 Corinthians 15:3–7, in which the Gospel is defined as the death, burial, resurrection, and appearances of Christ, shows that this understanding of the Gospel goes right back to the very beginning of the church in Jerusalem.

Thus, the origin of Christianity hinges on the belief of the earliest disciples that God had raised Jesus from the dead. But the question is: How does one explain the origin of that belief? As R. H. Fuller says, even the most skeptical critic must posit some mysterious X to get the movement going.[7] But what was that X?

Summary

Now we're ready to summarize all three of our points:

First, we saw that numerous lines of historical evidence indicate that the tomb of Jesus was found empty by a group of his women followers.

Second, we saw that several lines of historical evidence establish that on numerous occasions and in different places various individuals and groups saw appearances of Jesus alive from the dead.

And finally, we saw that the very origin of the Christian faith depends on the belief of the earliest disciples that God had raised Jesus of Nazareth from the dead.

One of the things that most astonished me after completing my doctoral research on Jesus' resurrection at the University of Munich was the realization that these three great, independently established facts represent *the majority view* of New Testament critics today. The only point of serious disagreement would be on the physical nature of the resurrection appearances. But the state of current scholarship strongly supports the three facts as I have stated them.

These are not the conclusions of conservative or evangelical scholarship; these are the conclusions of mainstream New Testament criticism. As we saw, three-quarters of scholars who have written on the subject accept the fact of the empty tomb; virtually no one today denies that the earliest disciples experienced post-mortem appearances of Jesus; and far and away most scholars agree that the earliest disciples at least believed that God had raised Jesus from the dead. It is the critic who would deny these facts that today finds himself on the defensive.

It's worth noticing that the historicity of these three facts is not affected by inconsistencies in the circumstantial details of the Gospel accounts. The three facts are well-established even given conflicts in the secondary details. Historians expect to find inconsistencies even in the most reliable sources. No historian simply throws out a source because it has inconsistencies. Otherwise we'd have to be skeptical about all secular historical narratives which also contain such inconsistencies, which is wholly unreasonable. Moreover, in the case of the four Gospels the inconsistencies aren't even within a single source; they're between independent sources. But obviously, it doesn't follow from an inconsistency between two independent sources that both sources are wrong. At worst, one is wrong if they can't be harmonized. Minor discrepancies in the narratives thus don't affect the historicity of the three facts as I have stated them.

Actually, the Gospels are largely consistent. All four Gospels agree that:

> Jesus of Nazareth was crucified in Jerusalem by Roman authority during the Passover Feast, having been arrested and convicted on charges of blasphemy by the Jewish Sanhedrin and then slandered before the governor Pilate on charges of treason. He died within several hours and was buried Friday afternoon by Joseph of Arimathea in a tomb, which was shut with a stone. Certain women followers of Jesus, including Mary Magdalene, having observed his interment, visited his tomb early on Sunday morning, only to find it empty. Thereafter, Jesus appeared alive from the dead to the disciples, including Peter, who then became proclaimers of the message of his resurrection.

All four Gospels attest to these facts. Many more details can be supplied by adding facts which are attested by three out of four.

The remaining question, then, is how the three established facts I've stated are best explained.

Explaining the Evidence

We come, then, to the second step: determining which explanation of the evidence is the best. Historians weigh various factors in assessing competing hypotheses. Some of the most important are as follows:[8]

> 1. The best explanation will have greater *explanatory scope* than other explanations. That is, it will explain more of the evidence.

2. The best explanation will have greater *explanatory power* than other explanations. That is, it will make the evidence more probable.

3. The best explanation will be *more plausible* than other explanations. That is, it will fit better with true background beliefs.

4. The best explanation will be less *contrived* than other explanations. That is, it won't require adopting as many new beliefs which have no independent evidence.

5. The best explanation will be *disconfirmed by fewer accepted beliefs* than other explanations. That is, it won't conflict with as many accepted beliefs.

6. The best explanation will meet conditions 1–5 so much better than the others that there's little chance that one of the other explanations, after further investigation, will do better in meeting these conditions.

Since a hypothesis may do really well in meeting some conditions but not so well in meeting others, figuring out which hypothesis is the best explanation may often be difficult and requires skill. But if the explanatory scope and power of a hypothesis are very great, so that it does a much better job in explaining a wide variety of facts, then it's likely to be the true explanation.

So let's apply these tests to the typical hypotheses which have been offered down through history to explain the empty tomb, post-mortem appearances, and origin of the disciples' belief in Jesus' resurrection, and let's see if they do better or as well in explaining these facts as the Resurrection Hypothesis.

Conspiracy Hypothesis

According to this hypothesis, the disciples stole the body of Jesus and lied about his appearances, thus faking the resurrection. This was the very first counter-explanation for the empty tomb, as we've seen, and it was revived during the eighteenth century by European deists. Today, however, this explanation has been completely given up by modern scholarship. We can see why when we assess it by the standard criteria for testing historical hypotheses.

1. *Explanatory scope.* The Conspiracy Hypothesis does seem to cover the full scope of the evidence, for it offers explanations of the empty tomb (the disciples stole the body), the post-mortem appearances (the disciples lied about seeing Jesus), and the origin of the disciples' (supposed) belief in Jesus' resurrection (again, they lied).

2. *Explanatory power.* How probable is the evidence, given the Conspiracy Hypothesis? Here doubts begin to arise about the adequacy of the hypothesis.

First, consider the story of the empty tomb. If the disciples stole Jesus' corpse, then it would be utterly pointless to fabricate a story about *women* finding the tomb to be empty. Such a story would not be the sort of tale Jewish men would invent. Moreover, the simplicity of the story is not what one would expect given the Conspiracy Hypothesis—where are the scriptural proof-texts, the evidence of fulfilled prophecy? Why isn't Jesus described as emerging from the tomb, as in later forgeries like the Gospel of Peter? Neither is the dispute with nonbelieving Jews well-explained. Why isn't Matthew's guard already there in Mark's story? Even in Matthew's story the guard is set too late: the body could have already been stolen before the guard arrived on Saturday morning, so that they were guarding, unbeknownst to them, an empty tomb! For a fail-safe alibi against theft of the body, see again the forged Gospel of Peter, where the guard is set immediately upon interment of the corpse.

As for the appearance stories, similar problems arise. A fabricator would probably describe Jesus' resurrection appearances in terms of Old Testament visions of God and descriptions of the end-time resurrection (as in Daniel 12:2). But then Jesus should appear to the disciples in dazzling glory. And why not a description of the resurrection itself? Why no appearances to Caiaphas the high priest or to the villains on the Sanhedrin, as Jesus predicted? They could be then branded as the real liars for denying that Jesus did appear to them!

"Okay, so here's the plan: We get the body out of the tomb and stash it somewhere, and then we come back and tell a story that will probably get us all killed. So who's with me on this?"

But the explanatory power of the Conspiracy Hypothesis is undoubtedly weakest when it comes to the origin of the disciples' belief in Jesus' resurrection. For the hypothesis is really a denial of that fact; it seeks to explain the mere semblance of belief on the disciples' part. But as critics have universally recognized, you can't plausibly deny that the earliest disciples at least sincerely *believed* that Jesus was risen from the dead. They staked their very lives on that conviction. The transformation in the lives of the disciples is not credibly explained by the hypothesis of a conspiracy. This shortcoming alone has been enough in the minds of most scholars to sink the old Conspiracy Hypothesis forever.

3. *Plausibility*. The real Achilles' heel of the Conspiracy Hypothesis is, however, its implausibility. One might mention here objections to the unbelievable complexity of such a conspiracy or the supposed psychological state of the disciples; but the overriding problem that dwarfs all others is that it

is wholly anachronistic to suppose that first-century Jews intended to hoax Jesus' resurrection. The Conspiracy Hypothesis views the disciples' situation through the rearview mirror of Christian history rather than through the eyes of a first-century Jew.

In the first place, there was no expectation in Judaism of a Messiah who, instead of establishing David's throne and subduing Israel's enemies, would be shamefully executed by the Gentiles as a criminal. Moreover, the Jewish idea of resurrection was just unconnected with the idea of Messiah and even incompatible with it, since Messiah was not supposed to be killed. As N. T. Wright nicely puts it, if you're a first-century Jew, and your favorite Messiah got himself crucified, then you've basically got two choices: either you go home or else you get yourself a new Messiah.

Secondly, the Jewish conception of resurrection of the dead differed in at least two fundamental respects from the resurrection of Jesus.

First, in Jewish thinking the resurrection to glory and immortality always occurred *after* the end of the world. Jews had no idea of a resurrection within history. That's why, I think, the disciples had so much trouble understanding Jesus' predictions of his own resurrection. They thought he was talking about the resurrection at the end of the world. Look at Mark 9:9–11, for example:

> As they were coming down from the mountain, He gave them orders not to relate to anyone what they had seen, until the Son of Man rose from the dead. They seized upon that statement, discussing with one another what rising from the dead meant. They asked Him, saying, "Why is it that the scribes say that Elijah must come first?" (NASB)

Here Jesus predicts his resurrection, and what do the disciples ask? "Why is it that the scribes say that Elijah must come first?" In first-century Judaism it was believed the prophet Elijah would come again before the great and terrible Day of the Lord, the judgment day when the dead would be raised.

The disciples could not understand the idea of a resurrection occurring within history prior to the end of the world. Hence, Jesus' predictions only confused them.

Thus, given the Jewish conception of the resurrection, the disciples after Jesus' crucifixion would not have come up with the strange idea that he had been already raised. They would in all probability have looked forward to the resurrection at the last day and, in keeping with Jewish custom, perhaps preserved his tomb as a shrine where his bones could rest until the resurrection.

Second, in Jewish thinking the resurrection was always the resurrection of *all* the righteous dead. Jews had no idea of the resurrection of an isolated individual apart from the general resurrection. Moreover, there was simply no connection between the individual believer's resurrection and the prior resurrection of the Messiah. That's why we find no examples of other failed messianic movements claiming that their executed leader was risen from the dead. Wright has been insistent upon this point. "All the followers of those first century messianic movements were fanatically committed to the cause.... But in no case right across the century before Jesus and the century after him do we hear of any Jewish group saying that their executed leader had been raised from the dead, and he really was the Messiah after all."[9]

First-century Jews had no idea of the resurrection of an isolated individual, especially of the Messiah, in advance of the general resurrection at the end of the world. So the idea of stealing Jesus' corpse and saying that God had raised him from the dead is hardly one that would have entered the minds of these Jewish disciples of Jesus nor seemed to them a plausible strategy for evangelizing their fellow Jews!

> **TALK ABOUT IT**
>
> How does this historical background help you understand incidents such as those described in Mark 8:31–32 and Acts 17:16–18, 32?

But what about influences from outside Judaism? A suggestion widespread on the Internet today is that early Christians came up with the idea of

Jesus' resurrection through the influence of pagan mythology. This suggestion is an old one. Back around the turn of the nineteenth to the twentieth century, scholars in comparative religion collected parallels to Christian beliefs in other religious movements, and some even thought to explain Christian beliefs, including the belief in Jesus' resurrection, as the result of the influence of such myths. The movement soon collapsed, however, principally due to two factors:

First, scholars came to realize that the parallels are false. The ancient world was a virtual fruit basket of myths of various gods and heroes. Comparative studies in religion require sensitivity to their similarities and differences, or distortion and confusion inevitably result. Unfortunately, those who were eager to find parallels to Jesus' resurrection failed to exercise such sensitivity.

Many of the alleged parallels are actually stories of the *assumption* of the hero into heaven (Hercules, Romulus). Others are *disappearance* stories, which claim that the hero has vanished into a higher sphere (Apollonius of Tyana, Empedocles). Still others are *seasonal symbols* for the crop cycle, as the vegetation dies in the dry season and comes back to life in the rainy season (Tammuz, Osiris, Adonis). Some are *political expressions* of emperor worship (Julius Caesar, Caesar Augustus).

None of these ideas is parallel to the Jewish idea of the resurrection of the dead. Indeed, most scholars have come to doubt whether, properly speaking, there really were *any* myths of dying and rising gods at all. For example, in the myth of Osiris, which was one of the best-known symbolic seasonal myths, Osiris doesn't really come back to life but simply continues to exist in the realm of the dead.

Scholars have come to realize that pagan mythology is simply the wrong interpretive context for understanding Jesus of Nazareth. Jesus and his disciples were first-century Israelite Jews, and it is against that background that they must be understood. The collapse of the alleged parallels is just one indication that pagan mythology is the wrong interpretive context for understanding the disciples' belief in Jesus' resurrection.

Second, there is in any case no causal connection between the pagan myths and the origin of the disciples' belief in Jesus' resurrection. Jews were familiar with the seasonal pagan deities (Ezekiel 8:14–15) and found them abhorrent. That's why there is no trace of cults of dying and rising gods at all in first-century Israel. It's pretty unlikely that the original disciples would have come up with the idea that Jesus of Nazareth was risen from the dead because they had heard pagan myths about dying and rising seasonal deities. So scholars have universally abandoned this approach. Internet skeptics are more than a hundred years out of date.

Notice that this criticism undermines not only conspiracy theories, which suppose that the disciples *insincerely* proclaimed Jesus' resurrection, but also any theory which suggests that, on the basis of pagan or Jewish influences, they *sincerely* came to believe in and preached his resurrection.

4. *Less contrived.* Like all conspiracy theories of history, the Conspiracy Hypothesis is contrived in supposing that what all the evidence seems to point to is, in fact, mere appearance only, to be explained away by hypotheses for which there is no evidence. Specifically, it postulates motives and ideas in the minds of the earliest disciples and actions on their part for which there is not a shred of evidence. It can become even more contrived, as hypotheses have to be multiplied to deal with objections to the theory, for example, how to account for the appearance to the five hundred brethren or the women's role in the empty tomb and appearance stories.

5. *Disconfirmed by fewer accepted beliefs.* The Conspiracy Hypothesis tends to be disconfirmed by our general knowledge of conspiracies, their instability and tendency to unravel. Moreover, it is disconfirmed by accepted beliefs such as the sincerity of the disciples, the nature of first-century Jewish messianic expectations, and so on.

6. *Exceeds other hypotheses in fulfilling conditions 1–5.* This condition is obviously not met, since there are better hypotheses (such as the Hallucination Hypothesis), which don't dismiss the disciples' belief in Jesus' resurrection as a blatant lie.

No scholar would defend the Conspiracy Hypothesis today. The only place you read about such things is in the popular, sensationalist press or on the Internet.

Apparent Death Hypothesis

A second explanation was the Apparent Death Hypothesis. Critics around the beginning of the nineteenth century claimed that Jesus was not completely dead when he was taken down from the cross. He revived in the tomb and escaped to convince his disciples he had risen from the dead.

Today this hypothesis has also been almost completely given up. Once again, let's apply our criteria for the best explanation:

1. *Explanatory scope.* The Apparent Death Hypothesis also provides explanations for the empty tomb, post-mortem appearances, and origin of the disciples' belief in Jesus' resurrection.

2. *Explanatory power.* Here the theory begins to founder. Some versions of the Apparent Death Hypothesis were really variations on the Conspiracy Hypothesis. Instead of stealing the body, the disciples (along with Jesus himself!) were supposed to have conspired to fake Jesus' death on the cross. In such cases, the theory shares all the weaknesses of the Conspiracy Hypothesis. A nonconspiratorial version of the theory was that Jesus just happened to survive the crucifixion, though the guards thought he was dead. Such a version of the hypothesis is also saddled with insurmountable difficulties: How do you explain the empty tomb, since a man sealed inside a tomb could not move the stone so as to escape? How do you explain the post-mortem appearances, since the appearance of a half-dead man desperately in need of medical attention would hardly have elicited in the disciples the conclusion that he was the Risen Lord and conqueror of Death? How do you explain the origin of the disciples' belief in Jesus' resurrection, since seeing him again would lead them to conclude only that he had not died, not that he was, contrary to Jewish thought (as well as their own eyes), gloriously risen from the dead?

3. *Plausibility.* Here again the theory fails miserably. Roman executioners could be relied upon to ensure that their victims were dead. Since the exact moment of death by crucifixion is uncertain, executioners could ensure death by a spear thrust into the victim's side. This is what happened to Jesus (John 19:34). Moreover, what the theory suggests is virtually physically impossible. The Jewish historian Josephus tells of how he had three acquaintances who had been crucified removed from their crosses, but despite the best medical attention, two of the three died anyway (*Life* 75:420–21). The extent of Jesus' tortures was such that he could never have survived the crucifixion and entombment. The suggestion that a man so critically wounded then went on to appear to the disciples on various occasions in Jerusalem and Galilee is pure fantasy.

4. *Less contrived.* The Apparent Death Hypothesis, especially in its conspiratorial versions, can become enormously contrived. We're invited to imagine secret societies, stealthily administered potions, conspiratorial alliances between Jesus' disciples and members of the Sanhedrin, and so forth, all with not a scrap of evidence in support.

5. *Disconfirmed by fewer accepted beliefs.* The Apparent Death Hypothesis is massively disconfirmed by medical facts concerning what would happen to a person who has been scourged and crucified. It is also disconfirmed by the unanimous evidence that Jesus did not continue among his disciples after his death.

6. *Exceeds other hypotheses in fulfilling conditions 1–5.* This theory also is hardly a standout! For that reason it has virtually no defenders among New Testament historians today.

Displaced Body Hypothesis

In one of the few modern Jewish attempts to deal with the facts concerning Jesus' resurrection, Joseph Klausner in 1922 proposed that Joseph of Arimathea placed Jesus' body in his tomb temporarily, due to the lateness of the hour and the closeness of his own family tomb to the place of Jesus' execution. But then he moved the corpse later to the criminals' common graveyard. Unaware of the displacement of the body, the disciples upon finding the tomb empty inferred that Jesus was risen from the dead. Although no scholars defend Klausner's hypothesis today, I have seen attempts by popular authors to revive it. In light of what has already been said of other theories, its shortcomings are evident:

1. *Explanatory scope.* The Displaced Body Hypothesis has narrow explanatory scope. It tries to explain the empty tomb but says nothing about the post-mortem appearances and the origin of the disciples' belief in Jesus' resurrection. Independent hypotheses must be adopted to explain the full scope of the evidence.

2. *Explanatory power.* Klausner's hypothesis has no explanatory power with regard to either the appearances or the origin of the Christian faith. As for the empty tomb, the hypothesis faces an obvious problem: since Joseph and any servants with him knew what they had done with the corpse, the theory is at a loss to explain why the disciples' error wasn't corrected once they began to proclaim Jesus' resurrection—unless, that is, one resorts to contrived conjectures to save the day, such as Joseph and his servants' sudden deaths!

It might be said that Jesus' corpse would have no longer been identifiable. That is, in fact, not true. Jewish burial practices typically involved digging up the bones of the deceased a year later and placing them in an ossuary. So gravesites, even for criminals, were carefully noted. But, in any case, the objection misses the point. The point is that the earliest Jewish/Christian disputes about Jesus' resurrection were not over the location of Jesus' grave or the identity of the corpse but over why the tomb was empty. Had Joseph displaced the body, the Jewish/Christian controversy would have taken a quite different course.

3. *Plausibility.* The hypothesis is implausible for a number of reasons. So far as we can rely on Jewish sources, the criminals' graveyard was only fifty to six hundred yards from the site of Jesus' crucifixion. Jewish practice,

furthermore, was to bury executed criminals on the day of their execution, so that's what Joseph would have wanted to accomplish. Therefore, Joseph could and would have placed the body directly in the criminals' graveyard, thereby eliminating any need to move it later or defile his own family tomb. Indeed, Jewish law did not even *permit* the body to be moved later, except to the family tomb. Joseph had adequate time for a simple burial, which probably included washing the corpse and wrapping it up in a sheet with dry spices.

4. *Less contrived.* The theory is mildly contrived in ascribing to Joseph motives and activities for which we have no evidence at all. It becomes really contrived if we have to start inventing things like Joseph's sudden death in order to save the hypothesis.

5. *Disconfirmed by fewer accepted beliefs.* The theory suffers disconfirmation from what we know about Jewish burial procedures for criminals mentioned above.

6. *Exceeds other hypotheses in fulfilling conditions 1–5.* Again, no historian seems to share this estimation.

Hallucination Hypothesis

In his book *The Life of Jesus, Critically Examined* (1835), David Strauss proposed that the resurrection appearances were merely hallucinations on the part of the disciples. The most prominent defender of this view today is the German New Testament critic Gerd Lüdemann. How does the Hallucination Hypothesis fare when assessed by our criteria?

1. *Explanatory scope.* The Hallucination Hypothesis has narrow explanatory scope. First, it says nothing to explain the empty tomb. Therefore, one must either deny the fact of the empty tomb (and, therefore, the burial as well) or else conjoin some *independent* hypothesis to the Hallucination Hypothesis to account for the empty tomb.

Again, the Hallucination Hypothesis says nothing to explain the origin of the disciples' belief in Jesus' resurrection. Simply postulating post-mortem visions of Jesus on the part of the disciples does not explain why they believed that he was risen from the dead. In order to increase the plausibility of the Hallucination Hypothesis, some scholars have made a great deal out of the alleged similarities between the post-mortem appearances of Jesus and visions of recently departed loved ones on the part of the bereaved. But the overriding lesson of such intriguing stories is that the bereaved do *not* as a result of such experiences, however real and tangible they may seem, conclude that the deceased has returned physically to life—rather the deceased is seen in the afterlife. As Wright observes, for someone in the ancient world, visions of the deceased are not evidence that the person is alive, but evidence that he is dead!

Moreover, in a Jewish context other, more appropriate interpretations of such experiences than resurrection are close to hand. Given the current Jewish beliefs about life after death, the disciples, if they were to project hallucinations of Jesus, would have seen Jesus in heaven or in glory, where the souls of the righteous dead were believed to abide until the final resurrection. And such visions would not have led to belief in Jesus' resurrection. At the most, they would have only led the disciples to say that Jesus had been assumed into heaven, not raised from the dead.

In the Old Testament, figures such as Enoch and Elijah were portrayed as not having died but as having been taken directly into heaven. In an extrabiblical Jewish writing called *The Testament of Job* (40), the story is told of two children killed in the collapse of a house. When the rescuers clear away the rubble, the bodies of the children are nowhere to be found. Meanwhile, their mother sees a vision of the two children glorified in heaven, where they have been taken up by God. It needs to be emphasized that for a Jew an assumption into heaven is not the same as a resurrection. Assumption is the taking of someone bodily out of this world into heaven. Resurrection is the raising up of a dead man in the space-time universe. They are distinct ideas.

Given Jewish beliefs concerning assumption and resurrection, the disciples, having seen heavenly visions of Jesus, would not have preached that Jesus had been raised from the dead. At the very most, the empty tomb and hallucinations of Jesus would have caused them to believe in the assumption of Jesus into glory, for this was consistent with their Jewish frame of thought. But they wouldn't have come to believe that Jesus had been raised from the dead, for this contradicted Jewish beliefs about the resurrection of the dead, as we've seen in our discussion of the Conspiracy Hypothesis. Thus, even given hallucinations, belief in Jesus' resurrection remains unexplained. The Hallucination Hypothesis therefore has unacceptably narrow explanatory scope.

2. Explanatory power. The Hallucination Hypothesis does nothing to explain the empty tomb and the origin of the disciples' belief in Jesus' resurrection. But what about the appearances? It arguably has weak explanatory power even when it comes to the appearances.

Suppose that Peter was one of those individuals who experiences a vision of a deceased loved one or experienced a guilt-induced vision, as Lüdemann imagines. Would this suffice to explain the resurrection appearances? Not really, for the diversity of the appearances bursts the bounds of anything found in the psychological casebooks. Jesus appeared not just one

ASSUMPTION AND RESURRECTION

Resurrection is the raising up of a dead man in the space-time universe to glory and immortality. *Assumption* is the taking of someone bodily out of this world into heaven. *Revivification* is the return of a dead man to the mortal life. Second Kings 2:1–12 describes the assumption of Elijah into heaven. John 11:1–44 describes the revivification of Lazarus by Jesus. Note the differences between the two events and Jesus' resurrection.

time, but many times; not at just one locale and circumstance, but at a variety of places and under a variety of circumstances; not to just one individual, but to different persons; not just to individuals, but to various groups; not just to believers, but to unbelievers and even enemies. Positing a chain reaction among the disciples won't solve the problem because people like James and Paul don't stand in the chain. Those who would explain the resurrection appearances psychologically are compelled to construct a composite picture by cobbling together different unrelated cases of hallucinatory experiences, which only serves to underline the fact that there's nothing like the resurrection appearances in the psychological casebooks.

3. *Plausibility*. Lüdemann attempts to make his Hallucination Hypothesis plausible by a psychoanalysis of Peter and Paul. He believes they both labored under guilt complexes which found release in hallucinations of Jesus. But Lüdemann's psychoanalysis is implausible for three reasons: *First*, Lüdemann's use of depth psychology is based upon certain theories of Jung and Freud which are highly disputed. *Second*, there is insufficient data to do a psychoanalysis of Peter and Paul. Psychoanalysis is difficult enough to carry out even with patients on the psychoanalyst's couch, so to speak, but it's next to impossible with historical figures. For that reason historians reject any attempt to write psychobiographies of deceased historical figures. Finally, *third*, the evidence we do have suggests that Paul did *not* struggle with a guilt complex as Lüdemann supposes.

Nearly fifty years ago the Swedish scholar Krister Stendahl pointed out that Western readers have tended to interpret Paul in light of Martin Luther's struggles with guilt and sin. But Paul (or Saul) the Pharisee experienced no such struggle. Stendahl writes:

> Contrast Paul, a very happy and successful Jew, one who can say "As to righteousness under the Law (I was) blameless" ([Philippians] 3.6). That *is* what he says. He experiences no troubles, no problems, no qualms of conscience. He is

a star pupil, the student to get the thousand dollar graduate scholarship in Gamaliel's Seminary.... Nowhere in Paul's writings is there any indication ... that psychologically Paul had some problem of conscience.[10]

In order to justify his portrait of a guilt-ridden Paul, Lüdemann is forced to interpret Romans 7 in terms of Paul's pre-Christian experience. But this interpretation is rejected by almost all commentators since the late 1920s. So Lüdemann's psychoanalysis is positively implausible.

A second respect in which the Hallucination Hypothesis is implausible is its taking the appearances to be merely visionary experiences. Lüdemann recognizes that the Hallucination Hypothesis depends on the presupposition that what Paul experienced on the Damascus Road was the same as what all the *other* disciples experienced. But this presupposition is groundless. In including himself in the list of eyewitnesses to Christ's resurrection appearances, Paul is in no way implying that they were all just like the appearance to him. Many of Paul's opponents in Corinth denied that he was a true apostle, so Paul is anxious to include himself along with the other apostles who had seen Christ. Paul is trying to bring his experience up to the objectivity and reality of theirs, not to pull their experience down to merely visionary experiences.

So the Hallucination Hypothesis suffers from implausibility with respect to its psychoanalysis of the witnesses and its blanket reduction of the appearances to visionary experiences.

4. *Less contrived.* Lüdemann's version of the Hallucination Hypothesis is contrived in a number of ways: for example, it assumes that the disciples fled back to Galilee after Jesus' arrest, that Peter was so obsessed with guilt that he projected a hallucination of Jesus, that the other disciples were also prone to hallucinations, and that Paul had a struggle with the Jewish law and a secret attraction to Christianity.

5. *Disconfirmed by fewer accepted beliefs.* Some of the accepted beliefs of New Testament scholars today tend to disconfirm the Hallucination Hypothesis, at

TALK ABOUT IT

Why do you suppose the Hallucination Hypothesis is today the most prominent hypothesis among those who deny Jesus' resurrection?

least as Lüdemann presents it: for example, the beliefs that Jesus received an honorable burial by Joseph of Arimathea, that Jesus' tomb was discovered empty by women, that psychoanalysis of historical figures is not feasible, that Paul was basically content with his life under the Jewish law, and that the New Testament makes a distinction between a mere vision and a resurrection appearance.

6. *Exceeds other hypotheses in fulfilling conditions 1–5.* The Hallucination Hypothesis remains a live option today and in that respect has outstripped its rivals. But the question is whether it outstrips the Resurrection Hypothesis.

The Resurrection Hypothesis

We've seen how poorly the typical explanations of the empty tomb, the post-mortem appearances, and the origin of the disciples' faith fare when assessed by standard criteria for testing historical hypotheses. They're especially weak when it comes to explanatory scope and power and are often highly implausible.

But does the Resurrection Hypothesis do any better at explaining the evidence? Is it a better explanation than the implausible naturalistic explanations offered in the past? In order to answer these questions, let's apply our same criteria to the hypothesis that "God raised Jesus from the dead."

1. *Explanatory scope.* The Resurrection Hypothesis, we've seen, has greater explanatory scope than explanations like the Hallucination Hypothesis or the Displaced Body Hypothesis precisely by explaining all three of the main facts at issue, whereas these rival hypotheses explain at most one.

2. *Explanatory power.* This is perhaps the greatest strength of the Resurrection Hypothesis. The Conspiracy Hypothesis and the Apparent Death Hypothesis just do not convincingly account for the empty tomb, resurrection appearances, or origin of the Christian faith: on these theories the evidence

(for example, the transformation of the disciples) becomes very improbable. By contrast, on the hypothesis of Jesus' resurrection it seems extremely probable that the tomb should be empty, that the disciples should see appearances of Jesus alive, and that they should come to believe in his resurrection.

3. *Plausibility.* The plausibility of Jesus' resurrection grows exponentially once we consider it in its historical context, namely, Jesus' unparalleled life and radical personal claims, and in its philosophical context, namely, the evidence for God's existence. Once one embraces the view that God exists, the hypothesis that God would raise Jesus from the dead is no more implausible than its rivals.

4. *Less contrived.* The Resurrection Hypothesis possesses great explanatory scope and power, but some scholars have charged that it is contrived. Being contrived, you'll recall, is a matter of how many new suppositions a hypothesis must make which are not implied by existing knowledge.

So defined, however, it's hard to see why the Resurrection Hypothesis is extraordinarily contrived. It requires only one new supposition: that God exists. Surely its rival hypotheses require many new suppositions. For example, the Conspiracy Hypothesis requires us to suppose that the moral character of the disciples was defective, which is certainly not implied by already existing knowledge; the Apparent Death Hypothesis requires the supposition that the centurion's lance thrust into Jesus' side was just a superficial poke or is an unhistorical detail in the narrative, which again goes beyond existing knowledge; the Hallucination Hypothesis requires us to suppose some sort of emotional preparation of the disciples which predisposed them to project visions of Jesus alive, which is not implied by our knowledge. Such examples could be multiplied.

It should be noted, too, that scientific hypotheses regularly include the supposition of the existence of new entities, such as quarks, strings, gravitons, black holes, and the like, without those theories being characterized as contrived. Moreover, for the person who *already* believes in God, the Resurrection Hypothesis doesn't even introduce the new supposition of God's existence, since that's already implied by his existing knowledge. So the Resurrection

Hypothesis cannot be said to be contrived simply in virtue of the number of new suppositions it introduces.

If our hypothesis is contrived, then, it must be for some other reasons. Philosophers of science have found it notoriously difficult to explain what it is exactly that makes a hypothesis contrived. There seems to be an air of artificiality about a hypothesis deemed to be contrived, which can be sensed by those who are seasoned practitioners of the relevant science.

Now I think that the sense of discomfort which many people, *even Christians*, feel about appealing to God as part of an explanatory hypothesis for some phenomenon in the world is that so doing has this air of artificiality. It just seems too easy when confronted with some unexplained phenomenon to throw up one's hands and say, "God did it!" Is the hypothesis that "God raised Jesus from the dead" contrived in this sense?

I don't think so. A supernatural explanation of the empty tomb, the resurrection appearances, and the origin of the Christian faith is not contrived given the context of Jesus' own unparalleled life, ministry, and personal claims. A supernatural hypothesis readily fits into such a context. It's also precisely because of this historical context that the Resurrection Hypothesis does not seem contrived when compared to miraculous explanations of other sorts: for example, that a "psychological miracle" occurred, causing normal men and women to become conspirators and liars who would be willingly martyred for their lies; or that a "biological miracle" occurred, which prevented Jesus' dying on the cross (despite the spear thrust through his chest, and so forth). It is *these* miraculous hypotheses which strike us as artificial and contrived, not the Resurrection Hypothesis, which makes abundantly good sense in the context of Jesus' ministry and radical personal claims. Thus, it seems to me that the Resurrection Hypothesis cannot be characterized as excessively contrived.

5. *Disconfirmed by fewer accepted beliefs.* I can't think of any accepted beliefs which disconfirm the Resurrection Hypothesis—unless one thinks of, say, "Dead men do not rise" as disconfirmatory. But this generalization does nothing to disconfirm the hypothesis that *God* raised Jesus from the dead.

We may consistently believe *both* that men do not rise naturally from the dead *and* that God raised Jesus from the dead. By contrast, rival theories are disconfirmed by accepted beliefs about, for example, the instability of conspiracies, the likelihood of death as a result of crucifixion, the psychological characteristics of hallucinatory experiences, and so forth, as we have seen.

6. *Exceeds other hypotheses in fulfilling conditions 1–5.* There's certainly little chance of any of the rival hypotheses' ever exceeding the Resurrection Hypothesis in fulfilling the above conditions. The bewilderment of contemporary scholarship when confronted with the facts of the empty tomb, the resurrection appearances, and the origin of the Christian faith suggests that no better rival is anywhere on the horizon. Once you give up the prejudice against miracles, it's hard to deny that the resurrection of Jesus is the best explanation of the facts.

Conclusion

In conclusion, therefore, three great, independently established facts—the empty tomb, the resurrection appearances, and the origin of the Christian faith—all point to the same marvelous conclusion: that God raised Jesus from the dead. Given that God exists, this conclusion cannot be barred to anyone seeking for the meaning to existence.

1. John A. T. Robinson, *The Human Face of God* (Philadelphia: Westminster, 1973), 131.
2. Jacob Kremer, *Die Osterevangelien—Geschichten um Geschichte* (Stuttgart: Katholisches Bibelwerk, 1977), 49–50.
3. Gary Habermas, "Experience of the Risen Jesus: The Foundational Historical Issue in the Early Proclamation of the Resurrection," *Dialog* 45 (2006): 292.
4. C. H. Dodd, "The Appearances of the Risen Christ: A Study in the Form Criticism of the Gospels," in *More New Testament Studies* (Manchester: University of Manchester, 1968), 128.
5   Hans Grass, *Ostergeschehen und Osterberichte*, 4th ed. (Göttingen: Vandenhoeck & Ruprecht, 1974), 80.
6. Gerd Lüdemann, *What Really Happened to Jesus?*, trans. John Bowden (Louisville, KY: Westminster John Knox, 1995), 80.
7. R. H. Fuller, *The Formation of the Resurrection Narratives* (London: SPCK, 1972), 2.
8. C. Behan McCullagh, *Justifying Historical Descriptions* (Cambridge: Cambridge University Press, 1984), 19.
9. N. T. Wright (lecture, Asbury College and Seminary, 1999).
10. Krister Stendahl, "Paul among Jews and Gentiles," in *Paul among Jews and Gentiles* (Philadelphia: Fortress, 1976), 12–13.

I. Determining the evidence to be explained

   A. Jesus' tomb was found empty by a group of his women followers on the first day of the week following his crucifixion.

      1. The historical reliability of the story of Jesus' burial supports the empty tomb.

      2. The story of Jesus' empty tomb is independently reported in very early sources.

      3. Mark's story is simple and lacks legendary development.

      4. The tomb was discovered empty by women.

      5. The earliest Jewish response to the disciples presupposes the empty tomb.

   B. Various individuals and groups on different occasions and under varying circumstances experienced appearances of Jesus alive.

      1. Paul's list of eyewitnesses to Jesus' resurrection appearances guarantees that such appearances occurred.

      2. The gospel accounts provide multiple, independent reports of post-mortem appearances of Jesus.

      3. The resurrection appearances were physical, bodily appearances.

   C. The first disciples came sincerely to believe in Jesus' resurrection despite every predisposition to the contrary.

      1. Jews had no expectation of a Messiah who instead of triumphing over Israel's enemies would be shamefully executed by them as a criminal.

      2. Jewish beliefs about the afterlife preclude anyone's rising from the dead to glory and immortality before the resurrection at the end of the world.

II. Explaining the evidence

   A. Rival explanations do not fare well when assessed by the standard criteria for the best explanation, such as explanatory scope, explanatory power, plausibility, being contrived, disconfirmation by accepted beliefs, and outstripping its rivals in meeting these criteria.

1. Conspiracy theory
2. Apparent death theory
3. Displaced body theory
4. Hallucination theory

B. The resurrection theory when judged by these same criteria emerges as the best explanation.

CHAPTER 9

IS JESUS THE ONLY WAY TO GOD?

The Christian ideal has not been tried and found wanting.
It has been found difficult and left untried.
G. K. Chesterton, *What's Wrong with the World*

I often speak on university campuses on the existence of God. I typically present a cumulative case climaxing in Jesus' resurrection. After one of my talks at a major Canadian university, one slightly irate co-ed wrote on her comment card, "I was with you until you got to the stuff about Jesus. God is *not* the Christian God!"

This attitude is pervasive in Western culture today. Most people are happy to agree that God exists; but in our pluralistic society it has become politically incorrect to claim that God has revealed himself decisively in Jesus.

New Testament Teaching

And yet this is what the New Testament clearly teaches. Take the letters of the apostle Paul, for example. He invites his Gentile converts to recall their pre-Christian days: "Remember that you were at that time separated from Christ, alienated from the commonwealth of Israel and strangers to the covenants of promise, *having no hope and without God* in the world" (Ephesians 2:12 ESV).

It's the burden of the opening chapters of Paul's letter to the Romans to show that this desolate condition is the general situation of mankind. Paul explains that God's power and deity are made known through the created order around us, so that men are without excuse (1:20), and that God has written his moral law upon all men's hearts, so that they are morally responsible before him (2:15). Although God offers eternal life to all who will respond in an appropriate way to God's general revelation in nature and conscience (2:7), the sad fact is that rather than worship and serve their Creator, people ignore God and flout his moral law (1:21–32). The conclusion: all men are under the power of sin (3:9–12).

Worse, Paul goes on to explain that no one can redeem himself by means of righteous living (3:19–20). Fortunately, however, God has provided a means of escape: Jesus Christ has died for the sins of mankind, thereby satisfying the demands of God's justice and enabling reconciliation with God (3:21–26). By means of his atoning death, salvation is made available as a gift to be received by faith.

Perpetua was a young mother who was arrested in the early third century AD for refusing to acknowledge other gods besides Christ. She and several others were sentenced to be torn to pieces by wild animals. While in prison she wrote an account of her experience, which survives to this day.

The logic of the New Testament is clear: the *universality of sin* and the *uniqueness of Christ's atoning death* entail that there is no salvation apart from Christ. As the apostles proclaimed, "There is salvation in no one else, for there is no other name under heaven given among men by which we must be saved" (Acts 4:12).

This particularistic doctrine of salvation through Christ alone was just as scandalous in the polytheistic world of the Roman Empire as in contemporary Western culture. Early Christians were often subjected to severe persecution, torture, and death because they refused to embrace a pluralistic approach to religion and offer sacrifice to the Roman gods. In time, however, as Christianity grew and became the official religion of the Roman Empire, the scandal receded. Indeed, for medieval thinkers like Augustine and Aquinas, one of the marks of the true church was its universality. To them it seemed incredible that the great edifice of the Christian church, filling all of civilization, should be founded on a falsehood.

The Demise of the Traditional Doctrine

The demise of this doctrine came with the so-called "Expansion of Europe," that is, the three centuries of exploration and discovery from about 1450 until 1750. Through the travels and voyages of men like Marco Polo, Christopher Columbus, and Ferdinand Magellan, new civilizations and whole new worlds were discovered which knew nothing of the Christian faith. The realization that much of the world's population lay outside the bounds of Christianity had a twofold impact upon people's religious thinking.

First, it tended to relativize religious beliefs. People realized that far from being the universal religion of mankind, Christianity was largely confined to Western Europe, a corner of the globe. No particular religion, it seemed, could make a claim to universal validity; each society seemed to have its own religion suited to its peculiar needs.

Second, it made Christianity's claim to be the only way of salvation seem narrow and cruel. Enlightenment rationalists like Voltaire taunted the Christians of his day with the prospect of millions of Chinese doomed to hell for not having believed in Christ, when they had not so much as even heard of Christ.

In our own day, the influx into Western nations of immigrants from former colonies and the advances in telecommunications which have served to shrink the world to a global village have heightened our awareness of the religious diversity of mankind. As a result, religious pluralism—the view that there are many roads to God—has today become once again the conventional wisdom.

Henricus Martellus's 1489 world map showed increasing knowledge of Asia and of Africa's west coast. Soon the New World was added to such maps.

The Problem Posed by Religious Diversity

But what, exactly, is the problem posed by mankind's religious diversity? And for whom is this supposed to be a problem? When you read the literature on this issue, the recurring challenge seems to be laid at the doorstep of the person who affirms that Christ is the only way to God. Let's call this viewpoint Christian particularism. The phenomenon of religious diversity is taken to imply the truth of pluralism, and the main debate then becomes the question of which form of pluralism is the most plausible.

But why think that Christian particularism is indefensible in the face of religious diversity? What exactly seems to be the problem?

Fallacious Arguments for Pluralism

When you examine the arguments on behalf of pluralism, you'll find many of them to be almost textbook examples of logical fallacies.

Argument ad Hominem

For example, it's frequently asserted that it's arrogant and immoral to hold to any kind of religious particularism because you must then regard all persons who disagree with your own religion as mistaken.

This seems to be a textbook example of the logical fallacy known as "argument *ad hominem*," which is trying to invalidate a position by attacking the character of those who hold to it. This is a fallacy because the truth of a position is independent of the moral qualities of those who believe it. Even if all Christian particularists were arrogant and immoral, that would do nothing to prove that their view is false.

RELIGIOUS PARTICULARISM VERSUS RELIGIOUS PLURALISM

Particularism is the view that only one religion is a means of salvation. *Pluralism* is the view that many religions are means of salvation.

Recall the definitions of *formal* and *informal fallacies* from chapter 2.

Not only that, but why think that arrogance and immorality are necessary conditions of being a particularist? Suppose I've done all I can to discover the religious truth about reality and I'm convinced that Christianity is true, and so I humbly embrace Christian faith as an undeserved gift of God. Am I arrogant and immoral for believing what I sincerely think is true? What else can I do but believe it? I think it's *true*!

Finally, and even more fundamentally, this objection is a double-edged sword. For the pluralist also believes that *his* view is right and that all those adherents to particularistic religious traditions are *wrong*. Therefore, if holding to a view which many others disagree with means you're arrogant and immoral, then the pluralist himself would be convicted of arrogance and immorality.

TALK ABOUT IT

Do you think it's arrogant for a religious pluralist to believe that his view is right and all religious particularists are wrong? Explain.

Genetic Fallacy

Or to take another objection, it's frequently alleged that Christian particularism can't be correct because religious beliefs are culturally relative. For example, if you had been born in Pakistan, you would likely have been a Muslim. Therefore your belief in Christianity is false or unjustified.

But, again, this seems to be a textbook example of what is called the "genetic fallacy." This is trying to invalidate a position by criticizing the way a person came to hold that position. The fact that your beliefs depend upon where and when you were born has no relevance to the *truth* of those beliefs. If you had been born in ancient Greece, you would probably have believed that the sun orbits Earth. Does that imply that your belief that the Earth orbits the sun is therefore false or unjustified? Obviously not!

And once again, the pluralist pulls the rug from beneath his own feet: for had the pluralist been born in Pakistan, then he would likely have been a religious particularist! Thus, on his own analysis his pluralism is merely the product of his being born in late twentieth-century Western society and is therefore false or unjustified.

The Problem with Christian Particularism

Thus, some of the arguments you frequently hear against Christian particularism are pretty unimpressive. But don't think because such fallacious arguments are often given on behalf of religious pluralism that pluralism doesn't pose a serious challenge to Christian belief. On the contrary, I think it does. But clearing away these fallacious arguments can help us to get to the real problem which is lurking in the background.

The real problem, it seems to me, concerns the fate of unbelievers outside one's particular religious tradition. Christian particularism makes Christ the only doorway to eternal life, which pluralists take to be unconscionable.

Nowhere is this problem better illustrated than in the life of my own doctoral mentor at the University of Birmingham in England, John Hick. Professor Hick began his career as a relatively conservative Christian theologian. His first book was entitled *Christianity at the Centre*. But as he began to study the other world religions and to become acquainted with many of their saintly followers, he found it simply inconceivable that such good people should not be recipients of salvation. He realized what that meant. Somehow he had to get Jesus Christ out of the center. So long as Christ's incarnation and atoning death were retained, Christ could not be successfully marginalized. Hick therefore came to edit *The Myth of God Incarnate*, in which he argues that these central Christian doctrines are not true but mere myths. He wrote:

> The problem which has come to the surface in the encounter
> of Christianity with the other world religions is this: If Jesus
> was literally God incarnate, and if it is by his death alone that
> men can be saved, and by their response to him alone that

they can appropriate that salvation, then the only doorway to eternal life is Christian faith. It would follow from this that the large majority of the human race so far have not been saved. But is it credible that the loving God and Father of all men has decreed that only those born within one particular thread of human history shall be saved?[1]

This is the real problem raised by the religious diversity of mankind: the fate of those who stand outside the Christian tradition.

Is Hell the Problem?

But what exactly is the problem here supposed to be? What's the problem with holding that salvation is available only through Christ? Is the answer as simple as this: a loving God would not send people to hell?

I don't think so. The Bible says that God desires the salvation of every human being: "The Lord is ... not wishing that *any* should perish, but that *all* should reach repentance" (2 Peter 3:9 ESV). Or again, he "desires *all men* to be saved and to come to the knowledge of the truth" (1 Timothy 2:4 NASB). So God says through the prophet Ezekiel:

Have I any pleasure in the death of the wicked, says the Lord GOD, and not rather that he should turn from his way and live? ... For I have no pleasure in the death of any one, says the Lord GOD; so turn, and live.... Say to them, As I live, says the Lord GOD, I have no pleasure in the death of the wicked, but that the wicked turn from his way and live; turn back, turn back from your evil ways; for why will you die? (Ezekiel 18:23, 32; 33:11)

Here God literally pleads with people to turn back from their self-destructive course of action and be saved.

Thus, in a sense, God doesn't *send* anybody to hell. His desire is that everyone be saved, and he seeks to draw all persons to himself. If we make a free and well-informed decision to reject Christ's sacrifice for our sin, then God has no choice but to give us what we deserve. God will not send us to hell—but we shall send ourselves.

Our eternal destiny thus lies in our own hands. It's a matter of our free choice where we shall spend eternity: with God or apart from him. Those who are lost are self-condemned; they separate themselves from God despite God's will and every effort to save them, and God grieves over their loss.

Does the Punishment Fit the Crime?

Now the pluralist might admit that given human freedom God cannot guarantee that everyone will be saved. Some people might freely condemn themselves by rejecting God's offer of salvation. But, he might argue, it would be unjust of God to condemn such people *forever*. For even terrible sins like those of the Nazi torturers in the death camps still deserve only a finite punishment. Therefore, at most hell could be a sort of purgatory, lasting an appropriate length of time for each person before that person is released and admitted into heaven. Eventually hell would be emptied and heaven filled. Thus, ironically, hell is incompatible, not with God's love, but with his justice. The objection charges that God is unjust because the punishment does not fit the crime.

But, again, this doesn't seem to me to be the real problem. For the objection seems flawed in at least two ways:

First, the objection equivocates between *every* sin which we commit and *all* the sins which we commit. We could agree that every individual sin which a person commits deserves only a finite punishment. But it doesn't follow from this that *all* of a person's sins taken together as a whole deserve only a finite punishment. If a person commits an infinite number of sins, then the sum total of all such sins deserves infinite punishment.

Now, of course, nobody commits an infinite number of sins in the earthly life. But what about in the afterlife? Insofar as those who are separated from God continue to hate God and reject him, they continue to sin and so accrue to themselves more guilt and more punishment. In a real sense, then, hell is *self-perpetuating*. In such a case, every sin has a finite punishment, but because sinning goes on forever, so does the punishment.

Second, why think that every sin does have only a finite punishment? We could agree that sins like theft, lying, adultery, and so forth are only of finite consequence and so only deserve a finite punishment. But, in a sense, these sins are not what separate someone from God. For Christ has died for those sins; the penalty for those sins has been paid. One has only to accept Christ as Savior to be completely free and clean of those sins.

But the refusal to accept Christ and his sacrifice seems to be a sin of a different order altogether. For this sin repudiates God's provision for sin and so decisively separates someone from God and his salvation. To reject Christ is to reject God himself. And in light of who God is, this is a sin of infinite gravity and proportion and therefore plausibly deserves infinite punishment. We should not, therefore, think of hell primarily as punishment for the array of sins of finite consequence which we've committed, but as the just penalty for a sin of infinite consequence, namely, the rejection of God himself.

So the heart of the problem in religious particularism is not simply the doctrine of hell.

Is the Problem Lack of Information?

But perhaps the problem is supposed to be that a loving God would not send people to hell because they were *uninformed* or *misinformed* about Christ.

People who have never heard of Christ or have been given a distorted picture of Christ can't be expected to place their faith in Christ.

Again, this doesn't seem to me to be the heart of the problem. For according to the Bible, God doesn't judge people who have never heard of Christ on the basis of whether they've placed their faith in Christ. Rather God judges them on the basis of God's general revelation of himself in nature and conscience.

The offer of Romans 2:7 concerning those who have never heard the Gospel message is a bona fide offer of salvation: "To those who by patience in well-doing seek for glory and honor and immortality, he will give eternal life." Someone who senses his need of forgiveness through his guilty conscience and flings himself upon the mercy of the God revealed in nature may find salvation. This is not to say that people can be saved apart from Christ. Rather it's to say that the benefits of Christ's atoning death can be applied to people without their conscious knowledge of Christ.

Such persons would be similar to certain people mentioned in the Old Testament like Job and Melchizedek, who were saved only through Christ but who had no conscious knowledge of Christ. Being non-Jews, they were not even members of the covenant family of Israel, and yet they clearly enjoyed a personal relationship with God. Similarly, there could be modern-day Jobs living among that percentage of the world's population which has yet to hear the Gospel of Christ.

Unfortunately, the testimony of the New Testament, as we've seen, is that people don't generally

DANTE'S HELL

The medieval Italian poet Dante Alighieri wrote a poem called *Inferno* that depicts hell with gothic gruesomeness. But Dante carefully chose each type of suffering to illustrate his belief that the punishment for the sin is the sin itself. That is, each person's sin has formed his soul in such a way that he creates his own agony. For example, Satan stands at the bottom of hell encased chest-high in ice. What freezes the ice is the endless flapping of his bat-like wings. The flapping expresses his will: "I *will* fly to the heights of heaven and be equal to God on my own terms." If he could just humble himself and stop flapping, the ice would melt and he would be free. But he never does.

measure up even to these much-lower standards of general revelation. So there are little grounds for optimism about there being many people, if any at all, who will actually be saved through their response to general revelation alone. Nonetheless, the point remains that salvation is *universally accessible* through God's general revelation in nature and conscience. So the problem posed by religious diversity can't be simply that God would not condemn persons who are uninformed or misinformed about Christ.

The Real Problem

Rather it seems to me that the real problem is this: if God is all-knowing, then he knew who would freely receive the Gospel and who would not. But then certain very difficult questions arise:

1. Why didn't God bring the Gospel to people who he knew *would* accept it if they heard it, even though they reject the light of general revelation that they do have?

To illustrate: imagine a North American Indian living prior to the arrival of Christian missionaries. Let's call him Walking Bear. Let's suppose that as Walking Bear looks up at the heavens at night and sees the beauty of nature around him, he senses that all of this has been made by the Great Spirit. Furthermore, as Walking Bear looks into his own heart, he senses there the moral law, telling him that all men are brothers made by the Great Spirit and therefore we ought to live in love for one another.

But suppose that instead of worshipping the Great Spirit and living in love for his fellow man, Walking Bear ignores the Great Spirit and creates totems of other spirits and that rather than loving his fellow man he lives in selfishness and cruelty toward others. In such a case Walking Bear would be justly condemned before God on the basis of his failure to respond to God's general revelation in nature and conscience.

But now suppose that if only the missionaries had arrived, then Walking Bear would have believed the Gospel and been saved! In that case his salvation or damnation seems to be the result of bad luck. Through no fault of his own he just happened to be born at a time and place in history when the Gospel was not yet available. His condemnation is just; but would an all-loving God allow people's eternal destiny to hinge on historical and geographical accident?

> ### TALK ABOUT IT
>
> Do you think many people are saved without a conscious knowledge of Christ, because of their response to general revelation? What leads you to think that?

2. More fundamentally, why did God even create the world, when he knew that so many people would not believe the Gospel and be lost? Since creation is a free act of God, why not simply refrain from creating any free creatures at all?

3. Even more radically, why didn't God create a world in which everyone freely believes the Gospel and is saved? Such a world must be logically possible, since people are free to believe or not believe. So why didn't God create a world in which every person freely chooses to place his faith in Christ and be saved?

What should we say in answer to these questions? Does Christianity make God out to be cruel and unloving?

The Problem Analyzed

It's easy to let our thinking about such an emotionally charged subject become clouded by our feelings. In order to answer these questions objectively it will therefore be helpful to examine more closely the logical structure of the problem before us.

The problem seems to be very similar to the logical version of the problem of suffering, which we examined in chapter 6. The pluralist seems to be claiming that it's impossible for God to be all-powerful and all-loving and yet for some people to never hear the Gospel and be lost. That is to say, the following statements are logically inconsistent:

1. God is all-powerful and all-loving.
2. Some people never hear the Gospel and are lost.

Is There an Inconsistency?

So now we need to ask: Why think that 1 and 2 are logically inconsistent? After all, there's no *explicit* contradiction between them. But if the pluralist is claiming that 1 and 2 are *implicitly* contradictory, he must be assuming some hidden premises that would serve to bring out this contradiction and make it explicit. The question is, what are those hidden premises?

I must say that I've never seen any attempt on the part of religious pluralists to identify those hidden assumptions. But let's try to help out the pluralist a bit. It seems to me that he must be assuming something like the following:

3. If God is all-powerful, he can create a world in which everybody hears the Gospel and is freely saved.
4. If God is all-loving, he prefers a world in which everybody hears the Gospel and is freely saved.

Since, according to 1, God is both all-powerful and all-loving, it follows that he both can create a world of universal salvation and prefers such a world. Therefore such a world exists, in contradiction to 2.

Now both of the hidden assumptions must be necessarily true if the logical incompatibility of 1 and 2 is to be demonstrated. So the question is, are these assumptions *necessarily* true?

Consider assumption 3. It seems uncontroversial that God could create a world in which everybody hears the Gospel. That's no big deal. But so long as people are free, there's no guarantee that everybody in such a world would be freely saved. In fact, when you think about it, there's no reason to think that the balance between saved and lost in such a world would be any better than the balance in the actual world!

It is logically impossible to *make* someone *freely* do something. That's as logically impossible as making a round square or a married bachelor. Being all-powerful does not mean having the ability to do the logically impossible. So there's no guarantee that a possible world in which everyone hears the Gospel and is freely saved is feasible for God to create. For all we know, in any world of free people which God could create, some people would freely reject his saving grace and be lost. Hence, 3 is not necessarily true, and so the pluralist's argument is fallacious.

But what about assumption 4? Is it necessarily true? Let's suppose for the sake of argument that there are possible worlds which are feasible for God in which everyone hears the Gospel and freely accepts it. Does God's being all-loving compel him to prefer one of these worlds over a world in which some persons are lost?

Not necessarily! For the worlds involving universal salvation might have other, *overriding* deficiencies that make them less preferable. For example, suppose that the only worlds in which everybody freely believes the Gospel and is saved are worlds with only a handful of people in them, say, three or four. If God were to create any more people, then at least one of them would have freely rejected his grace and been lost. Must he prefer one of these sparsely populated worlds over a world in which multitudes believe in the Gospel and are saved, even though that implies that other persons freely reject his grace and are lost?

TALK ABOUT IT

Are people raised in Christian homes getting more grace for salvation than people raised in communities where the gospel is unknown? If not, why not? If so, is this a failure of love on God's part?

That's far from obvious. So long as God gives sufficient grace for salvation to all persons he creates, God seems no less loving for preferring a more populous world, even though that implies that some people would freely resist his every effort to save them and be damned. Thus, the pluralist's second assumption is also not necessarily true, so that his argument is revealed to be doubly fallacious.

So neither of the pluralist's assumptions seems to be necessarily true. Unless the pluralist can suggest some other premises, we have no reason to think that 1 and 2 are logically incompatible.

There Is No Inconsistency

But we can push the argument a notch further. We can show positively that it is entirely possible that God is all-powerful and all-loving and that many persons never hear the Gospel and are lost.

As a good and loving God, God wants as many people as possible to be saved and as few as possible to be lost. His goal, then, is to achieve an optimal balance between these, to create as few of the lost and as many of the saved as is feasible. But it's possible that the actual world (which includes the future as well as the present and past) has such a balance. It's possible that in order to create this many people who will be saved, God also had to create this many people who will freely reject him. It's possible that had God created a world in which fewer people go to hell, then even fewer people would have gone to heaven. It's possible that in order to achieve a multitude of saints, God had to accept a multitude of sinners.

It might be objected that an all-loving God would not create people who he knew *will be* lost, but who *would have been* saved if only they had heard the Gospel. But how do we know there *are* any such persons? It's reasonable to assume that many people who never hear the Gospel wouldn't have believed the Gospel even if they had heard it. Suppose, then, that God has so providentially ordered the world that *all* persons who never hear the Gospel are precisely such people.

In that case, anybody who never hears the Gospel and is lost would have rejected the Gospel and been lost even if he had heard it. No one could stand before God on the Judgment Day and complain, "All right, God, so I didn't respond to your general revelation in nature and conscience! But if only I had heard the Gospel, then I would have believed!"

For God will say, "No, I knew that even if you had heard the Gospel, you wouldn't have believed it. Therefore, my judgment of you on the basis of nature and conscience is neither unfair nor unloving."

Thus, it's possible that:

> 5. God has created a world which has an optimal balance between saved and lost, and those who never hear the Gospel and are lost would not have believed it even if they had heard it.

So long as 5 is even *possibly true*, it shows that there's no inconsistency between an all-powerful, all-loving God and some people's never hearing the Gospel and being lost.

On this basis we're now prepared to offer *possible* answers to the three difficult questions which prompted this inquiry. To take them in reverse order:

PROVIDENCE

Providence is the doctrine that God orders events in history so that his purposes are achieved. The challenge is doing this while respecting human freedom.

Some theologians abridge God's providence; some curtail human freedom. A better way is to say that God takes human free choices into account in his planning. He does this by knowing how every possible person would freely choose in whatever nondetermining circumstances God might place him in.

By creating certain persons in certain circumstances, God knows exactly how they will freely choose and can plan accordingly. On this view everything that happens is either directly willed by God or permitted by God, including where and when people are born.

(3) Why didn't God create a world in which everyone freely believes the Gospel and is saved?

Answer: It may not be feasible for God to create such a world. If such a world were feasible, then (all else being equal) God would have created it. But given his will to create *free* creatures, God had to accept that some would freely reject him and his every effort to save them and be lost.

(2) Why did God even create the world, when he knew that so many people would not believe the Gospel and be lost?

Answer: God wanted to share his love and fellowship with created persons. This is an incommensurable good. He knew this meant that many would freely reject him and be lost. But he also knew that many others would freely receive his grace and be saved. The happiness and blessedness of those who would freely embrace his love should not be precluded by those who would freely spurn him. Persons who would freely reject God and his love should not be allowed, in effect, to hold a sort of veto power over which worlds God is free to create. In his mercy God has providentially ordered the world to achieve an optimal balance between saved and lost by maximizing the number of those who would freely accept him and minimizing the number of those who would not.

(1) Why didn't God bring the Gospel to people who he knew would accept it if they heard it, even though they reject the light of general revelation that they do have?

Answer: There are no such people. God in his providence has so arranged the world that those who would respond to the Gospel if they heard it, do hear it. The sovereign God has so ordered human history that as the Gospel message spreads out from first-century Palestine, he places people in its path who would believe it if they heard it. Once the Gospel reaches a people, God providentially places there persons who he knew would respond to it if they heard it. In his love and mercy, God ensures that no one who would believe the Gospel if he heard it is born at a time and place in history where he fails to hear it. Those who don't respond to God's general revelation in nature and conscience and never hear the Gospel wouldn't respond to it if they did hear it. Hence, no one is lost because of historical or geographical accident. Anyone who wants *or even would want* to be saved will be saved.

These are just *possible* answers to the questions we posed. But so long as they're even possible, they show that there's no incompatibility between God's being all-powerful and all-loving and some people's never hearing the Gospel and being lost.

Furthermore, these answers are attractive because they also seem to be quite biblical as well. In his open-air address to the Athenian philosophers gathered on the Areopagus Paul declared:

> The God who made the world and everything in it is the Lord of heaven and earth and … gives all men life and breath and everything else. From one man he made every nation of men, that they should inhabit the whole earth; and he determined *the times* set for them and *the exact places* where they should live. God did this so that men would seek him and perhaps reach out for him and find him, though he is not far from each one of us. "For in him we live and move and have our being." (Acts 17:24–28 NIV)

This sounds exactly like the conclusions to which I have come through purely philosophical reflection on the question!

Plausibility of the Solution

Now the pluralist might concede the logical *possibility* of God's being all-powerful and all-loving and some people's never hearing the Gospel and being lost but insist that these two facts are nonetheless *improbable* with respect to each other. People by and large seem to believe in the religion of the culture in which they were raised. But in that case, the pluralist might argue, it's highly probable that if many of those who never hear the Gospel had been raised in a Christian culture, they would have believed the Gospel and been saved. Thus, the hypothesis I've offered is highly implausible.

Now it would, indeed, be fantastically improbable that by coincidence alone it just turned out that all those who never hear the Gospel and are lost are persons who would not have believed the Gospel even if they had heard it. But that's not the hypothesis! The hypothesis is that a provident God has so arranged the world. Given a God endowed with knowledge of how every person would freely respond to his grace in whatever circumstances God might place him, it's not at all implausible that God has ordered the world in the way described.

Such a world wouldn't look any different outwardly from a world where the circumstances of a person's birth are a matter of chance. We can agree that people generally adopt the religion of their culture and that if many of those born into non-Christian cultures had been born in a Christian society instead, they would have become nominally or culturally Christian. But that's not to say that they would have come into a saving relationship with God. It's a simple empirical fact that there are no distinguishing psychological or sociological traits between persons who become Christians and persons who don't. There's no way to predict accurately by examining a person whether and under what circumstances that person would believe in Christ for salvation. Since a world providentially ordered by God would appear outwardly identical to a world in which one's birth is a matter of historical and geographical accident, it's hard to see how the hypothesis I've defended can be said to be improbable apart from a demonstration that the existence of a God endowed with such knowledge is implausible. And I don't know of any such demonstration.

TALK ABOUT IT

We've seen that the logical argument for pluralism doesn't hold up, but what about the emotional problem of imagining millions of people consigned to hell, some of whom have lived admirable lives? How do we address that emotional problem?

Conclusion

In conclusion, then, pluralists haven't been able to show any logical inconsistency in the biblical view that Christ is the only way of salvation. On the contrary, we've been able to prove that such a position is logically coherent. More than that, I think that such a view is not only possible, but plausible as well. Therefore mankind's religious diversity doesn't undermine the Christian Gospel of salvation through Christ alone.

In fact, for those of us who are Christians, I think that what I've said helps to put the proper perspective on Christian mission: it's our duty as Christians to proclaim the Gospel to the whole world, trusting that God has so providentially ordered things that through us the Good News will come to persons who God knew would accept it if they heard it.

For those who have not yet come to saving faith in Christ, I hope that what I've said leads to the realization that God has providentially arranged the world in order that you might hear the life-giving message of the Gospel and so place your faith in Christ. Amazing, isn't it? Eternal life and a relationship with God are within your grasp, if only you will seize them. The choice is yours. God will not compel you to believe. But he has arranged for you to hear the Gospel and has given you sufficient reasons to believe.

> Then Jesus came to them and said, "All authority in heaven and on earth has been given to me. Therefore go and make disciples of all nations, baptizing them in the name of the Father and of the Son and of the Holy Spirit, and teaching them to obey everything I have commanded you. And surely I am with you always, to the very end of the age." (Matthew 28:18–20 NIV)

1. John Hick, "Jesus and the World Religions," in *The Myth of God Incarnate*, ed. John Hick (London: SCM, 1977), 179–80.

RELIGIOUS PLURALISM OBJECTION

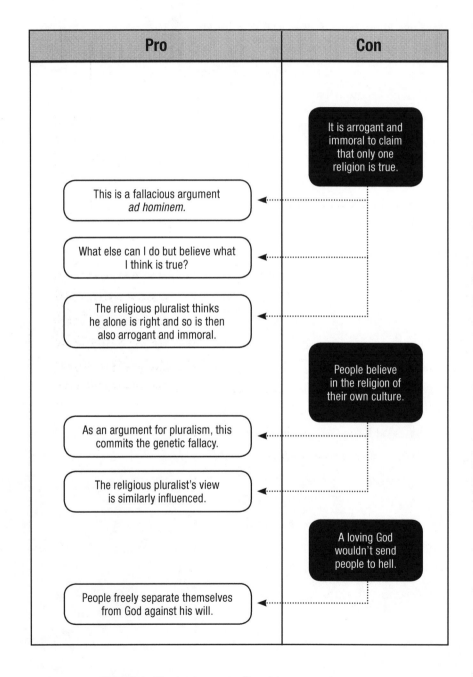

Pro	Con
	It is arrogant and immoral to claim that only one religion is true.
This is a fallacious argument *ad hominem*.	
What else can I do but believe what I think is true?	
The religious pluralist thinks he alone is right and so is then also arrogant and immoral.	
	People believe in the religion of their own culture.
As an argument for pluralism, this commits the genetic fallacy.	
The religious pluralist's view is similarly influenced.	
	A loving God wouldn't send people to hell.
People freely separate themselves from God against his will.	

RELIGIOUS PLURALISM OBJECTION (cont.)

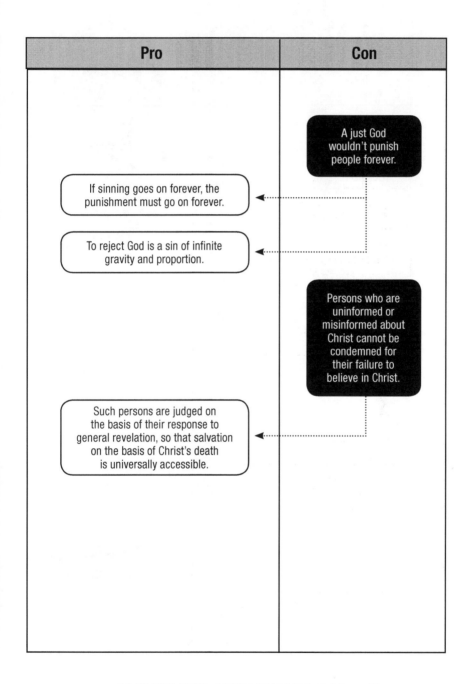

Pro	Con
	A just God wouldn't punish people forever.
If sinning goes on forever, the punishment must go on forever.	
To reject God is a sin of infinite gravity and proportion.	
	Persons who are uninformed or misinformed about Christ cannot be condemned for their failure to believe in Christ.
Such persons are judged on the basis of their response to general revelation, so that salvation on the basis of Christ's death is universally accessible.	

RELIGIOUS PLURALISM OBJECTION (cont.)

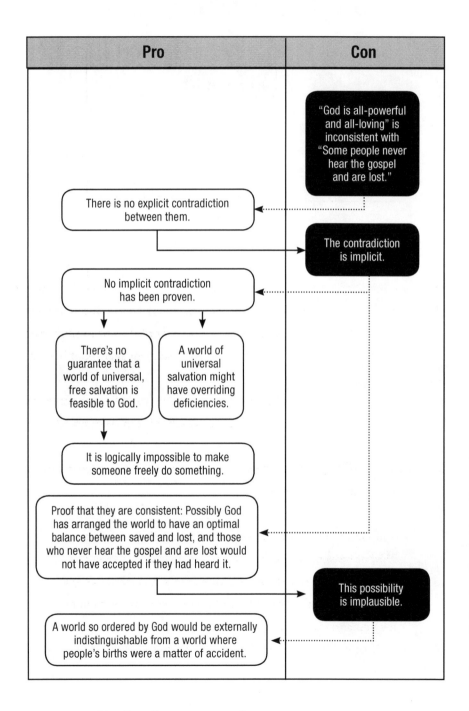

Pro	Con
	"God is all-powerful and all-loving" is inconsistent with "Some people never hear the gospel and are lost."
There is no explicit contradiction between them.	
	The contradiction is implicit.
No implicit contradiction has been proven.	
There's no guarantee that a world of universal, free salvation is feasible to God.	A world of universal salvation might have overriding deficiencies.
It is logically impossible to make someone freely do something.	
Proof that they are consistent: Possibly God has arranged the world to have an optimal balance between saved and lost, and those who never hear the gospel and are lost would not have accepted if they had heard it.	
	This possibility is implausible.
A world so ordered by God would be externally indistinguishable from a world where people's births were a matter of accident.	

AFTERWORD

HOW TO KNOW GOD AS A PERSONAL REALITY IN YOUR LIFE

This is eternal life, that they may know you, the only true God, and Jesus Christ whom you have sent.

Jesus of Nazareth, John 17:3 NRSV

The book is finished, and we've surveyed some of the evidence for Christian theism. Having read the book, some of you may be ready to put your trust in Jesus Christ. But you wonder how. In this afterword, I want to shift gears and share in a very personal way what the New Testament says about how we can come to know God.

There's not really all that much that you have to believe in order to become a Christian (the rest is in-house discussion!). It can be summed up as four basic truths.

Truth #1: God loves you and created you to know him personally.
The Bible says:

> The God who made the world and everything in it is the
> Lord of heaven and earth.... From one man he made all the
> nations, that they should inhabit the whole earth.... God
> did this so that they would seek him and perhaps reach out
> for him and find him, though he is not far from any one of
> us. "For in him we live and move and have our being." (Acts
> 17:24, 26–28 NIV)

It's worth pausing to emphasize that on the biblical view, God's existence is an objective fact, as real as the existence of this book, or of the Grand Canyon. The Bible knows nothing of the fashionable idea that God's existence may be "true for you, but not true for me." That idea is as misconceived with regard to God as it is with regard to the Grand Canyon. Can you imagine a wagon train crossing the American frontier and the scout rides up in a panic saying that there's a mile-wide canyon ahead stretching as far as you can see in either direction, and the wagon master says, "That may be true for you, but it's not true for me! Push on!" God is even more real than the Grand Canyon.

People who say that God's existence may be "true for you, but not true for me" are confusing something's being real *in one's experience* with something's being *actually real.* For a little child Santa Claus or the Tooth Fairy may seem real in the sense that they are real in his experience. Nevertheless, such characters are not actually real, that is to say, they don't have existence outside of your mind. Something that is actually real exists independently of whether anybody believes in it or not. For example, molecules are actually real because they exist, and they always have existed, even before scientists developed the technology to discover them. Something that is actually real exists whether anybody believes in it or not.

Now the Bible presents God as an actual reality who may or may not be real in your experience. He wants you to experience his love, but his existence doesn't depend on whether or not you experience him. Long before mankind ever existed, God created the universe out of nothing and fine-tuned it for the existence of intelligent, interactive life. As we've seen, these truths have been amazingly confirmed by scientific discoveries during the past century, so that it is eminently rational to believe in God. His existence is an objective fact, supported by the evidence.

Now a lot of people believe that God exists, but if you question them further about who God is, you find that in their thinking God is just a nebulous sort of higher power, maybe just an impersonal force. Therefore I think it's important to say a word about the biblical concept of God, or we may be using the same word "God" and yet talking about two entirely different things, just as a railroad engineer and a young bride might use the word "train" to refer to totally different things.

The God of the Bible is the infinite, personal God. This concept is nearly unique among the world's religions. The God or Absolute of Eastern religions like Hinduism or Buddhism is infinite, but it is not personal. The mythological gods of Greece and Rome like Zeus or Mercury were certainly personal, but they were not infinite. The God of the Bible, on the other hand, is both infinite and personal.

When we say that God is infinite, we mean, for example, that God is *uncaused*: he doesn't depend on anyone or anything for his existence. Rather everything else depends on him. He is utterly distinct from his creation: we are creatures; he is Creator. We also mean that God is *eternal*: he never began to exist and will never cease to exist. We mean that he is *all-present*: there is nowhere in the universe where you can go to escape his notice or his power. In fact, if, as the evidence suggests, time and space began to exist in the Big Bang, then God transcends time and space in the sense that he existed without time and space and then brought them into being at the moment of creation. We mean that God is *incorporeal*: that is to say, he is not physical or material. This is already implied by his transcending space and time. Just as you are a soul or spirit conjoined to a body, so God is mind or spirit without a body—only he is an infinite, uncreated mind. We mean that God is *all-powerful*: he can do anything that is logically possible for him to do. The most spectacular displays of his power are his creation of the universe out of nothing and his raising Jesus from the dead. God is an infinite being.

On the other hand, God is also a personal being. When we say that God is personal, we mean that he possesses all the qualities essential to personhood: he is an intelligent, moral agent. Now some people say they cannot understand how God can be both personal and infinite. They equate personhood with being finite. But this is a false assumption. God has all the qualities of personhood, only to an unlimited degree. For example, he is *all-knowing*:

there are no facts which are unknown to him; he knows every truth. He is also *morally perfect*: he is not only without any trace of evil, but he himself is the source and standard of ultimate moral goodness. More specifically, God's moral nature comprises both love and justice. God is as loving as he is just. His justice means his perfect righteousness: evil is dispersed from his presence just as darkness is dispersed by light. His love means his unconditionally seeking the good of others, which is expressed in his kindness and generosity and compassion. God is a personal being.

But God is more than just personal: on the biblical view he is tri-personal. That is to say, God is not a solitary individual existing eternally alone. Rather God is three persons. Perhaps the best way to think of this is by means of a comparison: just as my human nature has associated with it one center of self-consciousness, which I call "I," God's nature has associated with it three centers of self-consciousness. These three persons are all equal in power, knowledge, glory, and every other respect, but we refer to them as the Father, Son, and Holy Spirit because of the different roles they play in God's relations to humanity.

Thus, prior to his creation of the world, God wasn't lonely or wanting for company. Rather in the tri-unity of his own being, he was enjoying the fullness of the love relationship between the three persons of the Trinity. But then why did God create the world? Certainly not because of any need in himself; rather, as Truth #1 states, God created us so that we might know the joy and fulfillment of knowing God personally. He invites us, as it were, to share the intra-Trinitarian love relationship as adopted children, not because he needed us, but because he loves us! Thus, creation, as much as salvation, is sheerly an act of God's grace.

Now the message of the Bible is like one of those "good news–bad news" stories. For the Bible also teaches:

Truth #2: Man is sinful and separated from God, and thus his relationship with God is broken.

The Bible says:

Ever since the creation of the world his invisible nature, namely, his eternal power and deity, has been clearly perceived in the things that have been made. So they are without excuse; for although they knew God they did not honor him as God or give thanks to him, but they became futile in their thinking and their senseless minds were darkened.... And since they did not see fit to acknowledge God, God gave them up to a base mind and to improper conduct. They were filled with all manner of wickedness, evil, covetousness, malice. Full of envy, murder, strife, deceit, malignity, they are gossips, slanderers, haters of God, insolent, haughty, boastful, inventors of evil, disobedient to parents, foolish, faithless, heartless, ruthless. Though they know God's decree that those who do such things deserve to die, they not only do them but approve those who practice them. (Romans 1:20–21, 28–32)

There's probably no other truth in the Bible that is more confirmed empirically than the fallen, sinful state of mankind. Near the close of the nineteenth century, in the heyday of classical liberal theology, a magazine was founded with the cheery title *The Christian Century*. That's what they expected the twentieth century to be! Now as we look back on the twentieth century, we look back on a century that brought two world wars which claimed well over fifty million lives, a disastrous seventy-year social experiment predicated on human perfectibility called Soviet communism which resulted in incalculable suffering and loss of human life, and decades of civil war and strife in the Third World which have claimed over thirty million lives. If anyone in the history of the world ought to be free of the illusion of human goodness and perfectibility, it ought to be us.

Moreover, what's interesting about that catalog of sins which I just quoted from the book of Romans is that it is such a mixture of sins.

Seemingly insignificant sins like disobedience to parents or gossip stand cheek to jowl with horrendous sins like murder and adultery. There isn't any attempt to discriminate between little sins and big sins. All sin is disobedience to God and an affront to God. Any sin is therefore serious. It renders us morally guilty before God and ruptures our relationship with him.

Again, we need to emphasize the objectivity of this fact. Our problem is not guilt *feelings*; our problem is *guilt itself*. No psychotherapy, no Scientology, no human-potential program can remove the objective guilt each of us bears before God for our moral wrongdoing, even if they could succeed in removing our guilt feelings. We don't need God as a psychotherapist to help us feel better about ourselves; we need God to pardon and cleanse us of the stain of guilt we bear.

Because we are objectively morally culpable for our sins, we find ourselves spiritually separated from God. That's why God seems so distant and unreal to most people. Groping in spiritual darkness and sensing the spiritual void in our own hearts, we try to get back to God by our own efforts: pilgrimages, penances and prayers, mind-emptying meditation and yoga, self-denial and asceticism; even self-mutilation and human sacrifice characterize the various religions of the world which people have invented to find God. But all in vain. The great German philosopher Immanuel Kant said that it would take an eternity for a man to bring his life into conformity with God's moral law. And even if he succeeded, he would still be guilty of all the sins he had committed along the way in his infinite striving for perfection. Thus, there can be no salvation through religion and human effort.

That's why people who say that we just need to obey the Golden Rule or the Ten Commandments are so tragically mistaken. The most disastrous thing that could happen to us would be for God to judge us by our performance. For no one can earn his way to heaven; no one is good enough. C. S. Lewis once remarked that we do not realize how bad we are until we have truly tried to be good. We cannot make ourselves acceptable to God. That is why the ethical life, as the Danish philosopher Søren Kierkegaard saw, ultimately ends in despair over one's inextricable guilt.

If we were to die in this condition, we would go into eternity forever separated from God. That's what hell really is. Hell is not torture racks and pincers and red-hot tongs, but the state of eternal separation from the source of all goodness and joy and life. It is a sort of living death, being cut off from everything good that you know.

So Truth #2 is the bad news: man is sinful and separated from God, and thus his relationship with God is broken. Now these two truths present God with a dilemma. He loves us and created us to know him, but he finds us in rebellion to him and poisoned with evil, deserving only his justice. His perfect justice demands punishment for sin, rightly deserved; but his love demands reconciliation and compassion. Both are essential to his nature; neither can be compromised.

What is God to do in this dilemma? The answer comes in our next truth.

Truth #3: Jesus Christ is God's solution to man's sin. Through him a relationship to God is restored.

Truth #3 is the good news! In the greatest invasion in history, God entered into human history in the form of a Jewish baby. The second person of the Trinity took on human nature and in the person of Jesus of Nazareth lived the righteous life before God that each of us should have. He submitted to and did God the Father's will perfectly. He therefore had no penalty for personal sin to pay. Nevertheless, he voluntarily chose to die in our place, to pay the death penalty of sin that we deserve.

The crucifixion of Jesus was thus no accident of history, no unforeseen tragedy. The Bible says that God had planned it before the foundation of the world. He foreshadowed its significance in the system of animal sacrifices in the Old Testament. Jesus was called the Lamb of God, not because he was meek and mild, but because, like the sacrificial Passover lamb (Exodus 12), he was slain on our behalf.

When Jesus celebrated his final Passover with his disciples on the eve of his crucifixion, he took some of the unleavened bread and tore it and said, "This is my body which is given for you." Then he took a cup of wine and said, "This cup is the new covenant in my blood, which is poured out for many." Jesus understood his death as a sacrificial offering which inaugurated a new covenant between God and man. At the cross he took upon himself my guilt and died in my place, thereby meeting the demands of God's justice and freeing up God's love to forgive and cleanse and restore me.

What transpired at the cross was the greatest transaction in history. My sin for his righteousness! The Bible says, "God was in Christ reconciling the world to Himself, not counting their trespasses against them.... He made Him who knew no sin to be sin on our behalf, so that we might become the righteousness of God in Him" (2 Corinthians 5:19, 21 NASB).

I was once trying to explain this concept to a businessman, and he said, "Oh, I understand this. It's imputation." I was shocked! Since "imputation" is a theological term, I was surprised to hear him use it. But he said, "We use imputation all the time in the insurance business." He explained that under certain insurance policies, if someone else were to drive my car and have an accident, he would not be held responsible; rather the responsibility would be imputed to me. I would be the one at fault.

Now it's just the same with Christ. My sin and guilt are imputed to Christ; more than that, in return his perfect righteousness is imputed to me. Do you see why I said this is the greatest exchange in history?

God ratified Jesus' dying for us by raising him from the dead. The resurrection, an event which has remarkable historical credibility, as we have seen, confirms that Jesus' sacrifice was effective and valid. Moreover, it broke the power of sin and death and hell, which had held sway over us.

Jesus Christ is thus God's solution to human sin. Apart from the cross of Christ, there is no forgiveness of sin. Of all the religious leaders of the world, Christ alone is divine, Christ alone died in our place for our sins, and Christ alone rose from the dead in confirmation of his sacrifice. Other religions don't even claim such things for their founders. They represent man's best efforts to reach up to God; Christ is God's best effort to reach down to man.

Finally, the fourth truth tells us how we can appropriate what God has done on our behalf:

Truth #4: We must receive Jesus Christ as our Savior and Lord; then we can know God personally.

Many people sincerely believe the first three truths I've shared, and yet their lives remain spiritually empty. They may go to church and even be quite religious, but it is evident by the way that they live that their lives have not been changed by God. They are Christians in name only. They have never received Christ as Savior and Lord and come to know him.

What, then, does it mean to receive Christ? I asked this once of a college student, and he said, "Receive the Eucharist?" Given his Catholic background, this answer was perfectly logical. Since Catholics believe that in the Mass, the bread and wine are literally changed into the body and blood of Christ, the communicant does take in Christ. But that's not what I'm talking about. According to Jesus, when he returned to his Father after the resurrection, the Holy Spirit, the third person of the Trinity, would stand in Jesus' place. Thus, it would be technically more correct to say that we must receive the Holy Spirit. Over and over again in the New Testament you find that a person is not truly a Christian unless and until he receives God's Holy Spirit. It is the presence of the Holy Spirit in a person that makes him a Christian. Since the Holy Spirit stands in Christ's place and continues his ministry, he becomes so closely identified with Christ himself that one speaks of receiving Christ.

Look in the following passage how the apostle Paul uses the terms "Spirit of God," "Spirit of Christ," and "Christ" interchangeably. He says:

> You do not live as your human nature tells you to; you live as the Spirit tells you to—if, in fact, the Spirit of God lives in you. Whoever does not have the Spirit of Christ does not belong to him. But if Christ lives in you, although your body is dead because of sin, your spirit is alive because of righteousness. (Romans 8:9–10 TEV)

Do you notice the progression from "Spirit of God" to "Spirit of Christ" and finally to simply "Christ"? Did you also notice that the presence of the Holy Spirit is the decisive factor determining whether you are a Christian? Paul said, "Whoever does not have the Spirit of Christ does not belong to him."

Why is the presence of the Holy Spirit so crucial? Simply because we are spiritually dead apart from him. When the Holy Spirit comes into you, he makes you spiritually alive again, so that you can know and experience God. To give an analogy, there are radio waves all around us all the time, even passing right through our bodies, but if your radio is dead, you can't hear the broadcast. The problem isn't with the transmitter; the problem is with the receiver. If you get a new receiver, then you can tune into the broadcast loud and clear. In the same way, our spiritual receivers are dead because of sin, and so we don't experience God's presence. When the Holy Spirit comes into a person, he takes the dead receiver and makes it alive so that the person can tune in to God.

This "making alive again" is called *regeneration*. We need to be spiritually regenerated, or born anew. Thus, when Jesus was talking once with a Jewish leader named Nicodemus, he said to him:

> "Truly, truly, I say to you, unless one is born anew, he cannot see the kingdom of God." Nicodemus said to him, "How can a man be born when he is old? Can he enter a second time into his mother's womb and be born?" Jesus answered, "Truly, truly, I say to you ... that which is born of the flesh is flesh, and that which is born of the Spirit is spirit. Do not marvel that I said to you, 'You must be born anew.'" (John 3:3–7)

Here Jesus makes it clear that he's talking about the necessity of an individual, spiritual rebirth which is produced by the Spirit of God. Moreover, he emphasizes that this new birth is the essential entrance requirement into God's Kingdom.

In order to find God as a spiritual reality in our lives, then, we need to be spiritually born anew by receiving Christ, or the Holy Spirit. But notice that Truth #4 says we must receive Christ "as our Savior and Lord." What does that mean? To receive Christ *as Savior* means trusting God to forgive our sins solely on the basis of Christ's sacrificial death. It means that we are not trusting in any way in our good works to save us or make us acceptable to God. Salvation is by grace alone. There's nothing we can do to earn God's pardon; we can only humbly and gratefully receive it.

To receive Christ *as Lord* means that you are giving your whole life to Christ to follow and obey him. Trusting in Christ is not just some sort of fire insurance. It is a commitment of all that you are and have to him. This is no more than his due, for he is God incarnate, and God alone is worthy of worship.

Now this can seem like a pretty daunting step to take. I remember when I, as a non-Christian, was contemplating this commitment, and I said to my Christian friends, "I don't know if I can do this. Somehow I can't look ahead five years from now and see Bill Craig as a Christian." It just seemed unimaginable. But my friends wisely said to me, "Don't think about five years from now, Bill. Just trust God for the present moment, and he'll take care of the future." So I did, and he has! Now it has been over forty years that I've walked with him, one day at a time, day by day. Paul says, "It is no longer I who live, but Christ who lives in me; and the life I now live … I live by faith in the Son of God, who loved me and gave himself for me" (Galatians 2:20).

So in summary, we've seen four biblical truths that can change your life:

1. God loves you and created you to know him personally.
2. Man is sinful and separated from God, and thus his relationship with God is broken.
3. Jesus Christ is God's solution to man's sin. Through him our relationship to God is restored.

4. We must receive Jesus Christ as our Savior and Lord; then we can know God personally.

As we come to the close of this book, I want to give you the opportunity to respond personally to what I've shared. The message which I've just shared with you was called by the early Christians "the Word of God." Perhaps you've sensed that God has been speaking to you, drawing you to him, and now it's time for you to respond. There's no set formula or recipe for how to receive Christ. Receiving Christ involves believing the four truths I've shared, turning to God from self, and opening your heart to him and making that commitment. One way to express this is by just talking to God and inviting Christ to be your Savior and Lord. If you want to make that commitment, I'd encourage you make the following prayer your own:

> God, I really need you. I've made a mess of my life. I've thought and said and done things that are wrong. I believe that you exist and that you sent Jesus to die for my sins. So right now, in the best way I know how, I commit myself to him as my Lord and Savior. Come into my life, forgive my sins, cleanse me, and make me into the person you want me to be. Thank you for hearing this prayer. Amen.

Let me be the first to congratulate you on the momentous step you've just taken. You have begun a new life with God. Like a newborn baby you now need to grow into spiritual maturity. So let me offer a few suggestions to help you grow in your relationship with God.

1. Read the Bible and pray daily. We speak to God through prayer, and he speaks to us through his Word, the Bible. I suggest you begin to read the Gospels in the New Testament, for these contain the story and teachings of Jesus. Seek to apply in your life what you read there. Talk to God in prayer constantly throughout the day. When you slip up and do something wrong,

don't try to sweep it under the rug, but confess it immediately to him and ask his forgiveness and cleansing.

2. Join in worshipping God with other believers. Find a church where the pastor faithfully preaches the Bible and Christ is honored. Tell others of your decision to follow Christ. You will gain great strength from being in the company of worshipping believers. Tell the pastor that you would like to be baptized as a public proclamation of your newfound faith in Christ. Baptism is the culminating act of your conversion, for in it you publicly identify with Christ's death and resurrection. Then get involved in the church by using whatever talents and abilities you have to serve others. This will help you to become others-oriented instead of self-oriented.

3. Expect trouble. The Christian life is a battleground where all sorts of negative cultural and spiritual forces are lined up against you. You may be belittled or persecuted for choosing to follow Christ. Hardships may come into your life. Things may not go as you hoped. Don't be discouraged. Jesus told his followers that they were to expect such trials and to ask God for the strength to persevere.

4. Ask the Holy Spirit to empower and guide you each day. The Holy Spirit of God, who lives within you, is your power source. You cannot live the Christian life on your own strength. So each day when you get up, take a moment in silent prayer to yield your life to the Holy Spirit and ask him to guide and empower you. As you yield your life to him, he will gradually change you from the inside out to become a better person.

I'm excited to think that some reader of this book may find new life in Christ through its contents. You have begun a great journey that will last for the rest of your life and on into eternity. *Bon voyage!*

Made in the USA
Columbia, SC
22 January 2024

30797881R00174